DREAM POETRY & MINOR WORKS

DREAM POETRY & MINOR WORKS

GEOFFREY CHAUCER

ᚖᛒᛟ

EDITED AND TRANSLATED
BY GERARD P. NECASTRO, PH.D.

Library of Congress Control Number: 2016961856.

Author: Geoffrey Chaucer
Editor: Gerard P. NeCastro
Translator: Gerard P. NeCastro

ISBN-10: 0-9894263-4-3
ISBN-13: 978-0-9894263-4-3
http://www.primaverapress.com

To all of my Chaucer students, past, present, and future.

CONTENTS

PREFACE

This volume, the third in this series of four volumes of Chaucer's works in modern English, began with my sister Christina, who was puzzled at my fascination with reading books in ancient languages that most people could not read and would not care to read. For her I set out to translate into modern English the works of Geoffrey Chaucer, which had brought me such joy for many years. There were already available many translations, old and new, into verse, but, I thought that they were not the best choices for modern readers. Because many people have difficulty following verse and because the clarity and accuracy of translations into verse are often compromised in order to make lines fit the rhyme and meter, I chose to translate his works into prose. My goal was to make my prose as true to Chaucer's original meaning and as approachable as possible.

The original project, to set the entire works into a readable translation, took nearly three years, and, after a hiatus of several years, it has taken a year each to polish the lines of each of the first three volumes. Any success I have had in completing this project is owed to the University of Maine System for its financial support, to countless teachers, students, and scholars for their encouragement along the way, and to my family, especially my wife, for humoring me though thousands of lines of poetry, though they could see that my eyes were "entirely dazed."

It is an honor to have the opportunity to present to you the works of one of the great geniuses our world has known.

About Geoffrey Chaucer

Geoffrey Chaucer was born between 1340 and 1343 to a middle-class merchant family. Though his father and grandfather were wine merchants, his name indicates that earlier generations were probably shoemakers, perhaps of French origin. In his early career, he served at court as a page and then as a soldier. It is well known that he was captured in 1360 at the Siege of Rheims (in the Hundred Years War) and was ransomed by King Edward III for £16, but not before the young poet lost his thumb and forefinger, the typical punishment for enemy archers.

In 1366 he was married to Philippa de Roet, a lady-in-waiting to Philippa of Hainault, Queen Consort to Edward III, and together the Chaucers had four children, Thomas, Elizabeth, Agnes, and Lewis (to whom Chaucer's *Treatise on the Astrolabe* is addressed). During the early years of their marriage, Chaucer seems to have studied law at The Inns of Court and traveled on several diplomatic missions, though usually only as a valet. Philippa seems to have died around 1387.

Though he was entrusted with several diplomatic missions to France and Italy, much of his career through the 1380s was as Controller of the Customs House in the London, a position of great responsibility in the bustling port city. He also served as a Commissioner of Peace in Kent and Clerk of the King's Works under King Richard II, and represented Kent in Parliament in 1386. After Richard's deposition and murder in 1399, there are practically no records of Chaucer's life. Perhaps impoverished and disheartened, he died in 1400 and was buried at Westminster Abbey, the first person buried in Poets' Corner.

Chaucer probably started writing poetry at a young age.

Many of his shorter poems may have been composed in his early career, among them a poem about Mary Magdalene that the God of Love in the Prologue to *The Legend of Good Women*, written in the mid-1380s, says Chaucer wrote "long ago." His first major composition was *Book of the Duchess*, a sort of memorial of Blanche, Duchess of Lancaster, for her widower, John of Gaunt, the brother of Edward III and uncle of Richard II. It seems that for this poem Chaucer was granted a "tun" of wine (about 250 gallons) each year for the rest of his life. He also translated early in his career Boethius' *Consolation of Philosophy* and Jean de Meun and Guillaume de Lorris' *Romance of the Rose*, both works of which were very influential in Chaucer's own poetry.

Before he started writing in earnest his most famous work, *The Canterbury Tales,* he attempted several other major compositions: *The Parliament of Fowls*, the first Valentine's Day poem in English, in which the birds gather to choose their mates; *The House of Fame*, a literary investigation of fame, rumor, and reputation; *The Legend of Good Women*, a collection of legends, or quasi-saints' lives, of women from classical antiquity, retold by the fictional Chaucer as a sort of penance for defaming women in his *Troilus and Criseyde*. By the time he composed his *Troilus and Criseyde*, perhaps the first novel in the English language, Chaucer had reached full maturity as a poet, creating a work that is beautifully crafted, philosophically challenging, and delightfully human. The culmination of Chaucer's career, *The Canterbury Tales*, written in his later years, is a collection of tales told by twenty-five pilgrims on their way from the outskirts of London to Canterbury. Though it, like his *Anelida and Arcite*, *The House of Fame*, and *The Legend of Good Women*, was left incomplete at his death, it has long been considered as one of the very best works of literature throughout the world. Perhaps because it is brimming with variety, believable characters, and memorable plots (as John Dryden remarked, it contained "God's plenty"), its popularity and its relevance to generation after generation of readers has never decreased.

The poems in the present volume, though not as renowned as *The Canterbury Tales*, are equally enjoyable for Chaucer's observations on human nature, his inventive use of language, and his sense of humor.

THE BOOK OF THE DUCHESS

❦

INTRODUCTORY NOTES

Geoffrey Chaucer's *The Book of the Duchess* is the first major poem by the first major author of the English language. Years before he conceived of *The Canterbury Tales*, Chaucer seems to have written a fair number of minor or short poems, and these called his talents to the attention of John of Gaunt, the Duke of Lancaster (1340-1399), who was the son of King Edward III of England, uncle of Richard II, and father of Henry IV. Gaunt was married three times, first and most famously to Blanche of Lancaster in 1359, second to Constance of Castile in 1371, and third to Katherine Swynford in 1396.

Gaunt seems to have maintained a lifelong patronage of Chaucer, who composed *The Book of the Duchess* as a memorial to Gaunt's first wife Blanche (1345-1368), the mother of Henry IV. As noted above, Gaunt was so pleased with the work that he granted Chaucer a yearly "tun" of wine in thanks for his composition of this poem. Eventually, Chaucer and Gaunt were cousins through marriage, as Chaucer's wife Philippa de Roet was the sister of Gaunt's third wife Katherine.

The exact date of the poem as a memorial to Blanche, the Duchess of Lancaster, is a bit tentative. Blanche died on September 12, 1368, and the poem is usually dated somewhere between that date and some point in 1372 when Chaucer was likely at work on *The Parliament of Fowls* and on an ambassadorial mission to Italy. We have three other pieces of information that might set the date at 1374, 1380, or 1376: in 1374 Gaunt commissioned a double tomb and monument for himself and Blanche; in 1380 the work on these was completed;

and the poem itself describes how the dreamer (who arguably is Gaunt himself) has been unable to sleep for eight years, which might set the date at 1376. Though most Chaucerian scholars now tend to favor an earlier date of composition, it is hard to resist a scenario for presentation at court of this poem at a memorial service for Blanche.

Whatever the particulars of its composition may be, the poem offers us a memorable glimpse of the sorrowing Gaunt and his attempt to recall Blanche and his courtship with her. We see also how his struggle is underlined as the dreamer (a version of Chaucer, Gaunt himself, or some combination of the two) attempts to understand the grief of the knight, whose name is simply "Black," over the loss of his beloved "White." ("Blanche," of course, is French for white.) *The Book of the Duchess*, though an early work of Chaucer, is no minor accomplishment. The poignancy of the woeful Gaunt is balanced not only by Chaucer's masterful handling of a framing device of a restless narrator who reads the tale of Ceyx and Alcyone, a parallel to that of Gaunt and Blanche, but also by his adept portrayal of the relationship between the narrator/dreamer and the woeful knight. Likewise, Chaucer is able to describe Blanche in such a sympathetic but honest fashion that she is brought back into the lives of the members of court who loved her. Though Chaucer may have been as young as twenty-five at the time he wrote *The Book of the Duchess*, he was able to offer us a masterpiece about love and loss that is among the finest works of its kind ever written.

THE BOOK OF THE DUCHESS
ಠ

I wonder and wonder, by the light of the moon, how I stay alive, for I can hardly sleep at all, day or night. I have so many idle thoughts, all for lack of sleep, that, I swear, I care about nothing at all – whether anything comes or goes. There is nothing dear nor despised for me – it's all alike to me – joy or sorrow, it doesn't matter. For I feel nothing about anything, as if I am some sort of dazed thing, always on the brink of falling over; for sorrowful visions and images are always and everywhere fully in my mind.

And well you should know, it is against nature to live this way, for nature would not allow any earthly creature to endure for such a long time to be without sleep and in sorrow. And as I can not sleep, neither by night nor morning, I am melancholy and afraid that I shall die. Lack of sleep and heaviness[1] have slain my spirit of liveliness, so that I have lost all joy and vigor. My head is so full of fantasies that I don't know what's best to do.

But one might ask me why I can not sleep and what is wrong with me. But nonetheless, whoever asks this truly wastes his question. I, myself, can not tell why. But surely, the truth is that I maintain it is a sickness, I suppose, that I have suffered these eight years; and yet my remedy is never the nearer, for there is but one physician who can heal me. But enough about that. Let's pass over this until later. (What will not come about must be left behind.) It's best to return to our first subject.

So, recently, the other night, when I saw that I could not sleep, I sat up in my bed and bid someone to bring me a book,[2] a romance. And he brought it to me to read and drive the night away; for it seemed to me a better activity than playing either at chess or backgammon. And in this book were written fables that scholars and other poets had in old times (when people loved the law of nature) put into rhyme to be read and remembered. This book spoke primarily of the lives of queens and kings as well as many other smaller matters.

Among all this I found a tale that seemed to me an amazing thing. This was the tale. There was a king named Ceyx, and he had taken a wife, the best who ever lived, and this queen was named Alcyone. So it happened soon thereafter, this king would venture over the sea. To tell it shortly, when he was thus at sea, such a tempest rose up that their mast was broken and it toppled. It cleft their ship in two and drowned them all. They were never found, as the book says, ship nor man nor anything else. In this way this King Ceyx lost his life.

Now, to speak of Alcyone, his wife: this lady, who was left at home, wondered why the king didn't come home, for it was a long time. Soon her heart began to grieve, as she be-

[1] Heaviness. Spiritual heaviness (melancholy).
[2] Book. Probably *The Metamorphoses* by Ovid (43 BC – 18 AD).

4

lieved more and more that he did not fare well. She so longed for the king that it is a pitiful thing to tell the exceedingly sorrowful life that she, this noble wife, had, for, alas, she loved him best of all.

Soon she sent messengers to seek him both east and west, but they found nothing. "Alas!" she said, "that I was created! If only I could know whether or not my lord, my love, is dead. Surely, I will never eat one crumb of bread, I make a vow to my god here, unless I might hear of my lord!" Such sorrow this lady took to herself that, truly, I, the person who wrote this book, had such pity and such sorrow to read of her sorrow that, I swear, I fared all the worse the entire morning afterwards to think about her sorrow.

So when this lady received no word and as no man had found her lord, very often she swooned and cried "Alas!" When she was nearly out of her mind for sorrow, she could think of only one plan of action; she set down on her knees and wept so tenderly that it was a pity to hear. "O, mercy, sweet lady dear!" she said to Juno,[3] her goddess, "Help me out of this distress, and give me grace to see my lord soon, or to know where he may be, or how he fares, or in what manner, and I shall make you a sacrifice and with good will become wholly yours, body, heart, and all. And, if you would, lady sweet, please send me grace to sleep and to dream in my sleep a clear vision whereby I may know for certain whether my lord is alive or dead."

With that word she hung down her head and fell a-swoon, as cold as stone. Her women caught her up quickly, undressed her, and brought her to bed, and she, exhausted from weeping and lack of sleep, was so weary that a dead sleep fell on her before she noticed, thanks to Juno, who had heard her prayer and made her fall straight asleep. For as Alcyone prayed, just so was the deed done; for Juno immediately called her messenger[4] to do her errand, and he came without hesitation.

---

[3] Juno. The goddess of women and the wife of Jupiter. Also known as Hera.

[4] Messenger. Probably Iris, as mentioned in Chaucer's sources.

When he had come, she instructed him thus: "Go quickly," said Juno, "to Morpheus – you know him well, the god of sleep. Now listen carefully and remember well! Say this on my behalf: that he must go fast into the Great Sea,[5] and bid him that, above all, he take up Ceyx, the king's, body, which lies so pale and lacking all color. Bid him creep into that body and make it go to Alcyone the queen, where she lies alone, and show it to her briefly, so that there is no denying how he was drowned days ago. And make the body speak just as it used to do when it was alive. Go now quickly, and hurry!"

This messenger took leave, went upon his way, and never stopped until he came to the dark valley that stood between two rocks where there never grew wheat nor grass nor trees nor nothing that was anything. There was no beast, man, or anything else, but there were, running down from the cliffs, a few springs which made a lifeless, sleeping sound. And the waters ran down next to a cave that was carved under a rock amidst the deep valley. There these gods, Morpheus and Eclympasteyr (the god of sleep's son), who sleep and do no other work, lie and sleep. This cave was also as dark as the pit of hell all around. They had the fine leisure to snore away, as if to contend over who could sleep best. Some hung their chin upon their breast and slept upright, their head hidden, and some lay undressed in their bed and slept all day long.

This messenger came flying fast and cried, "Awake! Awake now!" It was all for nothing: nobody heard him there. "Awake!" he said, "who is lying there?" And then he blew his horn right in their ears and cried "Awake!" extremely loud.

This god of sleep looked up with his one eye and asked, "Who calls there?"

"It is I," said this messenger. "Juno instructed that you should go." And he told him what he should do (as I have told you before – there is no need to rehearse it again) and went his way when he had said this. Immediately this god of sleep

---

[5] Great Sea. The Mediterranean.

jumped out of his slumber and started to go, and did as he had been bidden to do: he took up the drowned body and bore it forth to Alcyone, his wife the queer, where she lay, exactly three hours before dawn, and stood at the foot of her bed.

And he called her by her very name and said, "My sweet wife, awake! Leave your sorrowful life, for in your sorrow there lies no remedy; for, surely, sweet, I am surely dead. You shall never see me alive. But, good sweet heart, see that you bury my body, for at a certain time you can find it beside the sea. Farewell, sweet, my world's bliss! I pray to God to lessen your sorrow. Our bliss lasts for so short a time!"

With that she cast up her eyes and saw nothing. "Alas!" she said for sorrow, and died within the third morning. But what else she said in that anguish I may not tell you now – it would be too long to dwell on it.

I will return you to my original subject, the reason why I have told this story of Alcyone and Ceyx the king, for I dare say this much: I would have been entirely buried and dead, because of lack of sleep, if I had not read and heeded this tale. And I will tell you why: for I could not, for comfort or suffering, sleep before I had read this tale of this drowned Ceyx the king and of the gods of sleeping. When I had read this tale well and looked over every bit of, it seemed amazing to me that it would be so, for I had never heard mention before then of any gods that could make people sleep, nor to wake, for I had known only one god.

Rather than I should so die through lack of sleep, I wished to make a gift to this Morpheus, or his goddess, Lady Juno, or some other creature, I cared not who. And in my amusement (and yet I had little desire to play) I said then, "Make me sleep and have some rest, and I will give him, or her, the best gift anyone ever hoped to receive. And into his possession, immediately, if he will make me sleep a little, I will give him a feather-bed of down of pure white doves, arrayed with gold and finely covered in fine black satin from abroad, and many pillows, and every pillowcase of linen from Reynes,[6] to sleep softly – he will not need to toss and turn so often. And I will give him everything that belongs to a bedchamber, and all his rooms I will have painted with pure gold and arrayed with many matching tapestries. All this shall he have (if only I knew where his cave is) if he can make me sleep soon, as he did for the goddess, queen Alcyone. And thus this same god, Morpheus, may gain from me more rewards than he ever won; and to Juno, who is his goddess, I shall so do, I believe, whatever will please her."

I had hardly said that word, exactly as I have told it to you, that suddenly, I know not how, such a desire overtook me to sleep that I fell asleep right on my book, and then I dreamed so inwardly sweet a dream, so wonderful a dream that I believe that no one has ever had the insight to interpret my dream correctly. No, not Joseph of Egypt,[7] without a doubt, who interpreted the Pharaoh's dream – no more than could the least of us; no, not even Macrobius[8] (who wrote all of the vision that he dreamed, about King Scipio the African, the noble man, of such marvels that happened then), could even interpret my dreams, I believe. Lo, thus it was; this was my dream.

It seemed this way to me: that it was May, and in the dawning of day I lay (I dreamed this) in my bed all undressed and looked about, for I was waked by a great heap of small birds that had startled me out of my sleep through the sound and sweetness of their song. And, as I dreamed, they sat together upon my chamber roof outside, upon the tiles, all over,

---

[6] Reynes. In France. Famous for its textiles.

[7] Joseph of Egypt. Interpreted the Pharaoh of Egypt's dreams. See Genesis 41.

[8] Macrobius. *The Dream of Scipio* was originally written by the Roman Cicero in the sixth book of *On the Commonwealth* and later expanded via lengthy commentary by Macrobius. In the dream the Roman general Scipio Aemilianus (185 BC – 129 BC), visited by the spirit of his grandfather, Scipio Africanus (236 BC – 183 BC), victor of the Second Punic War, is shown a vision of the universe. The topic of the work is the discordant and limited nature of human existence in a world which is otherwise harmonious. Scipio appears also in *Parliament of Fowls.*

and sang, each one in its own manner, the most solemn service, in harmony, that ever a person, I believe, has heard, for some of them sang low, some high, and all of one accord. In short, in a word, there was never heard so sweet a voice unless it had been a creation of heaven – so merry a sound, so sweet the tunes, that surely I would not have believed it for all the town of Tunis[9] unless I had heard them sing. For all of my chamber began to ring through the singing of their harmony. There was nowhere to be heard a sound half so sweet in instrument or voice, nor half as agreeable. For none of them pretended to sing, as each of them made great pains to find merry and skillful notes. They spared not their throats.

And the truth be told, my chamber was carefully decorated with pictures, and with glass were all the windows brightly glazed, not a flaw in any of them, so that to behold them it was a great joy. For the entire story of Troy[10] was wrought in the glasswork thus: of Hector and of King Priam, of Achilles and of King Laomedon, and also of Medea and of Jason, of Paris, Helen, and of Lavinia. And on all the walls were painted with fine colors the entire Romance of the Rose,[11]

---

[9] Tunis. He is punning: Tunis, tunes, towns. Tunis is in northern Africa.

[10] Troy. Of the Trojan War. The ancient war between the Greeks (or Achaeans) and the Trojans, which was fought over Helen, wife of Menelaus, the King of Sparta, whose wife was seduced and taken by the Trojan prince Paris back to Troy. The story is best-known from its telling in Homer's *Iliad* and *Odyssey* and Vergil's *Aeneid*. Hector was the military champion of Troy and son to Priam, king of Troy, who was the son of Laomedon. Achilles was the military champion of the Greeks who eventually slew Hector. Aeneas was the Trojan prince, nephew of Priam, who, upon the fall and destruction of Troy, sailed to Italy and founded what eventually became the Roman Empire. There he married Lavinia. Medea, magician and princess of Colchis, who married Jason, leader of the Argonauts who sought and won the Golden Fleece (with Medea's help), but later, after they were married and had two children, he deserted her. Eventually she killed Jason, his lover, and her own two children by Jason.

[11] *Romance of the Rose.* The most famous medieval French poem (which Chaucer translated). Written by Guillaume de Lorris (1200 – c . 1240) and Jean de Meun (c. 1240 – c. 1305), it encompasses "all the art of love."

both text and gloss.[12] My windows were all shut, and through the glass the sun shone upon my bed with bright beams, with many pleasant golden streams. And the sky was so fair, blue and bright, the air was clear and truly temperate, for it was neither too hot nor too cold, and there was not a cloud in the sky.

And as I lay thus, I thought I heard a hunter attempt to blow his horn tremendously loud to tell if the horn were clear or hoarse in its sound. And I heard men, horses, hounds, and other things going up and down, and all the men speaking of hunting – how they would slay the hart with their strength, and how the hart would at length become exhausted from the hunt – I don't remember what else.

As soon as I heard that, how they would go a-hunting, I was rather glad, and right away I took my horse and went forth out of my chamber. I never stopped until I came to the field outside. There I overtook a great company of hunters and foresters, with many chasing hounds and tracking hounds. They rushed to the forest, and I, with them. So finally I asked one of them who led a tracking dog: "Say, fellow, who shall hunt here?" I said.

And he answered, "Sir, the Emperor Octavian,[13] and he is near here."

"In God's name, in good time!" I said, "Let's go quickly!" and began to ride. When we came to the edge of the forest, every man right away went about doing what hunters are supposed to do. The master-hunter then, without delay, blew three notes with a great horn at the release of his hounds. Within a while the hart was sought, halooed after, and pursued for a great time; and so, at last, this hart deceived them and stole away from all the hounds a secret way. The hounds had overshot him completely and were defeated because of the

---

[12] Gloss. A footnote or commentary on the text.

[13] Octavian. Augustus Caesar (63 BC – 14 AD), adopted son of Julius Caesar and first emperor of the Roman Empire, which he ruled from 27 BC until his death in 14 AD.

lack of a scent. And so, at last, the hunter quickly blew his horn.

I walked away from my assigned tree,[14] and as I went, there came near me a whelp, that fawned on me as I stood there. It had followed me and did not know what to do. It came and crept toward me humbly, just as if it had known me. He held down his head and put back his ears and laid his hair down all smooth. I wanted to catch him, but quickly he fled from me and was gone. And I followed him, and it went forth down by a flowery green path, soft under my feet, thick with grass, soft and sweet, with many flowers, and rarely tread upon. So it seemed, for both Flora and Zephirus[15] – the two who make flowers grow, had made their dwelling there, I believe; for it was, to behold it, as though the earth would contend to be more ornate than the heavens, as it had more flowers, seven times as many, as there are stars in the sky. It had forgotten the poverty that Winter, through his cold mornings, had made it suffer, and the sorrows he brought; all was forgotten, and that was visible, for all the woods had grown green; the sweetness of the dew had made it grow.

There is no need to ask me if there were many green branches or thickets of trees full of leaves; every tree stood by itself, ten to twelve feet from the next. Such great trees, such immense strength; of forty or fifty fathoms high, neatly maintained, without a stray bough or twig, with crowns equally broad and thick – they were not an inch apart, so that it was entirely shady underneath. And many harts and hinds[16] were both before me and behind. The wood was full of fawns, sorrels, bucks, and does, as were there many roes, and many squirrels that sat high upon the trees and ate, making many feasts in their own fashion. In short, it was so full of beasts

---

[14] Tree. He was posted, for the purpose of the hunt, at a tree, towards which, supposedly, the hart would be driven.

[15] Flora and Zephirus. The beginning of Spring: when Chloris, the cold earth, is warmed by Zephirus, the West Wind, the flowers (Flora) return(s).

[16] Hart and Hind. Male and female deer.

that, even if Algus, the noble mathematician,[17] were to sit in his counting house and calculate with his ten numerals – for by those numerals all may learn, if they are sharp enough, to count and calculate – he would still fail to calculate correctly the wonders I dreamed in my dream.

But I roamed very quickly through the wood, until at last I became aware of a man in black, who had turned his back to a huge oak tree and sat. "Lord," thought I, "who may that be? What ails him to sit here so?" Quickly I drew up close to him; then I found him sitting upright, a striking, attractive knight – so was my impression of him – well-proportioned, and moreover rather young, twenty-four years old,[18] with little hair in his beard, and he was clothed all in black.

I stalked directly behind him and I stood there as still as possible, so that, to tell the truth, he didn't see me; so he hung his head down, and with a deadly sorrowful sound he made a complaint[19] of ten or twelve rhymed verses to himself, the most pitiful, the most doleful, I ever heard; for, I swear, it is a great wonder that Nature might allow any creature to have such sorrow and not be dead. So piteously pale[20] and lacking any ruddiness, he spoke his lay, a kind of tune, without music, without song; and this was it, for I can repeat it word for word – it began like this:

"I am by sorrow so much undone
That I get joy forever none,
Now that I see my lady bright,
Whom I have loved with all my might,
Is from me dead and is gone.

---

[17] Algus. The ninth-century inventor of Arabic numerals.

[18] Twenty-four years old. John of Gaunt was twenty-eight at the time of Blanche's death.

[19] Complaint. A type of poetry which expresses sorrow or hardship.

[20] Pale. This may signify that he, like the figure on whom he was based, was gaunt, or Gaunt.

"Alas, death, what so ails thee,
That thou wouldn't have taken me,
When thou took my lady dear,
That was so fair, so fresh, so free,[21]
So good that all may well see
Of all good folk she had no peer!"

When he had thus made his complaint, his sorrowful heart quickly became faint and his spirits grew dead; his blood had fled, for pure dread, down to his heart, to make him warm – for well it felt the heart had grief – to learn also why it was terrified, by nature, and to make it glad again, for it is the principal organ of the body. And this rush of blood made his entire hue change and grow green and pale, for there was no blood to be seen in any of his limbs.

As soon as I saw this – he fared so poorly, as he sat there – I went and stood right at his feet and greeted him; he spoke nothing, but argued with his own thoughts, and in his mind disputed firmly why and how his life might continue, as his sorrows seemed to him so painful and lay so coldly on his heart. So, his sorrow and gloomy thoughts made him so that he did not hear me – for he had pretty nearly lost his mind; even Pan,[22] whom we call the god of nature, was never so disturbed for his sorrows.

But at last, to tell the absolute truth, he became aware of me, as I stood before him and took off my hood, and had greeted him courteously and humbly, as best I knew how. He said, "I pray you, be not upset. I heard you not, to tell the truth, nor did I see you, sir, truly."

"Ah, good sir, it does not matter," I said, "I am quite sorry if I have at all disturbed you from your thought. Forgive me, if I have made a mistake."

"Yes, but it is easy to make amends," he said, "for no of-

---

[21] Free. Noble.
[22] Pan. Lost his beloved Syrinx when she was turned into the reeds. He then created a musical instrument (the pan-flute) by twining together seven reeds.

fense has been taken; nothing wrong has been said or done."

Lo, how well this knight spoke, as if it had been another person; he presented himself as neither blunt nor strange. As I noticed this, I began to acquaint myself with him, and he seemed to me, for all his suffering, so agreeable, so very knowledgeable and reasonable. Straightaway I began to search, to look where I might, for a worthy subject for discussion, so that I could get to know him better.

"Sir," I said, "this game is done. I maintain that this hart is gone; these hunters can find him nowhere."

"I do not care about that," he said; "my thoughts are not the least bit on that."

"By our Lord," I said, "I believe you well; that seems plain to me in your face. But, sir, will you listen to one thing? It seems to me I see you in great sorrow; but surely, sir, if you would reveal to me your woe, I would remedy it, if I can or may. You can test it by trying; for, by my word, to make you whole and well, I will give it all of my power. Please tell me of your painful sorrows; by chance it may ease your heart, which seems so sick within."

With that he looked on me askance, as one who says, "No, that will not be."

"Grant mercy, good friend," he said, "I thank you for wishing it so, but it may not be done so soon. No one may lighten my sorrow, which makes my hue to lessen and fade, and which has made me to lose my understanding, so that I am woeful that I was ever born! Nothing can make my sorrows slide away, not all the remedies of Ovid,[23] nor Orpheus,[24] the god of music, nor Daedalus with his ingenious

---

[23] Ovid. Roman author (43 BC – 18 AD) of the *Remedies of Love*, more famous for his *Metamorphoses*.

[24] Orpheus. Well-known for his love of Euridice, who, bitten by a snake, is taken to the underworld, Hades, where she is rescued by Orpheus, whose beautiful lyre music pleases (or puts to sleep) the god of the underworld. As they exit the underworld, Orpheus looks back at his wife, and she must return to Hades, where Orpheus later joins her after his own death. In the

inventions;[25] no physician may heal me, not Hippocrates nor Galen.[26] Woe is me that I should live even another twelve hours! But whoever wishes to try his hand to see if his heart can have pity for my sorrow, let him see me. I am a wretch whom death has stripped naked of all the bliss that ever I had and made lowest of all creatures, so much so that I hate all my days and my nights!

"All my pleasures, indeed, my whole life, are loathsome to me, for myself and my welfare are at odds. Death itself is so surely my foe that if I would say I want to die, he would say no; for when I pursue him, he flees; I wish to have him, but he will not have me. This is my pain without comfort, always dying and not dead, and so much so that not even Sisyphus,[27] who lies in hell, has no more sorrow to tell. And whosoever might come to know all my sorrow, I swear, unless he should sympathize and take pity on my painful sorrows, that man has a fiendish heart. For whosoever sees me tomorrow may say he has met with Sorrow, for I am Sorrow, and Sorrow is I.

"Alas! And I will tell you why: why my song is turned to lament, my laughter to weeping, my glad thoughts to sad ones; why all my work is also my idleness and my rest; why my wellness is woe, my good is harm; and why my joyful pastimes are turned into wrath, my delight into sorrow. So too my good health is turned into sickness, my security into dread, all my light to dark; my wit is folly, my day is night, my love is hate, my sleep waking, my mirth and meals are fasting; my self-confidence is turned to foolishness and I am entirely disconcerted, wherever I may be; my peace is turned into lawsuits and war.

---

medieval version of *Sir Orfeo*, she was snatched by the fairy king, and, after the descent to the underworld, Orfeo and Heurodis live happily ever after.

[25] Daedalus. Mythical inventor (whose name means "cunning inventor"). Invented wings with which his son Icarus could fly. But Icarus flew too close to the sun, the wax on them melted, and he plunged to his death.

[26] Hippocrates, Galen. Famous Greek and Roman physicians. (Thus the Hippocratic Oath.)

[27] Sisyphus. For his misdeeds on earth, his punishment in Hades, was to roll to the top of a hill a large stone, which then rolled down again.

"Alas, how would I ever fare in war? My boldness is turned to shame, for false Fortune has played a game of chess with me. Alas, the time it happened! The traitoress, false and full of guile, she who promises everything and delivers nothing, who walks upright and still limps, who squints so foully and still looks lovely, the disdainful and gracious one, who scorns so many creatures! She is an idol of false self-portraiture, for she would gladly deceive; she is the monster's head pleasantly disguised, like a dung-heap over-strewn with flowers. Her most innate and representative quality is her lying, for that is her nature; she is false – without sincerity, lawfulness, or moderation, as she is ever laughing with one eye, and weeping with the other. Whatever rises, she knocks down. I liken her to the scorpion, a false, flattering beast, for with his head he makes merry, but as he is flattering you, he will sting and envenom you. Fortune is the hostile charity, who is always false and seems true. So she turns her false wheel around, for it never remains stationary – at one moment you are being served at the table, at another you are a servant standing by the fire. She has blinded many: she is an enchantress, who seems to be one thing and is another.

"The false thief! What has she done? What do you suppose? By our Lord I will tell you: she began to play with me at chess; and with her various little cheating moves, she tricked me and stole away my queen. And when I saw my queen had been taken away, alas, I could not figure out how to continue playing, but said, 'Farewell, sweet, surely, and farewell everything, now and forever!'

"At that moment Fortune said, 'Check her!' And checkmated me, with an errant pawn, in the mid-point of the checker board! Alas, craftier at play was she than Attalus,[28] so was his name, who invented the game of chess. But I wish to God that I could have understood, just once or twice, the chess

---

[28] Attalus. Attalus Asiaticus or Attalus Philometor (c. 170 BC – 133 BC), king of Pergamon (modern Turkey).

problems the way that the Greek Pythagoras[29] might have. I should have played better at chess and thereby kept my queen better. But what does it matter? For truly, I say that wish isn't worth a straw! It would have turned out no better for me, for Fortune knows so many tricks that there are few who can beguile her; and she is also the less to blame; myself, I would have done the same, as God is my witness, had I been her; she ought, I suppose, to be more excused than me. For I must say a bit more about this: had I been God and might have done as I wished when she captured my queen I would have made the same move. For, as surely as God may give me rest, I dare well swear she took the best. But through that move I have lost my bliss; alas, that I was born!

"Forevermore, I truly believe, in spite of all my wishes, my joy is entirely reversed; but yet, what can I do? By our Lord, the only option seems to be to die soon. For I care nothing about anything, but live and die right in this thought; for there is no planet in the firmament, nor in the air nor in the earth or elements, that does not give me a gift of weeping when I am alone. For when I consider everything, how there is nothing owing to me in matters of sorrow, and how there exists no merriment that may relieve me of my distress, and how I have lost all my contentment, and how for all that I have no delight, then may I say I have absolutely nothing. And when all this comes into my mind, alas, then I am overcome! For whatever is done can not be changed. I have more sorrow than Tantalus."[30]

And when I heard him tell this tale so pitifully, as I have told you, hardly could I remain there longer, as it gave my heart so much woe. "Ah, good sir," I said, "do not say so!

---

[29] Pythagoras. Greek philosopher (c. 570 BC – c. 495 BC) and ruler who greatly advanced fields of mathematics and geometry.
[30] Tantalus. For stealing the nectar of the gods and for revealing their secrets, he was punished by being placed, hungry and thirsty, in Hades, under fruit trees which moved when he tried to pick them and in a river which receded when he tried to drink it.

Have some pity on Nature, which formed you as a creature. Remember Socrates,[31] for he considered anything that Fortune could do to be worth three straws."

"No," he said, "I don't think so."

"Why so, good sir? Yes, by God!" I said; "do not say so, for truly, even if you had lost twelve queens, and you murdered yourself for sorrow, you should be damned in this case, as was Medea, who slew her children on account of Jason;[32] and Phyllis, who was so desperate that she hung herself for Demophon,[33] for he had broken his appointed day to come to her. Another such rage had Dido, the queen of Carthage, who, because Aeneas was false to her, slew herself – for which she was a fool![34] And Echo died because Narcissus would not love her,[35] and likewise have many others done such folly; and Samson, who slew himself with a pillar, died for Delilah.[36] But there is no man alive today who would undergo such woe for a queen!"

"Why so?" he said, "it is not so. You know full little what you mean by your words; I have lost more than you think."

"Lo, tell me how that may be?" I said; "Good sir, tell me entirely, how, why, by what cause, and in what ways you have

---

[31] Socrates. Greek philosopher (470/469 BC – 399 BC) who argued that self-control, not Fortune, brought us pleasure.

[32] Medea and Jason. Knowing that her children would be slain by Jason's followers – since she had just slain Jason (unfaithful to her) and his bride – Medea slew her children.

[33] Phyllis…Demophon. Thracian princess who married this Athenian king. Their tragic tale is told in *The Legend of Good Women*.

[34] Dido and Aeneas. Their love is the topic of the opening books of Vergil's *Aeneid*. Though he pledged himself to Dido, Aeneas deserted her when he was reminded of his divine mission to found Rome.

[35] Echo and Narcissus. Narcissus, a beautiful youth, would love none but his own reflection in the water. Echo died of unrequited love for him.

[36] Samson and Delilah. Biblical story (twelfth century BC) in which the strong man Samson is betrayed by the enemy Delilah, who seduces him to find out the secret of his strength (his hair) and cuts his hair, enabling the Philistines to capture and blind him. When he later pulls down the pillars of the Temple of Dagon, he is killed along with many of the Philistines.

thus lost your bliss."

"Gladly," he said; "come sit down! I'll tell you upon the condition that you shall wholly, with all your wit, carry out your intention to listen carefully to it."

"Yes, sir."

"Swear your promise to do so."

"Gladly."

"Then you better keep your word."

"I shall, with great joy, God save me, wholly, with all the wit I have, listen to you as well as I can."

"In God's name!" he said, and began. "Sir," he said, "ever since I first could in my youth by learning or natural understanding in any way comprehend what love was, doubtless, I have ever since been a vassal to and paid tribute to Love, with entirely good intentions, and with great pleasure become his servant, body, heart, and soul, with good will. All this I committed to his service and did homage to him as my lord; and I prayed to him devoutly that he might employ my heart in such a way that it would be a delight to him and an honor to my dear lady.

"And I remained in his service many years before my heart was set anywhere in particular, and I knew not why; I believe it came to me naturally. Perhaps I was most capable in this respect, as is a white wall or slate, for it is ready to accept and receive anything that one will put there, whatever one wishes to paint or portray, no matter how elaborate the works may be.

"And at this time I fared well, so that I was able to have learned all about love, and I learned it as well or better than any other art or science; as love always came first in my mind, I never forgot it. I chose love as my first craft; therefore it has remained with me. Since I took it up at such a young age, my heart had no trouble with it, and time did not erase it, as I had studied too much for that to happen. Up to that time, Youth, my governess, instructed me in idleness; for it was in my early youth, and I knew very little worth knowing then, for all my works were impermanent at that time, and all my thoughts were changeable. Everything that I knew then was equally good; but that is how it was.

"It happened that I came one day into a place where I saw truly the fairest company of ladies assembled in one place that ever a man had seen with eye. Shall I call it chance or grace that brought me there? No, only Fortune, who is so accustomed to lie, the false perverse traitoress! I wish to God I could call her worse, for now she makes me woeful, and I will soon tell you why.

"Among these ladies, to tell the truth, I saw one who was like none of the rest; for I dare swear, without a doubt, that as the summer's bright sun is fairer, clearer, and has more light than any other planet in the heavens, the moon or the seven stars,[37] so had she, for all the world, surmounted them all in beauty, in demeanor, in graciousness, in stature, in cheerfulness – in short, in excellence so well bestowed upon her – what more can I say? By God and his twelve apostles, this was my sweet, her very self. She had such a steadfast countenance, such noble deportment and bearing, and Love, who had listened so carefully to my request, had looked upon me so quickly, that she was, so help me God, so swiftly caught in my mind that I didn't need to ask for advice from anywhere, but only looked to her and to my heart; for when her eyes so gladly beheld my heart, I believe, my own thought then, without a doubt, said it would be better to serve her for nothing than to serve another and be well-rewarded. And it was so, for I will tell you why right now in full detail.

"I saw her dance so becomingly, to sing and join in carols so sweetly, to laugh and play so womanly, to carry herself so graciously, and to speak so friendly and kindly, that surely I believe that never was seen so blissful a treasure as she. For every hair on her head, to tell the truth, was not red or yellow or brown; it seemed most like gold.

"And what eyes my lady had! Stately, kind, glad, sincere,

---

[37] Seven stars. Probably the seven other known heavenly bodies in the Milky Way; or, perhaps the Pleiades.

and true, well-proportioned, and not too wide. Thus her eyes looked directly, not aside or askance, but so carefully settled on things that they entirely ennobled everything they beheld. Her eyes seemed to say that she would have mercy[38] on me – fools would think so – but she would never do so hastily. But her look was not counterfeit; it was her own pure way of looking, a way in which the goddess, Lady Nature, had made her eyes open and close moderately; for even if she was delighted, her glances were not spread about foolishly or wildly, even if she was being playful; but, it seemed to me, her eyes said, 'By God, all of my ill-will is gone!'

"In this way she loved to live so fully that dullness was afraid of her. She was not too sober nor too glad; in all things she had more moderation, I believe, than any other creature. She hurt many men with her look, but that sat lightly on her heart, for she knew nothing of their thoughts; but whether she knew it or not, she nonetheless considered it as much as she would a piece of straw! To get her love, no nearer was he who dwelled at home than he who was in India; the first in line was always the last. But she loved good people, above all others, as one may love his brother; and she was very generous in this kind of love, especially in appropriate times and places.

"But what a face had she! Alas, my heart is so woeful that I can't describe it! I lack both the English and the wit to unfold it fully; and my spirits are also too dull for me to devise so great a thing. I have no wit that can suffice to comprehend her beauty. But I dare say this much, that she had a fresh, lively complexion, and every day her beauty renewed. And her face was nearly the best of all, for surely Nature had such desire to make her face so beautiful that truly she was the chief example and pattern of Nature's beauty – and of all her work; for though her image seems so dark and distant, I think I see her always. And, moreover, even if everyone who ever lived were now alive, they would be unable to discover any

---

[38] Mercy. In the language of courtly love, for a woman to have mercy on a man is to allow him fully into her heart.

fault, any wicked sign, in her face, for it was sincere, honest, and kind.

"And such a fine, soft voice had my sweet one, the savior[39] of my life! So friendly, and so well-instructed, so well-grounded in reason, and so agreeable to all good people that, I dare well swear, by the cross, there was never found such eloquent speech, nor so sweet a tongue, nor one that scorned others less, nor could heal them more nor less falseness in her word, that in her simple promise alone was found as true as any bond or oath from any man's hand; nor could she chide anyone, not even one word. (I swear by the holy mass – even if the Pope himself sang it – that there was never any man nor woman harmed by her tongue; and as for her, all harm was hidden from her.) The whole world knows this well.

"But such a lovely neck had that sweet one, every inch perfectly shaped, without a blemish. It was white, smooth, straight, and even, without hollows or collar-bone, as it seems she had none. Her throat, as I remember, seemed a round tower of ivory, full, but not too full.

"And she was called the good fair 'White.' Truly that was my lady's name. She was both fair and bright; there was nothing inaccurate about her name. She had nice soft shoulders and a long body, and arms as well; every limb was well-rounded and fleshy, but not too much so; nice white hands, and red nails; round breasts; and firm broad hips; and a straight, flat back. I knew of no other fault, as far as I could tell, other than her limbs were not perfectly in proportion.

"She knew how to present herself so well, when she pleased, that I dare say that she was like a bright lamp from which everyone might receive an abundance of light, and never less. In manners and behavior my lady was so excellent that anyone who caught a glimpse of her remembered her fully; for I dare well swear, if she had been one among ten thousand standing in a row at a feast, she would have been, at the least, a chief paragon in the eyes of all; for wherever peo-

---

[39] Savior. Chaucer uses the word "leche," which means physician or healer.

ple gathered together without her, it seemed to me that the company was entirely lacking, like a crown without gemstones. Truly she was to my eye the solitary Phoenix of Arabia,[40] for there is only one of those, and I know of none other like her.

"To speak of goodness, truly she had as much graciousness as ever had Esther[41] in the Bible, and more, if more were possible. And, to tell the truth, she had in this way a wit so congenial, so fully inclined to goodness, that all her thoughts were fixed, by the Cross, without malice and upon gladness; and thus I never saw one less harmful than she. I don't mean that she did not know what harm was, or else she would not have known so well what good was.

"And truly, speaking of truth, if she had not truth, it would have been a pity. She had such a great portion of truth – and I dare well swear it – that Truth himself had chosen her, over one and all, as his principal manor and resting place. And thus she gracefully and calmly persevered, reigning the most moderately I have ever seen, so kind and tolerant was her mind; and she gladly understood reason; and, of course, she knew goodness well. She would do good deeds gladly; these were her custom in everything.

"Since she loved justice so well, she would do no wrong to anyone. No creature could do any shame to her, as she loved and honored her own name. She would not encourage anyone with false hopes, nor, be sure of this, would she strive to hold any creature in suspense with half-truths or false-seeming – unless anyone would lie about her. She sent no men to Rumania, Prussia, Mongolia, Alexandria, or Turkey, nor bid him to rush off and go bare-headed into the Gobi Desert and come home the long way, by the Kara-Nor, and say, 'Sir,

---

[40] Phoenix. In legends of the Phoenix, the bird which consumes itself in fire then is reborn of its own ashes, there is much emphasis placed on its solitary nature.

[41] Esther. Ancient Persian ruler and Old Testament model of wifely virtue and bravery (fifth century BC).

be sure that you have praiseworthy deeds to report before you return here!' She used no such petty tricks.

"But why do I tell my tale? For this very reason, as I have said: my love was entirely set on her. For surely she was, this sweet wife, my source of contentment, my joy, my life, my good fortune, my health, and all my blessing, the welfare of the world, and my goddess, and I was wholly hers, body and soul."

"By our Lord," I said, "I well believe you! Assuredly, your love was well bestowed; I don't know how you might have done better."

"Better? No creature has ever done half so well," he said.

"I understand it well, sir," I said, "by God!"

"No, *believe* it well!"

"Sir, yes, I do; I believe you well, that truly you thought that she was the best, and the fairest of all to behold, for anyone who looked on her with your eyes."

"With *my eyes*? No, *all* saw her said and swore it was so. And even if they had not, I would still have loved my noble lady best. And even if I had had all the beauty that Alcibiades[42] ever had; all the strength of Hercules; all the worthiness of Alexander;[43] all the riches that ever were in Babylon, Carthage, Macedonia, Rome, or Ninevah; all the courage of Hector[44] (whom Achilles slew at Troy, and so too was he slain in a temple, for both he and Antilochus were slain – so says Dares Frygius[45] – for the love of Polixena);[46] or all the

---

[42] Alcibiades. Athenian politician, orator, and military tactician (c. 450 BC – 404 BC), remembered also for his good looks.

[43] Alexander. Alexander the Great of Macedon (356 BC – 323 BC), ruler of much of the Eastern Mediterranean in the fourth century BC.

[44] Hector. Trojan hero. His death at the hands of Achilles is the climax of *The Iliad*.

[45] Dares Frygius. Trojan priest and author of *History of the Fall of Troy,* which claims to be an eye-witness account of the war, one of the sources of Chaucer's *Troilus and Criseyde*. Sometimes spelled Dares Phrygius.

[46] Achilles. For Achilles' killing of Troilus and Hector, Antilochus and Achilles were ambushed at the temple of Apollo, where Achilles had wished to marry Polixena.

wisdom of Minerva, I would forever, without a doubt, have loved her, for I must.

"'*Must?*' No, truly, I speak nonsense now; Not '*must*' – and I will explain why: because my heart *wished* it through good *will*, and because I was obliged to love her as the fairest and the best. She was as good, God rest my soul, as ever was Penelope[47] of Greece, or as the noble wife Lucrece,[48] who was the best (so says the Roman, Titus Livius).[49] She was as good, though nothing like her, except in goodness (though their stories are true); nonetheless she was as faithful as Lucrece.

"But why don't I tell you about the first time I saw my lady? I was rather young, to tell the truth, and still in great need of learning; when my heart would yearn to love, it was a great enterprise. As fitting with my young childlike mind, I boldly set all my mental energy, as well as my brain could manage, on loving her in the best way I knew how, to honor and serve her in the best way I knew at the time, I swear, without being false or slothful in any way, for I wished to see her more than anything. So greatly did seeing her affect me that when I first saw her in the morning I was cured of all my sorrow for the entire day; even into the evening it seemed nothing could grieve me, regardless of how painful my sorrows might be. And yet she sat so in my heart that, I swear, I would not for all the world leave this lady out of my thought; no, truly!"

"Now, I swear, sir," I said, "it seems to me you are in such a position to make your confession without repentance."

"Repentance? No, fy on that!" he said, "Should I now

---

[47] Penelope. Faithful wife of Odysseus, hero of *The Odyssey*. She waited him, though he was gone for twenty years and many men sought her hand.

[48] Lucrece. Faithful wife of Collatinus. Raped by Sextus Tarquinius, son of Lucius Tarquinius Superbus, the seventh and last king of Rome. Rather than endure the consequences, she took her life, c. 510 BC. She revealed the crime to her family and then took her life. Her revelation led to the deposing of the ruling family and the institution of the Roman Republic.

[49] Titus Livius. Livy (59 BC – 17 AD), author of *Ab Urbe Condita* (*From the Founding of the City*), which included the story of Lucrece, or Lucretia.

repent my love? No, surely! I'd be worse off than Achitophel,[50] or Antenor,[51] (the traitor who betrayed Troy), or the false Ganelon,[52] (who secured the treason of Roland and Oliver). No, while I am alive here, I will not forget her – nevermore."

"Now, good sir," I said then, "You have told me well before; there's no need to repeat again how you first saw her, and where. But would you tell me the manner in which you first spoke with her – this I ask you – and how she first came to know your thoughts, whether you loved her or not? And tell me also what you have lost, as I heard you mention earlier."

"Yes!" he said, "you know not what you mean by your words; I have lost more than you think."

"What loss is that?" I said then; "Will she not love you? Is it so? Or have you done something wrong, that she has left you? Is it this? For God's love, tell me everything."

"Before God," he said, "I shall do so. I say, just as I have said, on her was all my love bestowed, and yet she did not know it, not a bit, not for a long time, believe me! For be assured, I wouldn't dare, not for all this world, reveal my thoughts to her, nor would I have upset her, truly. Would you like to know why? She had control over my body: as she held my heart, I could not escape. But to keep myself from idleness, I went about my business in making songs, as best I knew how, and often I sang them aloud; and I made a great number of songs, although I could not make them so well, as I didn't know all the art of it, as did Lamech's son Tubal,[53] who

---

[50] Achitophel. Counseled Absalom to rebel against his father David. The rebellion failed, and Absalom was killed in the Battle of Ephraim Wood, tenth century BC. See 2 Samuel 17.

[51] Antenor. His treachery caused the downfall of Troy. As a peace offering, he sent the statue of Pallas Athene, the patron of Troy, to Ulysses.

[52] Ganelon. His treachery caused the great French hero Roland to be slain by the Saracens in the Battle of Roncevaux (or Roncesvalles), 778 AD, as told in *The Song of Roland*.

[53] Lamech's son Tubal. Actually Jubal: called the "father of all such as handle the harp and organ" (Genesis 4.21).

originated the art of song (according to the *Aurora*);[54]) for as his brother's hammers rang up and down upon the anvil, from this he took the first tune – though Greeks say it was Pythagoras[55] who was the founder of the art; but what does that matter? Nevertheless, I made songs from my feelings to gladden my heart. And listen, here was the first of all – and perhaps the worst of all:

'Lord, it makes my heart light
When I think on that sweet wight[56]
Who is so lovely to see;
And wish to God it might so be
That she would have me for her knight,
My lady, who is so fair and bright!'

"Now have I told you, to tell the truth, my first song. One day I thought to myself about the woe and sorrow I suffered to that point for her, and yet she knew nothing about it, nor did I yet tell her my thoughts.

"'Alas,' I thought, 'I know no remedy; unless I tell her, I am nothing but dead; and if I tell her, to tell the very truth, I am afraid she will be upset with me. Alas, what shall I do then?'

"I was so woeful in this debate, it seemed my heart would burst in two! So, at long last, to tell the truth, I determined that Nature never formed in any creature so much beauty, truly, and goodness, without mercy. In hope of that, I made my speech to her, but I told it badly and in a way that I never should have: for necessity, and against my own advising, I had to tell her, or die. I can hardly remember how I began; I can

---

[54] Aurora. Twelfth-century versified Latin paraphrase and commentary on parts of the Bible by Peter of Riga (1140-1209).
[55] Pythagoras. Greek philosopher (c. 570 BC – c. 495 BC) and ruler who greatly advanced fields of mathematics and geometry. He is reputed to have formulated Pythagorean tuning for reading and recording music.
[56] Wight. Creature, person.

retell it only hazily; and, so help me God, I think it was an unlucky day – there were *ten* wounds of Egypt that day[57] – for I skipped, out of pure fear, over many words in my speech, lest my words would be poorly said. With sorrowful heart and deadly wounds, quaking meekly for pure fear and shame, stammering in my speech, and growing entirely pale in hue – I often grew both pale and red – bowing to her, I hung my head; I dared not once to look on her, for my wits, manners, and everything were gone. I said 'Mercy!' and no more. It was not amusing; it sat sorely on me.

"So at last, to tell the truth, when my heart returned to me, to summarize, with all my heart I beseeched her to be my sweet lady; and swore, and promised her heartily to be always steadfast and true, and to love her always newly, freshly, and never have any other lady, and to preserve her honor, as best I could. I swore this to her: 'For your honor is all that ever there is for me evermore, my heart sweet! And I'll never be false to you, unless I am dreaming, so help me, dear God!'

"And when I had completed my speech, God knows, she valued it not so much as a straw, so it seemed. To be brief, her answer, truly, was this – I can not now counterfeit her words, but this was the main point of her answer: she utterly said 'No.' Alas, the sorrow and the woe I suffered that day, so much so that truly Cassandra,[58] who so bewailed the destruction of Troy and of Ilium,[59] never had such sorrow as I did then. I dared not say another word at that point, for pure fear, but stole away; and thus I lived many a day, so that truly I had no need to go further than the head of my bed to seek sorrow;

---

[57] Ten wounds of Egypt. According to a late medieval belief, there were two unlucky days (*di[e]s mal* in French) per month, on which people were afflicted with wounds or plagues (as were the Egyptians in the time of Abraham). Black is having ten of these days at once.

[58] Cassandra. Trojan prophetess, sister of Hector and Troilus. Was given the gift of prophesy by Apollo, who, when she spurned his love, condemned her to the fate that no one would believe her predictions.

[59] Ilium. Sometimes referred to as he citadel or fortress of Troy; other times, as the royal palace.

I found sorrow readily every morning, as my love for her never wavered.

"So it happened, another year passed, and I thought I would try once to let her know and comprehend my woe; and she came to understand well that I intended nothing but good, and honor, and to preserve her name above all things; and that I dreaded her disdain; and was so eager to serve her; and it would be a pity if I should die, since, surely, I intended no harm. So when my lady knew all this, she gave me the noble gift of her mercy entirely, without ever any offense to her honor. Without a doubt, I would have it no other way.

And with that she gave me a ring; I think it was the most memorable thing; of course, there's no need to ask if my heart grew glad! So help me God, I was quickly raised, as if from death to life; of all possible fortunes, I found the best of all, the gladdest, and the most enjoyable. For truly that sweet creature, when I was wrong and she was right, would always forgive me so kindly and graciously. In all my youth, in all events, she took me into her service. And there she was always so true, and our joy was ever renewed; our hearts were so equally paired that never would either of us be contrary to the other for any woe. For truly, both our hearts shared one bliss and one sorrow alike; they were both glad and sad the same; all was one for us, without a doubt. And thus we lived many years so well I can not tell how."

"Sir," I said, "where is she now?"

"Now?" he said, and stopped at once. With that he grew as dead as stone and said, "Alas, that I was born! That was the loss that I told you before that I had lost. Remember how I said earlier, 'You know full little what you mean by your words; I have lost more than you think.' God knows, alas! She was that very person!"

"Alas, sir, how? How may that be?"

"She is dead!"

"No!"

"Yes, by my word!"

"Is that your loss? By God, that is such a pity!"

And with that word they quickly began to sound the hunting signal to head home; all the hart-hunting was done for that time.

With that I thought that this king began to ride homeward to an adjacent place which was a short way from us – a long castle with white walls, by Saint John, on a rich hill,[60] so I dreamed; but thus it happened. I dreamed just as I tell you: in the castle there was a bell, and as it struck twelve, I awoke and found myself lying in my bed. And the book I had read, of Alcyone and Ceyx the king, and of the gods of sleep, I found wide open in my hand. I thought, "This is so strange a dream that I will, in the course of time, attempt to put this dream into rhyme as best I can, and do so soon."

This was my dream; now it is done.

---

[60] Long...hill. Chaucer may be punning with long castle (John of Gaunt was the Duke of Lancaster) and rich hill (his castle was at Richmond). In the same vein, Saint John was Gaunt's patron saint.

THE PARLIAMENT OF FOWLS

❧

INTRODUCTORY NOTES

Because Chaucer's *The Parliament of Fowls*, the shortest of his major works, contains the first mention in the English language of Valentine's Day and concerns the mating of birds at the end of winter, it is usually discussed as a celebration of love. If it is a celebration of love, it is not a typical one.

The poem contains many of the trappings of love, including a visit to the garden of love, the gathering of lover birds to select their mates, and the pledges of love by three suitors eagles to one young female eagle. The poem begins, however, with a discussion of the value of old books, a visit from a Roman general, a conversation on the importance of contributing to the general welfare of society (and what happens to those who do not contribute), and the entry gate into a place that might seem to be Hell itself. Likewise, later in the poem the wooing of the young eagle incites a heated discussion that nearly ends in a riot. These factors, along with an ending that one would not anticipate, might make us wonder if this poem is really about the virtue of love.

Despite the convoluted approach to love that Chaucer presents, we can assume without much hesitation that the poem is an allegory for a royal courtship. Most scholars have agreed that it reflects the courtship of Richard II and Anne of Bohemia, which culminated in their marriage in 1382. As the eldest daughter of Charles IV, Holy Roman Emperor, and Elizabeth of Pomerania, Anne (1366 – 1394) was well-sought by suitors. Though Anne was not received well by the court at first, she grew in the estimation of the court and in the love of Richard.

31

It is not clear when Chaucer wrote *The Parliament of Fowls*; it was surely written after the courtship began in 1380, but we do not know the status of the courtship at the time he completed the poem. We do know that, in Chaucer's inimitable way, we have a portrait of love that is not ideal, but true to life.

THE PARLIAMENT OF FOWLS

ౚ

The life so brief, the art so long in the learning, the attempt so hard, the conquest so sharp, the fearful joy that ever slips away so quickly – by all this I mean love, which so sorely astounds my feeling with its wondrous operation, that when I think upon it I scarce know whether I wake or sleep. For albeit I know not Love myself, nor how he pays people their wage, yet I have very often chanced to read in books of his miracles and his cruel anger. For certain, I have read that he will ever be lord and sovereign, and his strokes will be so heavy that I dare say nothing but, "May God save such a lord!" I can say no more.

Somewhat for pleasure and somewhat for learning I am in the habit of reading books, as I have told you. But why speak I of all this? Not long ago I chanced to look at a book, written in antique letters, and there I read very diligently and eagerly through the long day, to learn about a certain thing. For, as people say, out of old fields comes all this new wheat from year to year; and, in good faith, out of old books comes all this new knowledge that people learn. But now to my theme in this matter: it so delighted me to read on, that the whole day seemed to me rather short. This book of which I speak was entitled *Tully[1] on the Dream of Scipio*. It had seven chapters, on heaven and hell and earth, and the souls that live in those places. About this I will tell you the substance of Tully's wisdom, as briefly as I can.

The book first tells how, when Scipio had come to Africa, he met Masinissa,[2] who clasped him in his arms for joy. Then it tells their conversation and all the joy that was between them until the day began to end; and then how Scipio's beloved ancestor Africanus appeared to him that night in his sleep. Then it tells how Africanus showed him Carthage from a starry place, and disclosed to him all his good fortune to come, and said to him that any man, learned or unlettered, who loves the common profit[3] and is virtuous shall go to a blessed place where there is joy without end. Then Scipio asked whether people that die here on earth have a life and dwelling place elsewhere; and Africanus said, "Yes, without doubt," and added that our space of life in the present world, whatever way we follow, is just a kind of

---

[1] Tully. Roman orator, Cicero (Marcus Tullius, 106 BC – 43 BC), whose *Dream of Scipio*, the conclusion of his *Republic*, was preserved with a long commentary by Macrobius (Macrobius Ambrosius Theodosius, fifth century). The narrator is relating the Macrobius version. In the dream the Roman general Scipio the Younger (Aemilianus; 185 BC – 129 BC) meets his grandfather, Scipio the Elder (Africanus; 236 BC – 183 BC; victor of the Second Punic War) in a dream in which the younger is shown all the universe.

[2] Masinissa. King of Numidia (Libya; c. 238 BC – c. 148 BC). First fought with Carthage against Rome in the Second Punic War, but switched allegiance to Rome, which later helped to unify the Numidian tribes into one nation.

[3] Common profit. The common good.

death, and righteous people, after they die, shall go to heaven.

And he showed him the Milky Way, and the earth here, so little in comparison with the hugeness of the heavens; and after that he showed him the nine spheres.[4] And then he heard the melody that proceeds from those nine spheres, which is the fount of music and melody in this world, and the cause of harmony. Then Africanus instructed him not to take delight in this world, since earth is so little and so full of torment and ill favor. Then he told him how in a certain term of years every star should come into its own place, where it first was; and all that has been done by all mankind in this world shall pass out of memory.

Then he asked Africanus to tell him fully the way to come into that heavenly happiness; and he said, "First know yourself to be immortal, and always see that you labor diligently and give instruction for the common profit, and you shall not fail to come speedily to that dear place that is full of joy and of luminous souls. But breakers of the law, in truth, and lecherous people, after they die, shall forever be whirled about the earth in torment, until many ages have passed; and then, all their wicked deeds forgiven, they shall come to that blessed region, to which may God send you His grace to come."

The day began to end, and dark night, which withdraws beasts from their activity, bereft me of my book for the lack of light; and I set forth to my bed, full of brooding and anxious heaviness. For I both had that which I wished not and what I wished that I had not. But at last, wearied with all the day's labor, my spirit took rest and heavily slept; and as I lay in my sleep, I dreamed how Africanus, in the very same guise in which Scipio saw him that time before, had come and stood at the very side of my bed. When the weary hunter

---

[4] Nine spheres. Moving from the center, the Earth, outward: the Moon, Mercury, Venus, the Sun, Mars, Jupiter, Saturn, the Fixed Stars (Zodiac), and the Crystalline Sphere (Primum Mobile).

sleeps, quickly his mind returns to the woods; the judge dreams how his cases will fare, and the carter how his carts will go; the rich dream of gold, the knight fights his foes; the sick man dreams he drinks of the wine cask, the lover that he has his lady. I cannot say whether my reading of Africanus was the cause that I dreamed that he stood there, but thus he spoke: "You have done so well to look upon my old tattered book, of which Macrobius thought not a little,[5] that I wish to requite you for your labor."

Cytherea,[6] you sweet, blessed lady, who with your fire-brand subdues whomsoever you wish, and sends me this dream, be my helper in this, for you are best able! As surely as I saw you in the north-northwest[7] when I began to write my dream, so surely do you give me power to rhyme it and compose it!

---

[5] Macrobius…little. Understatement: Macrobius preserved the text and wrote a long commentary on it.

[6] Cytherea. Venus, the goddess of love.

[7] North-north-west. Reference to the position of the planet Venus in the night sky.

This aforesaid Africanus took me from there and brought me out with him to a gate of a park walled with mossy stone; and over the gate on either side, carved in large letters, were verses of very diverse senses, of which I shall tell you the entire matter:

> "Through me people go to that blessed place
> Where hearts find health and deadly wounds find cure,
> Through me men go unto the fount of Grace,
> Where green, lusty May shall ever endure.
> I lead them to blithe peace and joy secure.
> Reader, be glad; throw off your sorrows past.
> Open am I; press in and make haste fast."

On the other side it said:

> "Through me people go where mischance betides,
> Where is the mortal striking of the spear,
> To which Disdain and Coldness are the guides,
> Where trees no fruit or leaf shall ever bear.
> This stream shall lead you to the sorrowful weir
> Where fish in baleful prison lie all dry.
> To shun it is the only remedy."

These inscriptions were written, the one in gold, the other in black, and I beheld them for a long while, for at the one my heart grew hardy, and the other ever increased my fear; the first warmed me, the other chilled me. For fear of error my wit could not make its choice, to enter or to flee, to lose myself or save myself. Just as a piece of iron set between two load-stones of equal force[8] has no power to move one way or the other – for as much as one draws the other hinders.

So it fared with me, who knew not which would be better, to enter or not, until Africanus my guide caught and

---

[8] Two load-stones. Chaucer names these "adamantes," hard magnetic stones. The narrator is the epitome of indecision.

pushed me in at the wide gates, saying, "Your doubt stands written on your face, though you tell it not to me. But fear not to come in, for this writing is not meant for you or for any, unless he would be Love's servant. For in love, I believe, you have lost your sense of taste, just as a sick man loses his taste of sweet and bitter. Nevertheless, dull though you may be, you can still look upon that which you cannot do; for many a man who cannot complete a bout is nevertheless pleased to be at a wrestling match, and judges whether one or another does better. And if you have skill to set it down, I will show you something to write about."

With that he took my hand in his, from which I took comfort and quickly went in. But Lord, how glad and at ease I was! For everywhere I cast my eyes were trees clad, each according to its kind, with everlasting leaves in fresh color and green as emerald, a joy to behold: the builder oak, and the hardy ash, the elm the pillar and the coffin for corpses, the boxwood for making pipes, the holly for whip-handles, the fir to bear sails, the cypress to mourn death, the yew for the bowman, the aspen for smooth shafts, the olive of peace, the drunken vine, the victor palm, and the laurel for divination.

By a river in a green meadow, where there is at all points so much sweetness, I saw a garden full of blossomy boughs with white, blue, yellow and red flowers; and cold fountain-streams, teeming with life, full of small shining fish with red fins and bright silver scales. On every bough I heard the birds sing with the voice of angels in their melody. Some busied themselves to lead forth their young. The little bunnies ran off to play. Further on, I noticed all about the timid roe, the buck, harts and hinds and squirrels and small beasts of gentle nature. I heard stringed instruments playing harmonies of such ravishing sweetness that God, Maker and Lord of all, never heard better, I believe. At the same time a wind, which scarcely could have been gentler, made in the green leaves a soft noise that accorded with the song of the birds above. The air of that place was so mild that never was there discomfort on account of heat or cold. Every wholesome spice and herb grew there, and no person would age or sicken. There was a thousand times more joy than one can relate. And it was never night there, but always bright day in everyone's eye.

I saw our lord Cupid forging and filing his arrows under a tree beside a spring, and his bow lay ready at his feet. And meanwhile his daughter, Desire, well tempered the arrowheads in the spring, and by her cunning she piled them after as they should serve, some to slay, some to wound and pierce. Just then I noticed Pleasure and Clothing and Lust and Courtesy and Joy, as well as Deception, who has wit and power to cause a being to do foolish things. She was disguised, I deny it not. And under an oak, I believe, I saw Delight, standing apart with Gentle Breeding. I saw Beauty without any clothing, Youth, full of sportiveness and jollity, Foolhardiness, Flattery, Desire, Message-sending, Bribery, and three others – I will not tell their names.

And upon great high pillars of jasper I saw a temple of brass strongly stand. About the temple many women were dancing ceaselessly, of whom some were beautiful themselves and some beautiful in dress; only in their kirtles they went, with hair unbound – that was forever their business, year by year. And on the temple I saw many hundred pairs of doves sitting, white and beautiful. Before the temple door sat Lady Peace gravely, holding back the curtain, and beside her Lady Patience, with her pale face and wondrous discretion, sitting upon a mound of sand. Next to her were Promise and Cunning and a crowd of their followers within the temple and without.

Inside I heard a gust of sighs blowing about, hot as fire, engendered of longing, which caused every altar to blaze ever anew. And well I saw then that all the cause of sorrows that lovers endure is through the bitter goddess Jealousy. As I walked about within the temple I saw the god Priapus standing in sovereign position, his scepter in hand,[9] and in such attire as when the ass confounded him to confusion with its outcry by night. People were busily setting upon his head garlands full of fresh, new flowers of various colors.

In a private corner I found Venus, who was noble and stately in her bearing, sporting with her porter Riches. The place was dark, but in time I saw a little light – it could scarcely have been less. Venus reposed upon a golden bed until the hot sun should seek the west. Her golden hair was bound with a golden thread, but all untressed as she lay. And one could see her naked from the breast to the head; the remnant, in truth, was well covered to my pleasure with a filmy kerchief of Valence;[10] there was no thicker cloth that could also be transparent. The place gave forth a thousand

---

[9] Priapus...hand. Phrygian god of fertility and gardens, son of Aphrodite by Dionysus or Hermes. He is said to have argued with an ass over the relative size of their genitalia. Naked, they compared themselves, only to find that the ass' "sceptre" was larger.

[10] Valence. Medieval center of textile trades.

sweet odors. Bacchus, god of wine, sat beside her, and next was Ceres,[11] who saves all from hunger, and, as I said, the Cyprian woman[12] lay in the midst; on their knees two young people were crying to her to be their helper.

But thus I left her lying, and further in the temple I saw how, in scorn of Diana[13] the chaste, there hung on the wall many broken bows of such maidens as had first wasted their time in her service. And everywhere was painted many stories, of which I shall mention a few, such as Callisto[14] and Atalanta[15] and many maidens whose name I do not know.

[11] Ceres (Demeter). Goddess of grain, who gives the remedy for hunger.

[12] Cyprian woman. Venus.

[13] Diana. Goddess of the Moon, the hunt, and chastity. He sees many boughs offered to Diana by women in hopes that they might remain virgins.

[14] Callisto. Favorite hunting companion of Artemis (Diana), duped and ravaged by Zeus, who disguised himself as Artemis; then transformed into a bear by Hera (out of jealousy), or Artemis (for breaking her vow of chastity), or Zeus (to hide her from his wife, Hera).

[15] Atalanta, another virgin huntress, whose father, wanting only sons, left her in the forest where she was raised by bears and hunters.

There was also Semiramis,[16] Candace,[17] Hercules,[18] Biblis,[19] Dido,[20] Thisbe and Pyramus,[21] Tristram and Isolt,[22] Paris,[23] Achilles,[24] Helen,[25] Cleopatra,[26] Troilus,[27] and Scylla,[28] and the mother of Romulus[29] as well – all were portrayed on the other wall, and their love and by what plight they died.

When I had returned to the sweet and green garden that I

---

[16] Semiramis. Assyrian queen who succeeded her husband Ninus on the throne, built Babylon, and conquered Persia and Egypt. Known for beauty, valor, and lust.

[17] Candace. Queen of India (fourth century BC) who loved Alexander the Great.

[18] Hercules. Great Greek hero, son of Zeus and Alcmene, accidentally killed by his wife Deianeira.

[19] Biblis. Maiden who fell in love with her twin brother Caunus, but when she told him, he departed, horrified. She went mad and searched for him, but was eventually transformed into a spring.

[20] Dido. Queen of Carthage, lover of Aeneas (Trojan hero, later the pre-founder of Rome); she killed herself when she saw him depart.

[21] Thisbe and Pyramus. Star-crossed lovers who planned to meet at night at the tomb of King Ninus. Pyramus, having discovered her blood-stained cloak in the mouth of a lioness (from whom Thisbe had safely fled) killed himself because he believed that she had been eaten by the lioness; she then killed herself for loss of him.

[22] Tristram, Isolt. Famous lovers in the Arthurian tradition. Isolt, though married to King Mark of Cornwall, loved Tristram, who was Mark's most able and dedicated knight.

[23] Paris. Trojan son of Priam; his abduction of Helen from her husband, the Greek King Menelaus, was the immediate cause of the Trojan War.

[24] Achilles. Brooding Greek hero, invulnerable except for his heel (by which his mother held him when she dipped him into the River Styx), who slew the Trojan champion Hector and dragged his body around the city. In one version of his story, he died for the love of Polyxena.

[25] Helen. See note on Paris above.

[26] Cleopatra. Famous Egyptian queen, who died for the love of the Roman leader Antony.

[27] Troilus. Trojan son of Priam, and brother to Hector and Paris; his love affair with Criseyde is the topic for Chaucer's *Troilus and Criseyde*.

[28] Scylla. Daughter of Nisus, king of Megara. For love, she helped Minos to defeat her own father, though Minos left her soon afterward.

[29] The mother of Romulus. Rhea Silvia or Ilia, a priestess of Diana who was raped in the forest by Mars. She bore the twins Romulus and Remus, who founded Rome.

spoke of, I walked forth to comfort myself. Then I noticed
how there sat a queen who surpassed in beauty every other
creature, just as the brilliant summer sun passes the stars in
brightness. This noble goddess Nature was set upon a
flowery hill in a verdant glade. All her halls and bowers
were wrought of branches according to the art and
moderation of Nature.

And there was not any bird that is made through pro-
creation that was not ready in her presence to hear her and
receive her judgment. For this was Saint Valentine's Day,[30]
when every bird of every kind that people can imagine
comes to this place to choose its mate. And they made an

---

[30] Saint Valentine's Day. Valentine, a third-century figure who converted
many to Christianity, refused to renource his own faith, and, just before
his death, restored the sight and hearing of his jailer's daughter, is most
often remembered for marrying Christians against the will of the emperor
Claudius. This is the first reference to the holiday in the English language.
It is mentioned also in Chaucer's "Complaynt D'Amours" and "Complaint
of Mars," as well as his contemporary John Clanvowe's "The Cuckoo and
the Nightingale."

exceedingly great noise. And all earth and sea and trees and lakes were so full that there was scarcely room for me to stand, so full was the entire place. And just as Alan, in *The Complaint of Nature*,[31] describes Nature in her features and attire, so might people find her in reality.

This noble empress, full of grace, bade all the birds to take their station, as they were accustomed to stand always on Saint Valentine's Day from year to year. That is to say, the birds of prey were set highest, and then the little birds who eat, as nature inclines them, worms or other things of which I will not speak; and birds that live on seed sat upon the grass but water-fowls sat the lowest in the dale. There were so many that it was a marvel to see.

There one could find the royal eagle, which pierces the sun with his sharp glance; and other eagles of lower race, of which scholars can tell. There was that tyrant with dun gray feathers, I mean the goshawk, which harasses other birds with his fierce ravening. There was the noble falcon, which with his feet grasps the king's hand; also the bold sparrow-hawk, foe of quails; the merlin, which often greedily pursues the lark. The dove was there, with her meek eyes; the jealous swan, which sings at his death; and the owl also, which forebodes death; the giant crane, with his trumpet voice; the thieving chough; the prating magpie; the scornful jay; the heron, foe to eels; the false lapwing, full of trickery; the starling, which can betray secrets; the tame redbreast; the coward kite; the cock, timekeeper of little thorps; the sparrow, son of Venus;[32] the nightingale, which calls forth the fresh new leaves; the swallow, murderer of the little bees that make honey from the fresh-hued flowers; the wedded

---

[31] *The Complaint of Nature*. Work by Alain of Lille (c. 1128 – 1202) which dramatizes a remedy for humankind's straying from the laws of Nature, inspires the remainder of this work, especially the following description of the allegorical figure of Nature. In both Chaucer and Alain the birds seem to arise from her gown.

[32] Sparrow...Venus. The sparrow, a symbol of lechery, is typically named as an attribute or companion of Venus, not as her son.

turtle-dove, with her faithful heart; the peacock, with his shining angel-feathers; the pheasant, which scorns the cock by night; the vigilant goose; the cuckoo, ever unnatural;[33] the popinjay, full of wantonness; the drake, destroyer of his own kind; the stork, which avenges adultery; the greedy, gluttonous cormorant; the wise raven and the crow, with voice of ill-boding; the ancient thrush and the wintry fieldfare thrush.

What more shall I say? One might find assembled in that place before the noble goddess Nature birds of every sort in this world that have feathers and stature. And each by her consent worked diligently to choose or take graciously his lady or his mate.

But to the point: Nature held on her hand a formel[34] eagle, the noblest in shape that she ever found among her works, the gentlest and goodliest; in her every noble trait so had its seat that Nature herself rejoiced to look upon her and to kiss her beak many times. Nature, vicar of the Almighty Lord, who has knit in harmony hot, cold, heavy, light, moist, and dry in exact proportions, began to speak in a gentle voice: "Birds, take heed of what I say; and for your welfare and to further your needs I will hasten as fast as I can speak. You well know how on Saint Valentine's day, by my statute and through my ordinance, you come to choose your mates, as I prick you with sweet pain, and then fly on your way. But I may not, even if I were to win this entire world, depart from my just order, that he who is most worthy shall begin.

"The tercel[35] eagle, the royal bird above you in degree, as you well know, the wise and worthy one, trusty, true as steel, which you may see I have formed in every part as pleased me best – there is no need to describe his shape to you – he shall choose first and speak as he will. And after him each of you shall choose in order, according to your nature, each as

---

[33] Unnatural. Cuckoos left their eggs in unused nests built by other birds, and were thus considered unnatural.

[34] Formel. Female eagle.

[35] Tercel. A male eagle.

pleases you; and, as your fortune goes, you shall lose or win. But whichever of you love ensnares most, to him may God send her who sighs for him most sorely."

And at this she called the tercel and said, "My son, the choice is fallen to you. Nevertheless under this condition must be the choice of each one here, that his chosen mate will agree to his choice, whomsoever would choose her. From year to year this is always our custom. And whoever at this time can win grace has come here in blissful time!"

The royal tercel, with bowed head and humble appearance, delayed not and spoke: "As my sovereign lady, not as my spouse, I choose – and choose with will and heart and mind – the formel of so noble shape upon your hand. I am hers wholly and will serve her always. Let her do as she wishes, to let me live or die; I beseech her for mercy and grace, as my sovereign lady, or else let me die here presently. For surely I cannot live long in torment, for in my heart every vein is cut. Having regard only to my faithfulness, dear heart, have some pity upon my woe. And if I am found untrue to her, disobedient or willfully negligent, a boaster, or at any time love elsewhere, I pray you this will be my doom: that I will be torn to pieces by these birds, upon that day when she should ever know me untrue to her or guilty of faithlessness. And since no other loves her as well as I, though she never promised me love, she ought to be mine by virtue of her mercy; for I can fasten no other bond on her. Never for any woe shall I cease to serve her, however far she may roam. Say what you will, my words are done."

Just as the fresh red rose, newly blooming, blushes in the summer sun, so grew the color of this woman when she heard all this; she answered no word good or bad, so sorely was she abashed; until Nature said, "Daughter, fear not, I assure you."

Then spoke another tercel of a lower order: "That shall not be. I love her better than you, by Saint John, or at least I love her as well, and have served her longer, according to my station. If she should love for long being to me alone should be the reward; and I also dare to say, if she should find me false, unkind, a gossip, or a rebel in any way, or jealous, let me be hanged by the neck. And unless I bear myself in her service as well as my wit allows me, to protect her honor in every point, let her take my life and all the wealth I have."

Then a third tercel eagle said, "Now, sirs, you see how little time we have here, for every bird clamors to be off with his mate or lady dear, and Nature herself as well, because of the delay, will not hear half of what I would speak. Yet unless I speak I must die of sorrow. I boast not at all of long service; but it is as likely that I shall die of woe today as he who has been languishing these twenty winters. And it may well happen that a man may serve better in half a year, even if it were no longer, than another man who has served many years. I do not say this about myself, for I can do no service to my lady's pleasure; but I dare say that I am her truest man, I believe, and would be most glad to please her. In short, until death may seize me I will be hers, whether I wake or sleep, and true in all that heart can think."

In all my life since the day I was born never have I heard any man so noble make a plea in love or any other thing – even if a man had time and wit to rehearse their expression and their words. And this discourse lasted from the morning until the sun drew downward so rapidly. The clamor released by the birds rung so loud – "Make an end of this and let us go!" – that I well thought the forest would be splintered. They cried, "Make haste! Alas, you will ruin us! When shall your cursed pleading come to an end? How should a judge believe either side for yea or nay, without any proof?"

The goose, cuckoo, and duck so loudly cried, "Kek, kek," "Cuckoo," and "Quack, quack," that the noise reverberated in my ears.

The goose said, "All this is not worth a fly! But from this I can devise a remedy, and I will speak my verdict fair and soon, on behalf of the waterfowl. Let whoever wishes to do so, smile or frown."

"And I for the worm-eating fowl," said the foolish cuckoo; "of my own authority, for the common welfare, I will take the responsibility now, for it would be great charity to release us."

"By God, you may wait a while yet," said the turtle-dove. "If you are the one to choose who shall speak, it would be as well for him to be silent. I am among the birds that eat seed, one of the most unworthy, and of little wit – I know that well. But a creature's tongue would be better quiet than meddling with such doings about which he knows neither rhyme nor reason. And whosoever does so, overburdens himself in foul fashion, for often one not entrusted to a duty commits offence."

Nature, who had always an ear to the murmuring of folly at the back, said with ready tongue, "Hold your peace there! And straightway, I hope, I shall find a counsel to let you go and release you from this noise. My judgment is that you shall choose one from each bird-folk to give the verdict for you all."

The birds all assented to this conclusion. And first the birds of prey by full election chose the tercel-falcon to define all their judgment, and decide as he wished. And they presented him to Nature and she accepted him gladly. The falcon then spoke in this fashion: "It would be hard to determine by reason which best loves this gentle woman; for each has such ready answers that none may be defeated by reasons. I cannot see of what use are arguments; so it seems there must be battle."

"All ready!" then cried these tercel eagles.

"Nay, sirs," he said, "if I dare say it, you do me wrong: my tale is not done. For, sirs, take it not amiss, I pray, it cannot go thus as you desire. Ours is the voice that has the charge over this, and you must stand by the judges' decision. Peace, therefore! I say that it would seem in my mind that the worthiest in knighthood, who has longest followed it, the highest in degree and of gentlest blood, would be most fitting for her, if she wishes it. And of these three she knows which he is, I believe, for that is easily seen."

The waterfowl put their heads together, and after short considering, when each had spoken his large mouthful, they said truly, by one assent, how "the goose, with her gentle eloquence, who so desires to speak for us, shall say our say," and prayed God would help her.

Then the goose began to speak for these waterfowl, and said in her cackling, "Peace! Now every man take heed and hearken what argument I shall put forth. My wits are sharp, I love no delay; I counsel him; I say, even if he were my brother, leave him if she will not love him."

"Lo, here," said the sparrow-hawk, "a perfect argument for a goose – bad luck to her! Lo, thus it is to have a wagging tongue! Now, fool, it would be better for you to have held your peace than to have shown your folly, by God! But to do thus rests not in her wit or will; for it is truly said, 'a fool cannot be silent.'"

Laughter arose from all the birds of noble kind; and straightway the seed-eating fowl chose the faithful turtle-dove, and called her to them, and prayed her to speak the sober truth about this matter, and asked her counsel. And she answered that she would fully show her mind. "Nay, God forbid a lover should change!" said the turtle-dove, and grew all red with shame. "Though his lady may be cold for evermore, let him serve her always until he would die. In truth I praise not the goose's counsel, for even if my lady died I would have no other mate, I would be hers until death take me."

"By my hat, well jested!" said the duck. "That men should love forever, without cause! Who can find reason or wit there? Does one who is mirthless dance merrily? Who should care for him who is carefree? Yea, quack!" said the duck loud and long, "God knows there are more stars than a pair."

"Now fie, churl!" said the noble falcon. "That thought

came straight from the dunghill. You can not see when a thing is proper. You do as well with love as owls do with light; the day blinds them, but they see very well in darkness. Your nature is so low and wretched that you can not see or guess what love is."

Then the cuckoo thrust himself forward on behalf of the worm-eating birds and said quickly, "So that I may have my mate in peace, I care not how long you contend. Let each be single all his life; that is my counsel, since they cannot agree. This is my instruction, and there an end!"

"Yea," said the merlin, "as this glutton has well filled his paunch, this should suffice for us all! You murderer of the hedge-sparrow on the branch, the one who brought you up, you ruthless glutton! May you live unmated, you mangler of worms! It matters nothing to you, though your tribe may perish. Go, be a stupid fool, as long as the world lasts!"

"Peace now, I command here," said Nature, "For I have heard the opinions of all, and yet we are no nearer to our goal. But this is my final decision, that she herself shall have the choice of whom she wishes. Whosoever may be pleased or not, he whom she chooses shall have her immediately. For since it cannot here be debated who loves her best, as the falcon said, then I will grant her this favor, that she shall have him alone on whom her heart is set, and he who has fixed his heart on her shall have her. This judgment I, Nature, make; and I cannot speak falsely, nor look with partial eye on any rank. But if it is reasonable to counsel you in choosing a mate, then surely I would counsel you to take the royal tercel, as the falcon very wisely said; for he is noblest and most worthy whom I created so well for my own pleasure; that ought to suffice you."

The formel answered with timid voice, "Goddess of Nature, my righteous lady, true it is that I am ever under your authority, just as every other creature is, and I must be yours as long as my life may last. Therefore, grant me my first request, and immediately I will speak my mind to you."

"I grant it to you," said Nature; and this female eagle spoke immediately in this way: "Almighty queen, until this year comes to an end I ask for a period of delay, to take counsel with myself; and after that to have my choice free. This is all that I wish to say. I can say no more, even if you were to slay me. In truth, as for now I will in no manner serve Venus or Cupid"

"Now since it can happen no other way," Nature said then, "there is no more to be said here. Then I wish these birds to go their way each with his mate, so that they tarry here no longer."

And she spoke to them thus as you shall hear. "To you I speak, you tercels," said Nature. "Be of good heart, and continue in service, all three; a year is not so long to wait. And let each of you strive according to his degree to do well. For, God knows, she is departed from you this year; and whatsoever may happen afterwards, this interval is appointed to you all."

And when this work was all brought to an end, Nature gave every bird his mate by just accord, and they went their way. Ah, Lord! The bliss and joy that they made! For each of them took the other in his wings, and wound their necks about each other, ever thanking the noble goddess of Nature. But first were chosen birds to sing, as was always their custom year by year to sing a roundel[36] at their departure, to honor Nature and give her pleasure. The tune, I believe, was made in France. The words were such as you may here find in these verses, as I remember them.

> *Qui bien aime a tard oublie.*[37]
> "Welcome, summer, with sunshine soft,

---

[36] Roundel. (Or Rondeau.) Poem of ten to thirteen lines; the opening phrase or line is repeated as a refrain in the second and third stanzas.

[37] *Qui bien aime a tard oublie.* Who loves well forgets slowly. This line is included in some of the manuscripts of PF. It seems to be a consolation to the three suitors, and it may also indicate the source of the roundel or tune.

The winter's tempest you will break,
And drive away the long nights black!

"Saint Valentine, throned aloft,
Thus little birds sing for your sake:
Welcome, summer, with sunshine soft,
The winter's tempest you will shake!

"Good cause have they to glad them oft,
His own true-love each bird will take;
Blithe may they sing when they awake,
Welcome, summer, with sunshine soft,
The winter's tempest you will break,
And drive away the long nights black!"

And with the shouting that the birds raised, as they flew away when their song was done, I awoke; and I took up other books to read, and still I read always. In truth I hope so to read that some day I shall meet with something by which I shall fare the better. And so I will not cease to read.

Here ends the work of the Parliament of Fowls held on the day of Saint Valentine, according to Geoffrey Chaucer. Thanks be to God.

THE LEGEND OF GOOD WOMEN

❧

INTRODUCTORY NOTES

If Chaucer makes anything clear in his early poetry, it was that love does not come easily, and it often does not last long. In his *The Legend of Good Women* he continues to come to terms with love: he explores not only, as we might expect from the title, the lives of women "who were faithful in love," but also, and perhaps more so, the deeds of "false men who betrayed them."

This exploration is mandated in the *Prologue* by Queen Alceste (perhaps a mythological version of Anne of Bohemia, wife of Richard II), who sentences Chaucer to tell stories of good women because the poet has, as Love (Cupid) tells him, written "heresy against [his] religion," especially in his *Troilus and Criseyde*.

As with other works, such as *The House of Fame* and *Anelida and Arcite*, *The Legend of Good Women* was left unfinished. Scholars speculate that Chaucer, both as author and fictional narrator, got tired of the project. Perhaps he set it aside in order to begin *The Canterbury Tales*, which would give him the opportunity to write from varying points of view, not just one.

Though we can not be sure of Chaucer's attitude toward his work, it is clear that he is making a case that these women are martyrs for love. The word "legend" in the title of the work indicates that these women were saints, as a legend, or legendary, is a collection of saints' lives. As saints' legends were the most popular form of written entertainment in Chaucer's time, his audience would have known to read for the ways in which the women were tortured for love. One difference, of course, seems to be that the women in Chaucer's legends suffer for worldly love (*cupiditas*) while the women in saint's legends suffer for heavenly love (*caritas*). Another difference is that, though both types typically end in death, the lives of the Christian saints always end with a sort of victory over the evil forces of the world, whereas Chaucer's, or Cupid's, saints are defeated by the senseless acts of unfaithful lovers.

Though Chaucer borrows much in his creation of *The Legend of Good Women* (from several of his French contemporaries for the Prologue and from Ovid and Vergil for the legends), the cumulative effect is an original one, as we witness the emergence of a unique narrative voice exploring complex stories of love that do not end happily ever after.

THE LEGEND OF GOOD WOMEN

THE PROLOGUE

A thousand times I have heard it said that in heaven is joy and in hell pain; and I grant well that it is so. Nevertheless, I know this well, that there is no person dwelling in this land who has been in either hell or heaven, or who can know of them in any other way than as he has heard tell or found it written, for no person can put his knowledge to the test. But God forbid that people should believe far more than they have seen with their eyes! A man shall not deem all things false because he has not beheld them since long ago. God knows, a thing is nonetheless true, even if every creature cannot see it. Even Bernard the monk[1] did not see all things, by God!

Then in all reason must we give credence to the books we find, through which ancient things are kept in mind, and to the instruction of these wise ones from ancient times, and we must believe in these old and true histories of holiness, of kingdoms, of victories, of love, hate, and various other things that I cannot now recount And if old books were all gone, then the key of remembrance would be lost. Well ought we then to honor and believe old books, where we have no other way to test the truth.

As for me, though I know little, I delight to read in books and revere them in my heart. And to them I give full faith and credence, and I hold them so heartily in reverence that there is scarcely any activity that can draw me from my

---

[1] Bernard the monk. Bernard of Clairvaux (1090 – 1153), founder of the Cistercian order of monks, a major mystic and scholar in the medieval church.

books, unless it might be some festival, or else, of course, the lovely time of May, when I hear the little birds singing, and when the flowers begin to spring – then farewell to my books and my devotion!

Now I have also this disposition, that of all the flowers in the meadow I most love those white and red flowers, which people in our town call daisies. I have such affection for them, as I have said, that when May has arrived, no day dawns upon me in my bed, but I am up and walking in the meadow to see these flowers opening to the sun when it rises, in the bright morning, and through the long day thus I walk in the green.

That blissful sight softens all my sorrow, so glad I am for it, when I am in the presence of it, to give reverence to her. And I love it, and continually do, and ever shall, until my heart should die. I swear all this; I will not lie about this; no creature ever loved so passionately in his life. All day long I wait for nothing else, and I shall not lie, but to look upon the daisy, which well by reason people may call the "day's-eye," or else the "eye of day," the empress and flower of all the flowers.[2]

She is the brightness and the true light that in this dark world leads and directs me. The heart within my sorrowful breast fears and loves you[3] *so sorely that you are truly the mistress of my mind, and I am nothing. I give you my word, my work is knit so to your service that, just as a harp obeys the hand and makes sound according to its fingering, so too can you bring such a voice out of my heart, just as you wish, to laugh or lament. Be my guide and sovereign lady! As to my earthly god, I call to you as well, both in this work and in all my sorrows.*

And when the sun draws toward the west, then they close and take them to slumber until the morning when the day comes, so sorely they fear the night. This daisy, flower of all flowers, filled with all excellence and honor, always and alike fair and lusty of hue, fresh in winter as well as in summer, gladly would I praise it if I properly could. But I am filled with woe, for it lies not in my power!

For well I know that people have reaped the field of poetry before me and have harvested the wheat. I come after, gleaning here and there, and am very glad if perhaps I find an ear of any goodly words that they have left behind. And if I chance to recount again what they have said in their lusty songs, I hope that they will not be displeased, since all is said in furthering and worship of them who are followers of either the leaf or flower;[4] *but offer help, you who have*

---

[2] Flowers. There are two major versions of the Prologue to the LGW, known as F and G. This translation follows the G version, but adds in italics significant passages from the F version that are not included in G. In order to follow the logic of the narration, some minor rearrangement of material was necessary.

[3] You. Chaucer seems to conflate third person (she) and second person (you) in this passage.

[4] Leaf or Flower. The imagery of the flower and the leaf seems to have permeated court life in Chaucer's time, the flower signifying the glamour of the members of the court themselves and the leaf those who worked for

knowledge and power, you lovers who can write about emotions.

For trust well, I have not undertaken to sing in honor of the leaf against the flower, or of the flower against the leaf, any more than of the wheat against the chaff.[5] For to me neither is dearer; as yet I am retained by neither. I know not who serves the leaf, who the flower; that is in no way the object of my labor. For this work is all drawn out of another cask, of ancient story, before there was any such strife.

But the reason I spoke of giving credence to old books and revering them is that people should believe authorities in all things where there lies no other means of proof. Thus shall I say when the right time arises; I may not say everything at once in rhyme. For my intent is, before I go from you, to make known in English the naked text of many histories or many tales, just as authors tell them. Believe them if you wish.

When the month of May was almost gone, I roamed all the summer's day over the green meadow of which I have told you to gaze upon the fresh daisy. *My eager spirit, which always made me thirsty to see again this flower, so young, so fresh of hew, compelled me with such burning desire that in my heart I can still feel the fire that made me rise before it was day – and this was now the first morning of May – with dreadful heart and glad devotion, to be at the resurrection of this flower, when it should unclose itself in the light of the sun, which in the middle of the sign of the Taurus[6] rose as red as the rose that day, just as it did when it led Agenor's daughter[7] away.*

---

or supported them. There is also a contemporary poem by the name, *The Flower and the Leaf*, which follows the same idea.

[5] Chaff. Chaucer, following the Church Fathers, distinguishes between the wheat of the story, which is the essential truth, and the Chaff, which is the story's ornamentation.

[6] Taurus. The zodiacal sign from late April to late May.

[7] Agenor's daughter. Europa, who was seduced by Jupiter in the form of a bull. When she climbed on his back, he rode away into the sea with her.

And when the sun out of the south drew towards the west, and the flower had closed and gone to sleep, for darkness of the night which she feared, I sped swiftly home to my house; and in a little shady bower that I have, newly embanked with fresh-cut turfs, I asked people to lay my couch, and flowers to be strewn on it, for joy of the new summer. When I had laid me down and closed my eyes, I fell asleep within an hour or two.

Then I dreamed that I was in the meadow, and was roaming about to see that flower, just as you have heard me tell. This meadow was beautiful; it seemed to me to be entirely embroidered with sweet flowers. No herbs or trees or spicy resins could compare with it; for it utterly surpassed all odors and all flowers as well for its rich beauty. The earth had forgotten his poor estate of winter, which had made him naked and dejected, as the sword of cold had struck him so sorely.

Now the mild sun had relieved all of that, and clothed the earth in green all afresh. Rejoicing in the season, the little birds that had escaped the snare and the net mocked the fowler who had frightened them in winter and destroyed their brood. It eased their hearts to sing of him in scorn, and to flout the foul churl who for his greed had betrayed them with his tricks. This was their song, "The fowler we defy, and all his craft!"

On the branches some sang sweet songs of love and spring, in honor and praise of their mates, and for the new, joyous summer; it was a joy to listen. *Upon those branches full of soft blossoms, in their delight the birds often moved about and sang,*

"Blessed be Saint Valentine![8]

---

[8] Saint Valentine. Third-century figure who converted many to Christianity, refused to renounce his own faith, and, just before his death, restored the sight and hearing of his jailer's daughter. Best known for marrying Christians against the will of the emperor Claudius. Mentioned also in Chaucer's *Parliament of Fowls*, "Complaynt D'Amours," and "Complaint of Mars."

For on his day I chose you to be mine,
My sweetheart, and never have I repented."

And then they joined their beaks, and they paid honor and tenderness to each other, and then performed other ceremonies pleasing to love and nature. (I listened carefully to their song, for I dreamed I understood their meaning.)

And those that had been unfaithful – as the tydif bird is, for the sake of novelty – sought mercy for their trespassing, and humbly sang their repentance, and swore on the blossoms to be true, so that their mates would have mercy upon them, and at the last made their accord.

They all found a lord named Danger[9] for a time, yet Pity, through his strong gentle might, forgave them, and allowed Mercy to surpass Justice, through innocence and self-controlled Courtesy. But I do not call innocence folly, nor false pity, for virtue lies in the mean, as Etik[10] says. This is the manner to which I am referring.

And thus these birds, void of all malice, agreed to love, and gave up the vice of hate, and sang all of one accord, "Welcome, summer, our governor and lord!" And Zephyrus and Flora gently gave to the flowers, soft and tenderly, their sweet breath, and made them spread, as god and goddess of the flowery meadow. In this place it seemed to me I might, day by day, dwell always, the jolly month of May, without sleep or food or drink.

Then at last a lark sang on high. She said, "I see the mighty god of Love! Lo, yonder he comes! I see his wings spread!" Then I looked along the meadow and saw him come, leading by the hand a lady clothed in a royal habit of

---

[9] Danger. Refers here to the quality in a woman to resist a lover, if only temporarily, for the sake of her honor.

[10] Etik. The reference to "Etik" as the author of this commonplace idea that happiness comes through moderation is not clear. It might be a reference to the Roman poet Horace (65 BC – 8 BC), but is more likely to the *Ethics* of the Greek philosopher Aristotle (384 BC – 322 BC).

green. She had a net of gold around her hair, and over that a white crown with many flowers; for all the world,[11] just as the flower of the daisy is crowned with little white leaves, such were the flowers of her white crown, for it was made all of one fine oriental pearl; for this reason the white crown above the green, with the golden ornament in her hair, made her appear like a daisy.[12]

This mighty god of Love was clothed in silk embroidered full of green sprigs; on his head was a garland of rose-leaves, all set with fresh lilies. But the hue of his face I cannot tell, for truly his face shone so bright that the eye was dazzled by the gleam. For several minutes I could not look at him, but at last I saw that he held in his hands two fiery arrows, red as glowing coals. And he spread his wings like an angel. Albeit people say he is blind,[13] but it seemed to me that he could see well enough; for he looked sternly upon me, so that his look even now makes my heart cold.

He held by the hand this noble lady, crowned with white and clothed all in green, who was so womanly, benign, and gentle that, even if people should seek throughout this world, they should not find half her beauty in any being formed by nature. Her name was Alceste the gentle. May fair fortune ever come to her, I pray to God! For had it not been for the comfort of her presence, I would have been dead without help, for fear of Love's words and look, as you shall learn hereafter, when the time comes.

On the grass, behind this god of Love, I saw a company of nineteen ladies in royal garb coming at a gentle pace. And after them came such a train of women that I believed that all the possible women who had ever lived in this world

---

[11] For…world. Expression of exclamation, like, "I declare" or "Wasn't it amazing!"

[12] Pearl…daisy. Chaucer understands that the French word "marguerite" meant both pearl and daisy. In his day, the French poets (including Froissart, Machaut, and Deschamps) created a body of work known as Marguerite Poetry.

[13] Blind. Usually Chaucer and others understand this to mean blindfolded.

since God made Adam from earth composed only one third of them or one fourth. And every one of these women was faithful in love. Now was this a wondrous thing or not? For as soon as they perceived this flower that I call the daisy, they quickly stopped altogether and kneeled down by that very flower and sang with one voice,

"Hail and honor
To faithful womanhood, and this flower
That bears the symbol of our faithfulness!
Her white crown bears for us all the witness."

And after that they went in a circle slowly dancing around it, and sang, as it were in the fashion of a carol, this ballad which I shall tell you.

Ballad

"Hide, Absalom,[14] your bright golden tresses;
And Esther also, lay your meekness down;
And Jonathan, hide your friendly address;
And Penelope and Marcia Catoun,
Make of your wifehood no comparison;
Hide now your beauties, Isolt and Elaine,
Alceste comes, who makes all this pale and vain.

---

[14] Absalom...Alceste. Absalom, Tenth Century BC Biblical figure known for his beautiful hair, though he died when it was caught in a terebinth tree (sometimes misnamed as oak); Esther, Biblical wife of Ahasuerus, or Xerxes the Great, who was the model of patience in bringing victory to the Jews; Jonathan, Biblical figure, who, because of his kindness, was favored by King David, who had been Jonathan's rival for the throne of Israel; Penelope and Marcia Cato(un), the long-suffering wives of Odysseus, the Trojan War hero, and Cato the Younger, the Roman statesman; Isolt and Elaine, lovers of Tristram and Lancelot in Arthurian lore, both known for their beauty; Alceste, wife of Admetus, for whom Alceste gave her own life, when Apollo pleaded to the Fates to allow the soon-to-die Admetus to live, and they agreed, on the condition that someone would die in his place.

"Thy beautiful body, oh, let it not appear,
Lavinia;[15] and Lucrece too of Rome-town,
And Polyxena, who paid for love so dear,
And Cleopatra, with all your passion,
Hide your truth in loving and your renown,
And Thisbe, who for love had borne such pain;
Alceste comes, who makes all this pale and vain.

"Hero,[16] Dido, Laodamia together here,
And Phyllis, hanging for your Demophon,
And Canace, known ever by your heavy cheer,
Hypsipyle, who Jason falsely won,
Make now of your love-pledge no boast or moan,
Hypermnestra, Ariadne, cease complaint;
Alceste comes, who makes all this pale and vain."

This ballad may have been well sung, as I have said earlier,
about my noble lady; for certainly all these are not sufficient
to be equal with my lady in any way. For as the sun will
make the fire appear pale, so too my lady, who is so good, so

---

[15] Lavinia...Thisbe. Lavinia, last wife of Aeneas, founder of Rome; Lucrece, Roman noblewoman best known for taking her life after she was raped by Sextus Tarquinius, an Etruscan prince (son of the last Roman king), rather than living with the shame; Polyxena, Trojan princess, daughter of Priam and Hecuba, who was sacrificed so that the Greeks, following the advice of Achilles' ghost (she had fallen in love with him before his death), would have favorable winds for their journey home after the Trojan War; Cleopatra, Queen of Egypt, who was first the lover of Julius Caesar and later of Marcus Antony, and committed suicide when Antony, having been defeated by Octavian, took his life; Thisbe, ill-fated lover who committed suicide when she saw the lifeless body of her beloved Pyramus, who had taken his life when he thought that she had been killed by a lion.

[16] Hero...Ariadne. All women who had been left behind by their lovers; Hero by Lysander, Dido by Aeneas, Laodamia by Protesilaus, Phyllis by Demophon, Canace by Macareus, Hypsipyle by Jason, Hypermnestra by Lynceus, and Ariadne by Theseus. All of these stories are told in Ovid's *Heroides* (Heroines, first century BC).

fair, so gracious, surpasses all. I pray to God that goodness may come to her!

When this ballad was all sung, they sat full gently down upon the sweet and soft green grass, in order all in a circle about. First sat the god of Love, and then this lady clad in green with the white crown; and then near them all the rest sat courteously, according to their station. And then, for several minutes, in the entire place not a word was spoken.

Close by, reclining beneath a grassy slope, I waited, still as any stone, to learn what this group intended; until at last the god of Love turned his eyes on me and said, "Who is it who rests there?"

And I answered his question and said, "Sir, it is I." And I came nearer, and greeted him.

He said, "What are you doing here in my presence, and so boldly? For truly a worm would be more worthy to come into my sight than you."

"And why, sir," I said, "if it please you?"

"Because," he said, "you are in no way fit. My servants are all wise and honorable; you are my mortal foe, war against me, and speak evil of my long-time servants. And with your works of translation you plague them and hinder people's devotion in my service, and you maintain that it is folly to trust in me. You cannot deny it; for in text so plain that it needs no commentary you have translated *The Romance of the Rose*, [17] which is heresy against my religion. You also cause wise folk to withdraw from me, and you think in your cool wit that anyone is but a proper fool who loves with passion, too hard and hot. Well I know by this that you begin to drivel, like these old fools when their spirit fails, for in this way they abuse others, and know not what is amiss with themselves.

"Have you not also made in English the poem which tells

---

[17] Rose. Chaucer translated from French *The Romance of the Rose*, written by Guillaume de Lorris (1200 – 1240) and Jean de Meun (1240 – 1305), which encompasses "all the art of love."

how Criseyde forsook Troilus,[18] to show how women have gone astray? But nevertheless answer me this now, why would you not also speak well of women, as you have spoken evilly? Was there no good matter in your memory, and in all your books could you not find some story of good and faithful women?

"Yes, God knows! You have sixty books, old and new, all full of long stories, in which both Romans and Greeks tell about various women and what kind of life they led, and there is always a hundred good to one bad. This God knows, as well as all scholars who use them to explore such matters. What says Valerius or Livy or Claudian?[19] What says Jerome, in his treatise against Jovinian?[20] Jerome tells of pure maidens and faithful wives, of widows steadfast unto death; and he tells not of a few, but I dare say a hundred in succession, until it is piteous and sorrowful to read of the woe they endured for their faithfulness.

"For they were so true to their love that, rather than take a new mate, they chose death in various manners, and died just as the story will relate. Some were burned, some had their throats cut, and some were drowned, because they would not be false. For they all kept their maidenhood, or else widowhood or wedlock. And this was not only done for devoutness, but also for true virtue and purity, and so that

---

[18] Troilus. Chaucer's *Troilus and Criseyde,* Chaucer's lengthy tale (perhaps the first novel in the English language) of doomed love set against the backdrop of the Trojan War.

[19] Valerius…Claudian. Valerius: identity is uncertain, but likely the author (perhaps fourth century) of *Epistola Valerii ad Rufinum* (*Letter from Valerius to Rufinius*). Livy: Titus Livius (59 BC – 17 AD), the Roman historian, author of an extensive *History of Rome*. Claudian: Fourth century Roman poet, reputed as the last poet of classical Rome, author of *De Raptu Prosperina* (*On the Rape of Proserpine*). All three recorded stories of rapes or abuses of women.

[20] Jovinian. A treatise known as *Jerome against Jovinian*, which is the infamous attack of St. Jerome (347 – 420 AD) on marriage. The work does praise women in general, particularly those who gave their lives as Christian martyrs rather than marrying "heathens" or following their faith.

people should put no blame on them. And yet they were heathen, all of them, who so sorely dreaded all disgrace. These women of old so guarded their good name that I believe nobody shall ever find in this world a man who could be so true and kind as was the least woman in those days. Likewise, what do the epistles of Ovid[21] say about true wives and their travail?

"What says Vincent, in his *Historical Mirror?*[22] You may also hear the whole world of authors, Christian and heathen, discuss such matters. There is no need to write all day about them; but again I say, what ails you to write the chaff of stories and overlook the wheat?[23] By Saint Venus, by whom I was born, though you have rejected my faith, as other old fools have done in many days gone by, you shall repent your action in the sight of all humankind."

Then spoke Alceste, the worthy queen: "God, by your true courtesy, you must listen and see whether he can make any reply to these charges that you have made against him. A god should not thus be moved to anger, but being a deity he should be stable, and righteous and merciful as well. He cannot rightfully vent his ire before he has heard the other party speak. All that is carried to you in complaint is not the gospel truth; the god of Love hears many false tales. For in your court there are many flatterers, and many artful, tattling accusers, who drum many things in your ears out of hatred or jealous imaginings, or to have friendly talk with you. Envy – I pray God may give her bad luck! – forever washes the foul linen in a great court; out of the house of Caesar she

---

[21] Ovid. Publius Ovidius Naso (43 BC – 18 AD), Roman poet whose *Heroides* is a collection of letters written from famous women to the men who have left them.

[22] Vincent…Mirror. Vincent of Beauvais (1190 – 1264), whose *Speculum Historiale* (*Mirror of History*) was a comprehensive history which includes the story of Cleopatra, the first of the nine tales to follow.

[23] Chaff…wheat. Chaucer often distinguishes the kernel or fruit of the wheat, the essential matter, from the chaff, the full description (perhaps non-essential) of the matter.

departs neither by night nor day (thus says Dante).[24] No matter who departs, never will she be lacking. This man may be accused wrongly, and by rights should be absolved.

"Or else, sir, because this man is unwise, he might translate a thing not out of malice but because he is so used to writing books that he heeds not the substance of them; therefore, he wrote the *Rose* and *Criseyde* entirely innocently and knew not what he was saying. Or else he was told by some person to write those poems, and dared not refuse it, for before this he has written many books. In translating what old scholars have written, he has not sinned so grievously as if he should in malice write scornfully of love from his own point of view.

"A righteous lord should have this in mind, and not be like Lombard tyrants who practice willful tyranny;[25] for a king or lord by natural right ought not to be tyrannical or cruel like a tax collector, doing all the harm he can. He must bear in mind that they are his subjects, and that his true duty is to show all kindness toward his people, to hear their defenses readily, and their complaints and petitions in due time when they present them. This is the philosopher's[26] saying, that a king shall maintain his subjects through justice; that is his duty, in truth, and to this end a king is sworn deeply and has been for hundreds of years; and he shall maintain his lords in their station, as it is right and reasonable that they be exalted and honored and held most dear, for they are demigods here in this world.

"Thus shall he do to both rich and poor, albeit their conditions may not be alike, and have compassion on the poor. For behold the noble nature of the lion! When a fly annoys or bites him, he gently drives the fly away with his tail; for in his noble nature he does not stoop to avenge himself upon

---

[24] Dante. Dante Alighieri (Italian; 1265 – 1321), in his *Inferno*, 13.64-65.
[25] Lombard tyrants. A stereotype of the powerful men of fourteenth century Lombardy (Italy), though the stereotype may well be warranted.
[26] The Philosopher. The Greek philosopher Aristotle (384 BC – 322 BC).

a fly, as a dog and other beasts may do. A noble nature should show restraint and weigh all things by equity, and always maintain his own high station. For, sir, it is no noble act for a lord to condemn a man without speech or answer; in a lord that is a very foul practice. And if it should happen that the man cannot excuse himself, yet with sorrowful heart asks mercy, and humbly in his bare shirt yields himself up wholly to your judgment, then a god with brief consideration ought to weigh his own honor against the other's trespass. Since there is no cause for death here, you ought more readily to be merciful. Lay aside your wrath, and be a little yielding!

"This man has served you with his art and has furthered your religion with his poetry. While he was young he followed you; I do not know if he is now a renegade, but well I know that by what he has been able to write in praise of your name he has caused unlearned people to rejoice in serving you. He wrote the book called the *House of Fame*, and the *Death of Blanche the Duchess*[27] as well, and the *Parliament of Birds*, I believe, and all the love of Palamon and Arcite of Thebes,[28] though the tale is little known; and for your holy days many hymns, which are called Ballades, Roundels, and Virelays;[29] and to speak of other laborious works, he has translated Boethius[30] in prose, and *Of the Wretched Engendering of Mankind*,[31] which may be found in Pope Innocent;

---

[27] Death of Blanche the Duchess. Chaucer's *Book of the Duchess*.

[28] Palamon and Arcite of Thebes. Either Chaucer's *Palamon and Arcite* or *The Knight's Tale*.

[29] Hymns, Ballades, Roundels, and Virelays. Four types of formal poetry, the last two borrowed from the French tradition. Few of Chaucer's surviving poems, however, fit these descriptions.

[30] Boethius. Ancius Manlius Severinus (c. 475 – 525 AD), Roman philosopher, consul and minister to Theodoric, accused of treason. While awaiting execution he wrote *De Consolatione Philosphiae* (*The Consolation of Philosophy*), one of the most important books for the Middle Ages, which Chaucer translated into English (*Boece*).

[31] The Wretched Engendering of Mankind. This work is apparently lost, though it was presumably a translation of Pope Innocent III's *De miseria condicionis humane* (c. 1195).

and he also wrote the life of Saint Cecilia;[32] and also, a long while ago, *Origen upon the Magdalene*.[33] He ought now to have the lesser penalty, as he has written many lays[34] and other works.

"Now as you are a god and a king, I, your Alceste, once queen of Thrace,[35] ask you through your mercy never to harm this man so long as he lives. And he shall swear to you, and do so without delay, that he will sin no more thus. But just as you shall direct, so shall he write of women ever faithful in love, maidens or wives, whatsoever you wish. And he shall further you as much as he spoke amiss in the *Rose* or in *Criseyde*."

At this point the god of Love answered her thus: "Madame," he said, "it is long that I have known you to be so charitable and faithful that never, since the world was new, have I found any person who acted better toward me. Therefore, if I wish to safeguard my honor, I neither may nor will refuse your petition. All lies with you; do with him as pleases you, and forgive all, without further delay. For whosoever gives a gift or does an act of kindness, let him do it in good time, and his thanks will be greater for it. Judge, therefore, what he shall do. Go ahead now,[36] thank my lady here," he said.

I rose, got down on my knee, and then said, "Madame, may God on high reward you because you have made the god of Love forgive his wrath against me; and may He grant me the grace to live so long until I may truly know who you

---

[32] The life of St. Cecilia. The *Second Nun's Tale* in *The Canterbury Tales*.

[33] Origen upon the Magdalene. Usually regarded as a lost translation of the pseudo-Origen homily *De Maria Magdalena*, though *The Lamentation of Mary Magdalene*, included in the early printed editions of Chaucer, seems to be at least an approximation of this early work.

[34] Lays. Usually narrative poems of adventure and romance.

[35] Thrace. The southeast tip of the Balkan Peninsula, including northeastern Greece, Bulgaria, and Turkey.

[36] Go...now. Love, who has been speaking to Alceste, turns to the narrator for the last line of his speech.

are who have helped me and put me in such a hopeful state. But truly in this matter I thought not to have sinned or to have trespassed against love. For an honest man, in truth, has no part in the deeds of a thief; and a true lover ought not to blame me, though I speak in reproach of a false lover. He ought rather to remain on my side, because I wrote of Criseyde or of the Rose; whatsoever my author meant, it was my intention at least, God knows, to exalt faithfulness in love and to cherish it; and to warn people of falseness and evil by such examples. This was my intent."

And she answered, "Set aside your arguing, for Love will hear no pleas against himself, just or unjust: learn this from me. You have your pardon: hold yourself to that. Now will I say what penance you shall do for your trespass; understand it now. As long as you live, year by year you shall spend the most part of your life in writing a glorious legend of good women, maidens, and wives, who were ever faithful in love, and you shall tell of the false men who betrayed them, men who all their lives do nothing but see how many women they can shame – for in your world that is now seen as a sport. And though you care not to be a lover, speak well of love. This penance I give you. And I will so pray the god of Love that he shall charge his servants in any way to aid you and shall requite your labor. *And when this book has been completed, give it to the queen, on my behalf, at Eltham or at Sheene.*[37] Now go your way; your penance is only a small one."

The god of Love smiled, and then he said, "Do you know whether she is a maiden or wife, a queen or a countess, or of what degree, this woman who has given such a small penance to you who have deserved to suffer more sorely? But pity runs soon into a noble heart; that you can see. She manifests what she is."

And I answered, "No, sir, as I hope for happiness, I know

---

[37] Eltham...Sheene. Both were royal residences near London, the maintenance of which were under Chaucer's purview later in his career.

no more than that, as I can well see, she is kind."

"By my hood,"[38] Love said, "that is a true saying; and that you well know, by God, if you well consider. In a book that lies in your chest, do you not have the story of the great goodness of Queen Alceste, who was turned into a daisy? She who chose to die for her husband and to go to hell also instead of him? She whom Hercules rescued, by God, and brought out of hell back to happiness?"

And I replied, "Yes, now I recognize her! And is this the good Alceste, the daisy, mine own heart's repose? Now I feel well this woman's goodness, that both in her life and after her death her great goodness makes her renown double. Well has she requited me for my affection which I bear toward her flower, the daisy. It is no wonder that Jove should turn her into a star, as Agathon[39] tells, for her goodness. Her white crown bears witness of it; for she had as many excellences as there are small flowers in her crown. In remembrance and honor of her, Cybele[40] created the daisy, the flower all crowned with white, as people can see; and Mars gave its redness[41] to her crown, set amidst the white instead of rubies."

At this the queen grew somewhat red from modesty, when she was so praised in her presence. Then Love said, "It was a great negligence to write about the lack of steadfastness of women, since you know their goodness by experience and by old stories as well. Set aside the chaff, and write well of the wheat. Why would you not write of Alceste, and leave Criseyde sleeping in peace? For your writing should be

---

[38] By my hood. A simple commonplace oath.

[39] Agathon. This may refer to the Greek dramatist Agatone (c. 448 BC – c. 400 BC) named in Dante's *Pugatorio* 22.107; it more likely refers to Plato's *Symposium*, known as *Agatho's Feast*, given in honor of Agatone, which contains the story of Alcestis.

[40] Cybele. Goddess of fertility in ancient Phrygian; the Great Mother.

[41] Redness. Some have suggested that this refers to the red tips of the petals, but it likely refers to the gold in the center. (Red is still often used as the term to refer to gold today.)

of Alceste, since you know that she is a model of goodness; for she taught noble love, and especially how a wife ought to live, and all the bounds that she should keep. Your little wit was sleeping that time. But now I charge you on your life that in your Legend you write of this woman, after you have written of other lesser ones. And now farewell, I charge you no more.

"But before I go, this much I will tell you: no true lover shall go to hell. These other ladies sitting here in a row are to be in your ballad, if you will come to know them. In your books you shall find them all. Set them now all in mind in your Legend; I mean, those that are in your knowledge. For sitting here are twenty thousand more than you know, all good women, and true in love despite anything that may happen. The sun is drawing west. I must go home to paradise with this entire company. Make the verses of them as you wish, and serve always the fresh daisy.

"I wish you to begin with Cleopatra; and continue from there. And thus you shall gain my love. *For let us see now what sort of man that lover would be, who would endure so strong a pain for love as she. I know well that you may not set to rhyme all that such lovers did in their time; it would be too long to read and to hear. It will suffice me that you make it in this manner: that you retell the important part of all their lives, following what these ancient authors wish to treat. For whosoever shall tell so many stories, may he tell them shortly, or he shall dwell too long."*

And at these words I awoke from my sleep, and I began to write my Legend as follows.

Here ends the prologue.

I. THE LEGEND OF CLEOPATRA

ɛ̃

Here begins the Legend of Cleopatra,
Martyr, Queen of Egypt.

Afther the death of the king Ptolemy,[1] who had all
Egypt under his rule, Cleopatra his queen reigned;
until a certain time[2] when a certain situation arose
that from Rome there was sent a senator to win kingdoms
and honors for the town of Rome, as was their custom, and
to have the world under their obedience; and in truth his
name was Antony. As Fortune owed him a disgrace after he
had met with prosperity,[3] it so happened that he became a
rebel to the town of Rome; and moreover he falsely deserted
the sister of Octavian,[4] before she was aware, and at any cost
wished to have another wife. For these reasons he fell at
odds with Octavian[5] and with Rome.

Nevertheless this same senator was a worthy, noble war-
rior, in truth, and his death was a great pity. But Love had
brought this man into such a madness and so tightly bound
him in his snare, all for love of Cleopatra, that he set all the

---

[1] Ptolemy. Ptolemy XIV of Egypt (60 BC/59 BC – 44 BC), the brother-
husband of Cleopatra, who, with the assistance of Julius Caesar, forced
him from power.

[2] A certain time. Following the Battle of Philippi (42 BC), i.e., after
Marcus Antonius (Antony) and Augustus Caesar (Octavian) had defeated
the conspirators who had assassinated Julius Caesar. Antony, Octavian,
and Lepidus formed the Second Triumvirate of Rome.

[3] Fortune. As the wheel of Fortune continually turns, good and bad fortune
(or prosperity and disgrace) always follow one another.

[4] Sister of Octavian. Octavia, sister of Augustus Caesar (Octavain), the
fourth wife of Mark Antony

[5] Odds with Octavian. After Antony divorced Octavia and had an affair
with Cleopatra, Octavian declared war on Cleopatra, and thus on Antony.

world at no value. Nothing seemed to him so necessary as to love and serve Cleopatra. He cared not to die in arms in defense of her and her rights. And this noble queen in like fashion loved this knight, for his merit and his knighthood; and certainly, unless the books lie, he was in his nobility, discretion, and hardiness as worthy as any person alive. And she was as fair as the rose in May. And, as it is best to write briefly, she became his wife and had him as she desired.

To describe the wedding and the festival would take too long for me, who have undertaken such an enterprise as to put in verses so many stories, lest I should neglect things of greater weight and importance. (In such a way people might overload a ship or a barge.) Therefore I will skip lightly to the conclusion, and let the remains slip.

Octavian, maddened by this deed, raised a host of stout Romans, cruel as lions, to lead against Antony for his utter destruction. They went to their ship, and I leave them sailing thus. Antony was wary and would not avoid encountering these Romans if he could; he laid his plans, and on a certain day both he and his wife and his entire host went forth without delay to their ship; they waited no longer. Out at sea it happened that the foes met; the trumpet sounds on high, they shout and shoot and with the sun at their back make a fierce onset.

With a grisly sound out flies the huge shot, and furiously they hurtle together, and from the fore-tops down come the great stones. Among the ropes go grappling hooks full of claws. This man and that presses on with poleaxes; one flees behind the mast, and out again, and drives the other overboard. One pierces another upon his spear-point; one cuts the sail with hooks like scythes; another brings the wine-cup and bids them be glad; one pours peas upon the hatches to make them slippery; they rush together with pots full of quicklime.[6]

---

[6] Quicklime. Calcium oxide, used for a variety of purposes including mortar, in this case it would have burned the skin of the enemy.

And thus they pass the long day in battle, until at last (as everything has an end) Antony is defeated and put to flight, and all his people scatter as best they can.

The queen with all her purple sails fled likewise from the blows that went thick as hail-stones; no wonder she could not endure it. And when Antony saw that happen he said, "Alas the day that I was born! So on this day I have lost all my honor!" And in despair he started out of his wits, and stabbed himself to the heart at once, before he went further from the place.

His wife, who could get no mercy from Caesar, fled to Egypt in dread and anguish. But listen, all you who speak of devotion, you men who falsely swear by many oaths that you will die if your beloved should be so much as angered, behold what womanly faithfulness you may here see.

This woeful Cleopatra made such lament that no tongue can describe it; but in the morning she would delay no longer and commanded her skillful workmen to make a shrine out of all the rubies and fine gems that they could uncover in all

Egypt, and she filled the shrine with spices, had the body embalmed, and ordered that this dead corpse be enclosed in the shrine. And next to the shrine she had a pit dug, and put in it all the serpents she could find. Thus she spoke: "Now, beloved, whom my sorrowful heart so far obeyed that, from that blissful hour when I swore to be entirely and freely yours – I mean you, Antony, my knight – you were never out of my heart's remembrance as long as I was awake, day or night, in happiness or woe, in the carol or the dance.[7] And then I made this covenant with myself, that, whatever it was you felt, happiness or woe, the same would I feel, life or death, if it lay in my power for the honor of my wifehood. And I will fulfill that covenant while breath remains in me; and all shall see well that never was a queen truer to her love."

And at that word with a resolute heart she leaped naked into the pit among the serpents, and there she chose to be buried. Immediately the serpents began to sting her, and she received her death cheerfully, for the love of Antony who was so dear to her. And this is the truth of history; it is no fable.

Now, until I find a man this faithful and steadfast, who will so willingly die for love, I pray to God, may our heads never ache! Amen.

Here ends the Legend of Cleopatra, Martyr.

---

[7] Carol or dance. In the singing or in the dancing part of the festivity.

II. THE LEGEND OF THISBE OF BABYLON
ॐ

Here begins the Legend of Thisbe of Babylon, Martyr.

In Babylon, the town around which Queen Semiramis had built a moat and a very high wall with hard well-baked tiles,[1] this is what happened. In this noble town there dwelt two lords of high reputation; and they dwelt upon a green so close to each other that there was only a stone wall between them, as there often is in great towns. One of these men had a son, one of the most attractive in all that land; and the other had a daughter, the fairest who dwelt then in the eastern world. The name of each was brought to the other by women who were their neighbors. For in that country, even now in truth, maidens are closely and jealously guarded, lest they act foolishly.

This young man was called Pyramus, and the maiden called Thisbe; Ovid says thus. And so their praise was brought to each other by report, so that as they grew in years their love grew. And certainly, as for their age, there might have been marriage between them, except that their fathers would not agree to it. And both alike burned so sorely in love that none of their friends could hinder them from meeting secretly, sometimes by deceit, and speaking a bit about their longings. Cover the coals and the fire is hotter; forbid love, and it is ten times as raging.

This wall that stood between them was split in two, from the top right down, since long ago when it was built; yet this crack was so narrow and small that it was not visible to the

---

[1] Built...tiles. It is possible that this work was also undertaken by the Babylonian king Nebuchadnezzar (1125 BC – 1104 BC) nearly 1000 years after Semiramis. Babylon is modern-day Iraq.

tiniest extent. But what is it love cannot find? You two lov-
ers, to tell the truth, you first found this narrow little crack!
And they let their words, with voices as soft as any shrift,[2]
pass through the crack, and as they stood there, told all their
love-complaints and all their woe every time when they
dared. He stood upon the one side of the wall, Thisbe upon
the other, to hear the sweet sound of each other's voice; and
thus they would deceive their guardians. Every day they
would threaten this wall and wish to God it were beaten
down. Thus they would say: "Alas, you wicked wall!
Through your envy you hinder us entirely. Why will you not
split apart, or fall in two? Or at least, if you will not do so,
yet would you at least let us meet once, or once permit us to
kiss sweetly? Then would we be recovered from our painful
cares. But nevertheless we are indebted to you, inasmuch as
you allow us to send our words through your mortar and
stone. We still ought to be well pleased with you."

When these vain words were uttered, they would kiss the
cold stone wall and take their leave and depart. And they
were glad to do this in the evening or very early in the
morning, lest people saw them. And for a long time they did
thus, until one day, when Phoebus was clear and Aurora[3]
with her hot beams had dried up the dew on the wet herbs,
Pyramus came to this crack, as he was accustomed, and then
came Thisbe, and by their faith they pledged their honor to
steal away that same night, to beguile all their guardians, and
flee from the city; and, because the fields were so broad and
large, in order that they might meet at one place at one time,
they appointed their meeting to be under a tree where King
Ninus was buried. (For ancient pagans who worshipped idols
used then to be buried in fields.) And near this grave was a
spring. And, to tell this tale shortly, this covenant was very
strongly confirmed. To them it seemed that the sun delayed

---

[2] Soft as any shrift. As soft as any words spoken in the confessional cham-
ber in the Sacrament of Penance.
[3] Phoebus and Aurora. The sun and the dawn.

for a long time before it went down under the sea.

This Thisbe had so great a feeling and desire to see Pyramus that when she saw her time she stole away secretly at night with her face deceptively wimpled.[4] To keep her pledge she forsook all her friends. Alas! It is a pity that a woman should ever be so faithful to trust a man, unless she knew him better! She went to the tree at a swift pace, for her love made her so hardy; and down beside the spring she settled herself. Alas! Without more ado, a wild lioness, with its mouth bloody from strangling some beast, came out of the wood to drink at the spring where Thisbe was sitting. And when Thisbe saw that, she started up, with heart all terrified, and with fearful foot fled into a cave that she saw well by the moon. And as she ran she let fall her wimple and did not notice it, so sorely was she dismayed, and so glad of her escape as well. And thus she sat in hiding very quietly. When the lioness had drunk her fill, she roamed about the spring, and soon found the wimple, and tore it all to pieces with her bloody mouth. When this was done, she delayed no longer but made her way to the woods.

At last this Pyramus came, but, alas, he had stayed too long at home. The moon shone, and he could see well, and in his way, as he came speedily, he cast his eyes down to the ground, and as he looked down he saw the wide tracks of a lion in the sand, and he suddenly shuddered in his heart and grew pale and his hair stood on end; and he came nearer, and found the torn wimple. "Alas!" he said. "Alas, the day that I was born! This one night will slay both us lovers! How should I ask mercy of Thisbe, when I am the one who has slain her, alas! My prayer to you to come has slain you! Alas, to tell a woman to go by night to a place where peril might occur! And I so slow! Alas! If only I had been here in this place a furlong before you! Now may whatever lion or beast there may be in this forest tear apart my body! Now may it gnaw my heart!"

---

[4] Wimpled. With her face covered by a wimple (a headdress).

And with these words he sprang to the wimple, and kissed it often, and wept over it sorely and said, "Alas, wimple! There is nothing else, except that you shall feel my blood as well as you have felt the bleeding of Thisbe. And with these words he struck himself to the heart. The blood gushed out of the wound as broad as water when the pipe is broken.

Now Thisbe, who knew nothing of this, thought as she sat in fear, "If it so happens that my Pyramus has come here and cannot find me, he may hold me false and cruel as well." And she came out and searched for him both with her heart and with her eyes, and thought, "I will tell him about my dread both for the lioness and for all my behavior."

And at last she came upon her lover, all bloody, beating on the ground with his heels; and at this she started back, and her heart began to toss like the waves, and she grew pale as a boxwood tree. For a short moment she observed him and then well recognized that he was Pyramus, her dear heart.

Who could write what a deadly expression Thisbe had now, how she tore her hair, how she tormented herself, how she lay on the ground and swooned, how she wept his wound full of tears, how she mingled his blood with her lamentation and painted herself with his blood, and how she embraced the dead body, alas! How this woeful Thisbe acted then; how she kissed his frosty mouth so cold! "Who has done this! Who has been so ruthless, to slay my beloved! O, speak, my Pyramus! I am your Thisbe who calls you!" And at this she lifted up his head. This woeful man, in whom still remained some life, when he heard the name of Thisbe cried, cast his heavy, death-like eyes upon her and down again, and yielded up his spirit.

Thisbe arose without noise or outcry, and saw her wimple, along with his empty scabbard and his sword, which had put him to death. Then she spoke thus: "My sorrowful hand," she said, "is strong enough for such a task in my behalf, for love shall give me strength and boldness, I believe, to make my wound large enough. Dead I will follow you, and I will be the cause and partner also of your death," she said. "And though nothing except death alone could truly separate you from me, you shall now no more part from me than from death, for I will go with you. And now, you wretched, jealous fathers of ours, we who were once your children, we pray you that without more ill-will we may lie together in one grave, since love has brought us this pitiful end. And may the righteous God grant every lover, that truly loves, more prosperity than ever Pyramus and Thisbe had! And let no woman of gentle blood be so overconfident as to place herself in such hazard. Yet God forbid a woman may be only as true in loving as any man! And for my part I shall without delay make this plain."

And with these words she seized at once his sword, which was warm and hot with her lover's blood, and struck herself to the heart.

And thus are Pyramus and Thisbe gone. Of faithful men I find in all my books only a few more besides this Pyramus, and therefore I have spoken thus of him. For it is a rare delight to us to find a man who can be tender and true in love. Here you may see that, whoever her lover may be, a woman can only hope to find one as good as he.

Here ends the legend of Thisbe.

III. THE LEGEND OF DIDO, QUEEN OF CARTHAGE

ॐ

Here begins the Legend of Dido, Martyr.

May there be glory and honor, Vergil of Mantua,[1] to your name! I shall follow your lantern as well as I can, while you lead, in telling how Aeneas perjured himself to Dido. I will follow the main events of your *Aeneid,* and I will set forth the main idea from Ovid.[2]

When Troy was brought to destruction by the wiles of the Greeks, and especially by Sinon, pretending that the horse, through which many Trojans were to die, to be an offering to Minerva;[3] when Hector had appeared after his death, and fire so wild it could not be controlled raged through all the noble tower of Ilium, which was the chief fortification of the city; when all the land was brought low and Priam the king was slain and brought to nothing; and when Aeneas was charged by Venus to flee, he took his son Ascanius by his right hand, bore his aged father Anchises on his back, and fled; and on the way lost his wife Creusa.

He bore much sorrow in heart before he could find his companions. But at last, when he had found them, he prepared himself at a certain place, quickly pushed out to sea, and sailed forth with all his men toward Italy, as destiny directed. But it is not my point to speak of his adventures on the sea here, for it is not related to my subject matter; but, as I have

---

[1] Vergil of Mantua. Ancient Roman author (70 BC – 19 BC) of *The Aeneid,* the first four books of which relate the love story of Aeneas and Dido. Mantua is a city in the Lombardy region in central northern Italy.

[2] Ovid. Publius Ovidius Naso (43 BC – 18 AD), Roman poet, author of *The Heroides* (Heroines), which includes a letter from Dido to Aeneas.

[3] Minerva. Ancient goddess of wisdom and war, protector of the city of Troy; also known as Athena, for whom the Greek city of Athens is named.

said, my tale shall be of him and Dido, until I have finished.

So long he sailed the salty sea, until with difficulty he arrived in Libya with seven ships, and no larger fleet; and he was glad to rush to land, so shaken was he with the tempest. And when he had gained the haven, from all his fellowship he chose a knight called Achates to go with him to survey the land; he took with him no greater company. Forth they went, his comrade and he, without anyone to point the way, and left his ships riding at anchor.

So long he walked in the wilderness until at the last he met a huntress; she had a bow in hand, and arrows; her garments were cut short to the knee; but she was the fairest creature that ever Nature had formed. And she greeted Aeneas and Achates, and thus spoke to them, when she met them: "Have you seen walking near you," she said, "as you have gone wide and far, any of my sisters in this forest with garments tucked up and arrows in their quivers, with any wild boar or other beast that they have hunted?"

"Truly not, lady," said this Aeneas; "but it seems to me by your beauty you can not be a woman of this world, I would think, but are the sister of Phoebus.[4] And, if it is so that you are a goddess, have pity on our labor and woe.

"Truly, I am no goddess," she said; "for here in this land maidens walk with arrows and bow in this manner. This is the realm of Libya where you are, of which Dido is lady and queen." And briefly she told him all the reason of Dido's coming to those parts,[5] of which I wish not to write now;

---

[4] Sister of Phoebus. Diana, or Artemis, goddess of the moon, forest, animals, the hunt, and patron of women in childbirth and of virgins. As patron of virgins, she figures into much of Chaucer's work as the emblem of those who choose not to enter into the game of love.

[5] Dido's...parts. Born in Tyre (in modern-day Lebanon), Dido married the wealthy Sychaeus. After the death of Dido's father Belus, her brother Pygmalion slew Dido's husband Sychaeus, whose spirit came to her in a dream in which he related the story of his death. Dido then took his treasure and many followers to found what was to become the city of Carthage (in modern-day Tunisia).

there is no need, for it would be a waste of time. For this is the sum and substance: it was Venus, his own mother, who thus spoke with Aeneas; and she told him to turn toward Carthage, and without delay vanished out of his sight. I could follow Vergil word for word, but it would take entirely too long.

This noble queen named Dido, fairer than the shining sun and formerly wife to Sychaeus, had founded this noble town of Carthage, in which she reigned in such great glory that she was believed to be the flower of all queens in nobility, generosity, and beauty, so much so that anyone would be well who had seen her just once. She was so desired by kings and lords that her beauty had inflamed all the world, so well stood she in grace with every creature.

When Aeneas had come to that place, he made his way secretly to the chief temple of the whole town, where Dido was at her devotions. When he had come into the broad temple, I cannot say if it would be possible, but Venus made him invisible. Thus says the book, I promise you. And when Aeneas and Achates had been over this entire temple, they found depicted on a wall how Troy and all the land had been destroyed.

"Alas, that I was born!" said Aeneas, "our shame is known so far over the entire world that now it is depicted everywhere. We who were in prosperity are now defamed, and done so grievously that I care to live no longer." And with these words he burst out weeping so tenderly that it was pitiful to behold.

This lovely lady, queen of the city, stood in the temple in royal state, so splendid and so fair, so young, so joyous, with her glad eyes, that, if the god who made heaven and earth had desired a love, for beauty and goodness and womanhood and seemliness and fidelity, whom should he have loved but this sweet lady? There was no woman half so fitting.

Fortune, who governs the world, speedily brought forth so strange a chance that never yet was there so rare a case.

For all the company of Aeneas, which he deemed had been lost in the sea, had come to shore not far from that city. Therefore some of the greatest of his lords by chance came to the city to that same temple to seek the queen and entreat her for aid, for such renown of her goodness had spread. And when they had related all their woes, the tempest they had endured and all their distress, Aeneas showed himself to the queen and freely told who he was. Who could have been more joyful than his men at this moment, who had found their lord, their ruler?

The queen saw how they paid him such honor. She had often heard of Aeneas before that, and in her heart she had pity and woe that such a noble a man had so lost his heritage. And she could see that he was like a knight, well endowed in person and strength, and likely to be a courteous man; that he was articulate in his speech, had a noble face, and was well formed in brawn and bone. For, taking after Venus, he had such beauty that no man could be half so handsome, I believe. And he well seemed to be a lord. And because he was a stranger she liked him somewhat better; as – God save us – to some people a new thing is often sweet. Before long her heart pitied his woe, and with that pity love also came; and thus out of pity and courtesy he would need to be comforted in his distress.

She said that she was surely sorry that he had experienced such peril and such mishap. And in her friendly speech she spoke to him thus and said as you may hear: "Are you not the son of Venus and Anchises? In good faith, you shall have all the worship and assistance that I can rightly give you. Your ships and your followers I will protect." She spoke many courteous words and commanded her messengers to go that same day without fail to seek his ships and fill them with provisions; she sent many beasts to the ships, and presented them with wine as well. And she rushed to her royal palace, and she always had Aeneas near her.

What need is there to describe the feast to you? He was

never better at ease in his life. The festival was well provided with dainties and with splendor, with instruments of music, song and gladness; and many were the amorous glances and schemes. Aeneas had come into Paradise out of the mouth of Hell; and thus in bliss he recalled his state in Troy. After the meal, Aeneas was led to dancing-halls, full of fine hangings and rich couches and ornaments. And when he had sat down with the queen and spices had been served and wine passed around, he was led before long to his chambers to take his ease and have his rest, and all his men likewise, to do just as they wished.

There was no well bridled war horse, nor fine jousting steed, nor large easy-to-ride palfrey, nor jewel adorned all over with rich gems, nor fully weighted sacks full of gold, nor any ruby that shone by night, nor noble high-flying falcon for hunting herons, nor hound for hart or wild boar or deer, nor cup of gold, nor florins newly coined, which could be procured in the land of Libya, that Dido did not send to Aeneas. And all that he wished for, she provided for him. Thus could this honorable queen call upon her guests as one who knew how to surpass all in generosity.

Aeneas also sent Achates to his ship for his son, and for rich gear, including scepter, clothes, brooches and rings as well, some to wear, and some to present to her who had given him all these noble things. And he told his son to make the presentation and take the gift to the queen. This Achates returned, and Aeneas was eager and glad to see his young son Ascanius. But nevertheless, our author[6] tells us, that Cupid, who is the god of Love, at the prayer of his mother on high had taken on the likeness of the child, to enamor this noble queen of Aeneas. (But as to that text, be it as it may, I pay no attention to it.) But true it is that the queen made such to-do about this child that it is wondrous to hear of; and with good will she thanked him often for the gift that his father

---

[6] Our author. Chaucer typically refers to his source as his author, which in this case is Vergil, author of *The Aeneid*.

sent.

Thus was the queen in delight and joy with all these new, pleasant people of Troy. And she further inquired about the deeds of Aeneas and learned the entire story of Troy. And the two of them decided to converse and amuse themselves all long day. From this there was bred such a flame that luckless Dido had such a strong desire to become intimate with her new guest Aeneas that she lost her color and her health as well.

Now for the conclusion, the fruit of it all, the reason I have told this story, and shall continue it. Thus I begin; it happened one night, when the moon had lifted up her beams, that this noble queen went to her rest, sighed sorely, and tormented herself; she waked and tossed, started up many times as lovers usually do, as I have heard. And at last she made her moan to her sister Anna, and spoke thus: "Now, my dear sister, what can it be that makes me so horrified in my dream? This Trojan is so in my thoughts, because it seems to me that he is so well formed and so likely to be a worthy man, and that he know so much goodness as well, that all my love and life lie in his keeping. Have you not heard him tell of his adventures? Now surely, Anna, if you counsel me so, I would gladly be wedded to him. This is all; what more should I say? In him it all lies, to make me live or die."

Her sister Anna, as she saw her advantage, spoke as she thought and somewhat withstood her; but at this point there was so much discourse that it would be too long to retell. To sum it all up, the thing could not be withstood; love will love, it will hold back for no person. The dawn arose out of the sea; this amorous queen charged her attendants to prepare the nets and the spears broad and sharp. She wished to go hunting, this lusty, lovely queen, as this new sweet pain urged her.

On horse went all her lusty company, the hounds were led to the courtyard, and upon chargers swift as thought her young knights hovered all around, and a huge company of her women as well. Upon a stout palfrey white as paper, with a red saddle adorned delightfully, clearly embossed with bars of gold, sat Dido all covered with gold and gems, and she as fair as the bright morning that heals the sick of the night's sorrow. Upon a charger that leapt like flame (though one could turn him with a little bridle-bit) Aeneas sat, like Phoebus in his looks, so splendidly was he arrayed in his fashion; and governed his charger as he wished, by the foamy bridle with a golden bit.

And thus I let this noble queen ride forth in her hunting, with this Trojan by her. The herd of harts was found before long, with "Ho! Faster! Spur on! Loose the dogs! Loose them! Why won't the lion come, or the bear, so that I might meet him once with this spear?" Thus cried these young people, and on they went killing all these wild harts, and took them as they wished.

Amid all this the heavens began to rumble, and thunder roared with its grisly voice; down came the rain thick with hail and sleet and heaven's fire; so sorely it frightened this noble queen and her attendants as well that each was glad to flee away. And in brief, to save her from the tempest she fled into a little cave, and with her went Aeneas also. I know not if any more went with them; the author makes no mention of that.

And here began the deep devotion between the two of them; this was the first morning of their gladness, and the beginning of their sorrow. For there Aeneas so kneeled and revealed to her all his heart and his pain; and swore so deeply to be true to her in happiness or in woe, and to exchange her for no other – as a false lover so well knows how to make his complaint – that hapless Dido pitied his woe, and took him for a husband, to be his wife for evermore so long as they should live. And after this, when the tempest ceased, they came out in joy and went home.

Evil Rumor arose, and arose quickly, how Aeneas had

gone with the queen into the cave. And people judged as they wished. And when the king named Yrbas[7] knew of it, since he had always loved her and wooed her, to win her as his wife, he made such sorrow and sad expressions that it was pitiful and heart-rending to see. But in love it happens ever so, that one shall laugh at another's sorrow; now Aeneas laughs, and is in more bliss and wealth than ever he was in Troy.

O unfortunate woman, innocent, full of pity, faith, and tenderness, why did you so trust men? Had you such pity upon their pretended woe, even though you had before you so many old examples? Do you not see how they all perjured themselves? Where do you see one who has not forsaken his beloved or been unkind or done to her some mischief or robbed her or boasted of his acts to her? You can see this as well as you can read it.

Take heed now of this great gentleman, this Trojan, who so well knew how to please her, who pretended to be so true and yielding, so courteous and so discreet in his deeds; who knew so well how to perform all due observances, and attend her pleasure at dances and feasts and when she went to the temple and back again home; and who fasted until he had seen his lady, and wore in his heraldic devices I know not what for her sake; and who would compose songs, and joust and do many deeds at arms, and send her letters, tokens, brooches, rings. Now hear how he shall serve his lady! After he had been in peril of death from hunger and misadventures on the sea, and desolate, fugitive from his country, and all his company scattered by the tempest, she gave her body and her realm as well into his hand, when she might have been a queen of another land besides Carthage and lived in sufficiency of joy. What more would you want?

This Aeneas, who had vowed so deeply, was weary of

---

[7] Yrbas. Berber (North African) king who granted Dido the land that became Carthage when she arrived there. He later hoped for (perhaps demanded) her hand in marriage.

the business before long, and his hot earnestness had all blown by. Secretly he had his ships prepared and planned to steal away by night. This Dido suspected it and well thought that all was not right; for in the night he lay in his bed and sighed. Without delay she asked him what displeased him: "my dear heart, whom I love best?"

"Surely," he said, "this night my father's spirit has so sorely troubled me in my sleep, and Mercury as well has delivered a message, that it is my destiny to sail soon for I must conquer Italy. For this it seems to me my heart is broken." With this his false tears burst forth, and he took her in his two arms.

"Is that in earnest?" she said. "Will you do so? Have you not sworn to take me as your wife? Alas! What kind of a woman will you make of me! I am a gentlewoman and a queen! You will not thus foully flee from your wife? Alas, that I was born! What shall I do?"

To tell it briefly, this noble Queen Dido sought shrines and made sacrifices; she knelt and cried in such a way that it is pitiful to relate. She implores him and offers to be his slave, his servant of the lowest rank. She fell at his feet and swooned, her shining golden hair disheveled, and cried, "Have mercy! Let me go with you! These lords who are my neighbors will destroy me, left alone, because of you. Unless you will take me now as your wife, as you have sworn, then I will give you leave to slay me with your sword right now this evening, for then I shall die wedded to you. I am with child: grant my child life! Mercy, lord! Have pity in your thought!"

But all this was to no avail for her; for one night he let her lie sleeping and stole away to his followers, and as a traitor he sailed forth toward the great land of Italy. Thus he left Dido in woe and pain, and there he wedded a lady named Lavinia.

When he stole away from Dido in her sleep, he left a garment and his sword also standing right at the head of her bed, as he hastened to reach his ships. When hapless Dido awoke, she kissed this garment often for his sake, and said, "O you garment, so sweet while it pleased Jupiter, take my soul now, unbind me from this unrest! I have run through the whole course of fortune." And then she swooned twenty times, without any aid from Aeneas. And when she had made her lament to her sister Anna – of which I cannot write, such pity I have to tell of it – she bade her nurse and her sister to go fetch fire and other things right away, and said she wished to make a sacrifice. And when she saw her time, she leaped on the sacrificial fire, and with his sword she stabbed herself to the heart.

But before she was wounded, before she died, she did this, as my author tells: she wrote a letter without delay, which began in this way: "Just as the white swan," she said, "begins to sing at the time of his death, so to you I make my lament; not that I hope to get you back, for well I know that is all in vain, because the gods are contrary to me. But since my good name is lost through you, I may well lose a word or

a message upon you, albeit I shall be never better for that.
For the same wind that blew away your ship has blown away
your good faith." But whosoever wishes to know this entire
letter, let him read Ovid;[8] there one shall find it.

Here ends the Legend of Dido,
Martyr, Queen of Carthage.

---

[8] Ovid. I.e., in *The Heroides*.

IV. THE LEGEND OF HYPSIPYLE AND MEDEA

Here begins the Legend of Hypsipyle and Medea, Martyrs.

Duke Jason, you root of false lovers, you sly devourer and ruination of high-born women, tender creatures! You set your lures and your enticements for ladies with your stately appearance, your words stuffed with pleasantness, your pretended fidelity, your manner, your obsequiousness, your humble bearing, and your counterfeited woe and pain. Where others are false to one, you are false to two! Ah, often did you swear you would perish for love, when you felt no illness except foul delight, which you call love! As long as I live, your name shall be spread far in English, so that your deceitfulness shall be known! Take that, Jason!

Now the horn for the hunt is blown for you! But surely it is both a pity and a woe that love works in such a way with false lovers; for they shall find better love and better pleasure than he who has paid for his love dearly, or has suffered many bloody blows in fight. For the fox shall eat just as tender a capon, though he may be false and have deceived the fowl, as the head of the household shall, who has paid for that food. Although he may have claim to the capon in reason and justice, the false fox will get his share in the dark. This example well fits Jason, as he dealt with Hypsipyle and with Medea the queen.

In Thessaly,[1] as Guido[2] tells us, was a king named Pelias, who had a brother named Aeson; and when Aeson could scarcely walk on account of his age, he gave Pelias the

---

[1] Thessaly. Region of central Greece, bordering Macedonia to the north.

[2] Guido. Guido delle Collone, thirteenth-century Italian author of *Historia destructionis Troiae* (*History of the Fall of Troy*).

rule of his entire realm and made him lord and king. Of this
Aeson was begotten Jason, in whose time there was not in all
that land a knight so renowned for gentility, nobility,
strength, and vigor. After his father's death he so bore
himself that there was nobody who cared to be his foe, but
gave him all his honor and sought after him.

Pelias had great envy about this, imagining that Jason
might be so exalted and put in such position by the love of
the lords of his realm that he might remove him from his
own throne. And in his mind by night he plotted how Jason
might best be destroyed, without a scandal about his plot.
And at last he determined to send Jason into some far
country, where he might perish. This was his devious plan,
though he showed Jason all affection and loving appearance,
lest his lords should detect the plan.

Now it so happened, since fame spreads widely, that
there were great tidings everywhere and many reports that in
an island called Colchis,[3] eastward in the sea beyond Troy,
people might see a ram that had a fleece of gold so shining
that nowhere was there another such sight. But it was always
guarded by a dragon, by two fire-spitting bulls[4] made
entirely of brass, and by many other marvels all around. But
nevertheless this was the tale, that whosoever wished to win
that fleece must fight both the bulls and the dragon before he
could win it. And King Aeëtes[5] was lord of that island.

This Pelias contemplated this plot, to exhort his nephew
Jason to sail to that land to entertain himself. And so he said,
"Nephew, if such an honor might come to you as to win this
famous treasure and bring it into my land, it would be a great
pleasure and honor to me. Then would I be bound to requite

---

[3] Colchis. Region in the Southern Caucasus on the eastern coast of the
Black Sea; colonized by the Greeks from the sixth to second century BC.
[4] Dragon…bulls. Though dragons are typically depicted as fire-breathing,
in this case the bulls maintain this trait.
[5] Aeëtes. Born of Helios (god of the sun) and the Oceanid Perseis; brother
of Circe and Pasiphaë; and father of Medea, Chalciope and Absyrtus.

your labor. And I myself will pay all the expenses. Choose what people you wish to take with you. Let us see now, do you dare to take this voyage?"

Jason was young and eager at heart, and undertook this enterprise. Soon Argus[6] designed his ships. With Jason went the mighty Hercules and many others whom Jason chose as well. But whoever wishes to ask who went with Jason, read the *Argonautica*,[7] for that will tell a tale that is long enough.

Quickly Philoctetes hoisted the sail, when the wind was favorable, and they hastened themselves out of their country of Thessaly. Long they sailed the salty sea, until they arrived at the isle of Lemnos[8] (albeit this is not related by Guido, yet

---

[6] Argus. The name of the ship's designer, Argus, who was guided in his work by Athena, is the root of the word "Argonaut," who are generally categorized as the heroic band of Jason's followers.

[7] Argonautica. Chaucer may have known one or two versions: one by Apollonius of Rhodes (third century BC); the other by Valerius Flaccus (first century AD), who borrowed from Apollonius.

[8] Lemnos. Greek island in the northern Aegean Sea, near ancient Troy.

Ovid in his Epistles[9] says this), and of this isle the lady and queen was the fair young Hypsipyle, the shining-bright, who was daughter of Thoas, once the king.

Hypsipyle was walking to entertain herself and, roaming upon the cliffs by the sea, before long she discovered where under a bank the ship of Jason had arrived. In her goodness she speedily sent down a messenger to learn if any stranger had been blown there by storm during the night, so that she might bring him aid, as it was her custom to assist every creature and offer aid through her very kindness and courtesy This messenger hurried down and came upon Jason and Hercules as well, who had arrived on land in a small boat as they were refreshing themselves and catching their breath. The morning was mild and fine, and on his way the messenger met these two lords and very discreetly greeted them and gave his message, asking them without delay if they had suffered any damage, were in any way distressed, or had need of a pilot or food; for they should in no way lack aid, since aid was wholly the queen's will.

Jason answered mildly and gently; he said, "I heartily thank my lady for her goodness; truly, we need nothing now, except that we are weary and have left the sea to entertain ourselves until the wind blows nearer our course."

This lady was roaming with her attendants along the shore by the cliff to entertain herself, and found this Jason and the other standing speaking of their business, as I have said. This Hercules and Jason beheld how this lady was the queen, and greeted her kindly as soon as they had met her. And she noted well, and knew by their fashion, array, words, and looks that they were men of noble birth and high status. And she led these strangers to the castle with her, treated them with great honor, and asked them about their labor and travail on the salty sea; so that within one day or two she knew from the people who were in the ships that they were

---

[9] Epistles. In *The Heroides*, which is comprised of letters from women to the men who failed them.

Jason, full of renown, and Hercules, of great praise, that sought the adventures of Colchis. And she paid them more honor than before, and the more time passed, the more time she spent with them, for in very truth they were worthy people. And she spoke mostly with Hercules; to him her heart inclined, for he seemed to be steadfast, wise, true, discreet of speech, and without any wicked designs or other attachment in love.

This Hercules so praised Jason that he exalted him to the sun, saying that there was not under the high canopy of heaven a man half so true in love; and he was wise, hardy, trusty, and rich. In these three more points there was none like him: he surpassed all men, living or dead in character and enthusiasm; he was also truly nobly born; and he was likely to become king of Thessaly. He had no fault, except that he was afraid of love and shy in speech; he would rather murder himself and die than have anyone find him out to be a lover. "I wish to almighty God that I could give my flesh and blood, provided I would not die, if only he might find a wife somewhere, one of his status; for such a gallant life she should lead with this gallant knight!"[10]

And all this had been planned the day before by Jason and Hercules; by these two there was contrived a wicked fraud to become intimate with an innocent woman; for their agreement was to deceive this queen. And Jason was as coy as a maiden; he looked piteously but said nothing, and freely gave great gifts to her counselors and officers.

I wish to God that I had leisure to rhyme a full story of all his wooing! But if any false lover should be in this house,[11] just as that false lover now acts, so did Jason, with feigning and every act of trickery. You will get no more from me, unless you will read my author,[12] who tells the full story.

---

[10] Gallant knight. Presumably Hercules says these lines.

[11] This house. Perhaps a reference to the poem being read before an audience.

[12] Author. I.e., his source, which could mean Guido delle Collone, Ovid, or Apollonius of Rhodes (or Valerius Flaccus).

The sum of it is this, that Jason was wedded to this queen, and took of her substance whatever he wished for his provisions; and upon her he begat two children. And he hoisted his sail and never saw her again.

In truth she sent him a letter, which would be too long to write and tell, and reproached him for his great infidelity, and prayed to him to have some pity on her. And of his two children she told him this, that in truth they were like him in all things, except they did not know how to beguile others. And she prayed to God that before long the woman who had removed Hypsipyle from his heart might find him untrue to her also; and that she should be fated to slay both her children, and so might all those who allowed him to have his will with them. And all her days Hypsipyle remained true to Jason, and always remained chaste, as his wife; nor did she ever have joy in heart, but died for his love in bitter sorrows.

This Duke Jason, a dragon and devourer of love, had arrived in Colchis. Just as the appetite of matter[13] is always to take form, and may pass from form to form (or like a well that is bottomless), so also the false Jason could have no peace; for the craving of his appetite to work his will with women of gentle blood, this was all his delight and felicity.

Jason roamed forth to the town which once was called Jaconitos, which was the chief city of all Colchis; and he told the cause for his coming to Aeëtes, king of that land, praying him that he might have his trial to win the golden fleece if he could. To this petition the king agreed, and did him honor, as was fitting; and so much that he bid his daughter and heir, Medea, who was so wise and beautiful that never did a man see with his eyes a fairer woman, to keep Jason company at his meal and sit by him in the hall. Now Jason was a proper and lordly man, and had great renown; he was regal as a lion in his demeanor, pleasant and courteous in his speech, and knew without any book the

---

[13] Appetite of matter. The quality of a fluid to take the shape of its container.

trade and art of love entirely, and every ceremony of it. And as if Fortune owed Medea a foul misfortune, she became enamored of this man.

"Jason," she said, "for anything I see you have put yourself into great peril in this thing which you are about. For whoever wishes to achieve this adventure cannot well escape death, I believe, unless I would be his helper. But nevertheless," she said, "it is my will to assist you, so that you shall not perish but return home safe and sound to your Thessaly."

"My true lady," then said Jason, "I know well that my might and my travail all the days of my life do not merit your doing me this honor or that you would have any regard for my death or woe. May God thank you, for I can or may not thank you sufficiently. I am your man and humbly pray you, without more speech, to be my help; but surely I shall not hold back for fear of death."

Then this Medea made known to him from point to point the peril of the adventure and of his battle, and in what unequal combat he must stand, in which no creature except Medea herself could assure him of his life. And, to go shortly to the point, they were agreed between the two of them that Jason should wed her as a true knight. And the time was set for him to come in the evening to her chamber, and there take oaths by the gods that never for joy or woe, night or day, would he falsely fail her; that he would be husband as long as he lived to her who here had saved him from death. And upon agreement they met by night, and he took his oath and went to bed. And in the morning he hastened to arise, for she had taught him how he could not fail to win the fleece and achieve success in the conflict;[14] and thus she saved his life and his honor and got him a great name as a conqueror, even though it was through the wiles of her enchantment.

---

[14] Success...conflict. Medea gave Jason an herbal potion that put to sleep the sleepless guardian dragon, allowing Jason to gather the Golden Fleece.

Now Jason had the fleece and returned home with Medea and a great store of treasure. But it was unknown to her father that she went to Thessaly with her dear Duke Jason, who afterwards brought mischief upon her. For like a traitor he abandoned her, left with her his two young children, and falsely betrayed her, alas! Forever was he a chief of traitors in love and soon he wedded yet a third wife, the daughter of King Creon.[15]

This is the payment and reward that Medea received from Jason for her fidelity and kindness, as she loved him better than herself, I believe, and left her father and her heritage for him. And this is the prowess of Jason, that in his days no lover so false was found walking on earth. And therefore in her letter she began thus, when she upbraided him for his falseness: "Why did it please me more to look on your yellow hair than on the boundaries of my honor? Why did your youth, your comeliness, and the infinite graciousness of your tongue please me? Ah, had you died in your adventure, how much faithlessness would have died with you!" Well can Ovid compose her letter in verse, which would be too long for me to include here now.[16]

Here ends the Legend of Hypsipyle and Medea.

---

[15] Daughter of King Creon. Glauce, to whom Medea sent a poisoned dress and crown, which killed the new bride and her father Creon.

[16] Now. Chaucer leaves her story incomplete. Medea bore five sons to Jason. Two of her sons, Mermeros and Pheres, were killed in Corinth, assisting her in her revenge. She then murdered two other sons, Tisander and Alcimenes, leaving only Thessalus alive. With the aid of a golden chariot led by dragons (supplied by her grandfather Helios), she flew from Corinth to Athens where she married King Aegeus, bore a son, Medus, who lost his bid to the throne when the king's first son, Theseus, returned. No major sources name the manner in which she died.

V. THE LEGEND OF LUCRECE

ॐ

Here begins the Legend of Lucrece of Rome, Martyr.

Now I must speak of the exile of the kings of Rome by reason of their horrible deeds, and of the last king, Tarquin,[1] as Ovid and Titus Livy[2] relate. But it is not for that reason I tell this tale, but to praise and remember that true wife, the faithful Lucrece, for whose true wifehood and steadfastness not only do these pagans extol her but also he who is called in our legendaries the great Augustine[3] has great pity for this Lucrece, who died in Rome. And of the manner of her death I will treat but briefly, and touch upon only the important matter of this thing.

When Ardea[4] was besieged with Romans who were stern and stout, long lay the siege and accomplished little, so that they remained there half idle, as they judged. And in his sport the young Tarquin[5] began to jest, for he was loose tongued, and said that this was an idle existence, for no man there did more than his wife. He said, "And let us speak of wives; which is the best. Let every man praise his own as it pleases him, and let us ease our hearts with conversation."

A knight named Collatine arose and spoke thus: "Nay, there is no need to rely on words, but on deeds. I have a

---

[1] King, Tarquin. Lucius Tarquinius Superbus, the seventh and last king of Rome (reigned 535 BC – 509 BC; died 495 BC).

[2] Titus Livy. Titus Livius Patavinus, or Livy (59 BC – 17 AD), author of *Ab urbe condita libri*, commonly known as *The History of Rome*.

[3] Augustine. St. Augustine of Hippo (354 – 430 AD) uses Lucrece in *The City of God* as a defense of the virtue of Christian martyrs who had been raped by Romans but did not commit suicide.

[4] Ardea. Capital city of the Rutuli, in Latium about twenty miles south of Rome.

[5] Young Tarquin. Sextus Tarquinius, son of Lucius Tarquinius Superbus.

wife," he said, "who is held to be good by all who know her. Let us go to Rome tonight and see."

Tarquinius answered, "That is good."

To Rome Tarquin and Collatine came, went to the house of Collatine without delay, and alighted. The husband well knew the whole design of the house, and secretly they entered, for there was no porter at the gate. They stopped at the chamber door. This noble wife sat beside her bed with hair unbound, for she suspected no harm. She was working soft wool, our book says, to keep her from sloth and idleness, and she told her servants to perform their duties as well.

And she asked them, "What news do you hear? What do people say of the siege and how it shall end? Would to God the walls would fall! My husband has been so long away from this town; when I think of the siege of that place, for this reason the dread so sorely pains me that it stings to my heart just like a sword. God save my lord, I pray, in His mercy."

And at that she wept tenderly and paid no more attention to her work, but meekly let her eyes fall. And this demeanor well became her. And her tears, full of virtue, embellished her wifely chastity. Her look was worthy of her heart, for they accorded in sign and in truth. And at her words Collatine her husband came bursting in, before she was aware of him, and cried, "Fear not, for I am here!" And immediately she rose up with blissful countenance and kissed him, as wives used to do.

Tarquin, this proud king's son, considered her beauty and her demeanor, her blonde hair, her form, her manner, her hue, her words of lament, and saw that her beauty was not falsely created by any artifice. And he conceived such desire for this lady that it burned in his heart like a flame, so furiously that his wits were entirely forgotten. For he well imagined that she could never be won; and thus the more he coveted her and thought of her loveliness, the more he was in despair. His covetousness turned to blind lust.

In the morning, when birds began to sing, he returned secretly to the camp and walked sadly by himself, ever freshly recalling her image: "Thus lay her hair, and so fresh was her hue. Thus she sat, thus spoke, thus spun. This was her look, this was her beauty and her demeanor." His heart had now received all this thought. And as the sea, all tossed by a tempest, will yet heave for a day or two after the storm has fully departed, so too, though her form was absent, the pleasure of it was still present – but not pleasure, but rather evil delight or an unrighteous desire with evil intent. "For in spite of herself she shall be my mistress," he said; "chance always helps the hardy. However it ends, it shall be done."

And he buckled on his sword, departed, rode forth until he arrived at Rome, and all by himself took his way straight to the house of Collatine. The sun was down, and the day had lost its light. And he hid in a secret corner, and in the night stole out like a thief, when everyone had gone to their rest and none had a thought of such treachery. Whether it was by window or other sly means, he quickly entered and with sword drawn came speedily where this noble wife Lucrece was lying. And as she awoke she felt her bed pressed down. "What beast is that," she said, "weighing down my bed thus?"

"I am the king's son, Tarquin," he said; "but if you cry out or make a noise, or awaken any creature, by that God who formed man alive, I shall thrust this sword through your heart." And at that he leaped at her throat and set the sharp point on her heart.

She spoke no word, she had no strength; what should she say? Her wit had entirely fled. Just as when a wolf finds a solitary lamb, to whom should she lament or make moan? What! Shall she struggle against a powerful knight? Everyone well knows that a woman has no strength. What! Shall she cry? How shall she escape the man who has her by the throat, with his sword at her heart? She begged for mercy, and said all she could.

"If you do not yield to me," he said, this cruel man, "may Jupiter save my soul, I will slay your groom in the stable and lay him in your bed, and raise the alarm that I found you in such adultery. And thus you shall die, and also lose your good name, for you have no other choice."

Now at this time these Roman matrons so loved their fair reputation, and so dreaded shame, that, for fear of scandalous talk and fear of dying, she lost her wit and breath at once and lay in a swoon so deathlike that one could have smitten her arm or head off; she felt nothing, fair or foul.

Tarquin, heir to a king, who by lineage and justice should bear yourself as a lord and a true knight, why have you done dishonor to chivalry? Why have you basely wronged this lady? Alack! This was a villainous deed of yours!

But now to the point: I read in the history that after he departed, the misfortune that occurred was this. The lady sent for all her friends, father, mother, husband together; and with her shining hair all disheveled, in dress such as women then used to wear for the burial of their friends, she sat in the hall with a sorrowful look. Her friends asked what could ail her, and who was dead? And she sat continually weeping; for shame she could not fetch forth a word, nor did she dare to look upon them. But at last she told them of Tarquin, this sorrowful case, all this horrible thing. It would be impossible to tell the lament that she and all her friends made together. Had people's hearts been made of stone, it would have made them pity her, so wifely and so true was her heart. She said that for her guilt or infamy her husband should not have a foul name; she would not permit that in any way. And they all answered that upon their word they forgave her, as was just; it was no fault of hers, it lay not under her control. And they told her many examples.

But it was all for nothing, and thus she directly replied. "Be as it may," she said, "as to forgiving, I will by no means have forgiveness." And secretly she snatched forth a knife, and with it slew herself. And as she fell, she looked and still paid attention to her clothes; for as she fell down she still remained mindful lest her feet or the like would be bare, so well she loved purity and fidelity.

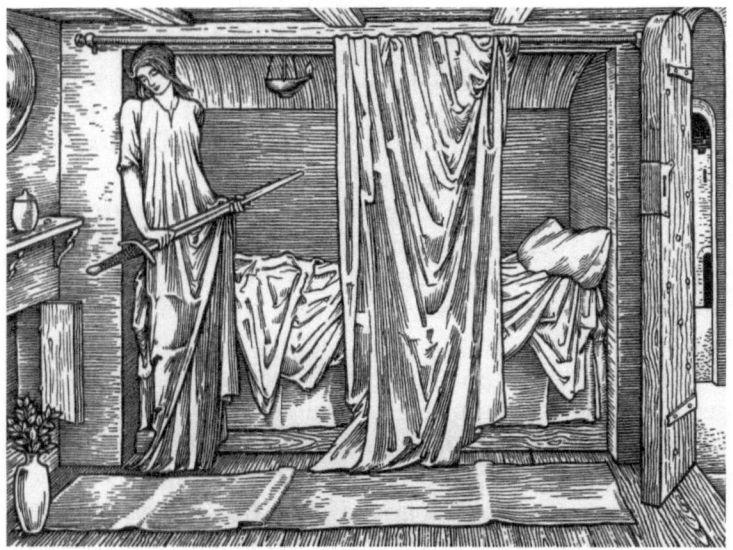

All the town of Rome felt pity for her, and Brutus[6] swore by her chaste blood that for that deed Tarquin should be banished, and all his kinsfolk; and he had the people summoned, and openly told the tale to them all, and openly had her carried on a bier through the entire town, so that the people might see and learn the horrible deed of her violation. And never since that day was there a king in Rome; and she was believed there to be a saint, and her day was always dearly worshipped in their law.

---

[6] Brutus. Lucius Junius Brutus (sixth century BC), a nephew of the reigning king, Lucius Tarquinius Superbus; already opposed to the king's extension of power, Brutus ceased the event of Lucrece's death to lead the nation to a bloodless change of regimes and the creation of the Roman Republic. Ancestor of Marcus Brutus, famous conspirator against Julius Caesar.

And thus ended Lucrece the noble wife, as Titus Livy[7] bears witness. I tell the tale because she was so faithful in love and never by her will did she turn to any new lover, and for the sake of the constant heart, steadfast and kind, which men may ever feel in these women; where they set their heart, there it remains. For well I know Christ himself tells that in all Israel, broad though the land may be, he found not so great faith as in a woman;[8] and this is no lie. And as for men, look what tyrannical deeds they do every day. Test them, whosoever may wish: even the truest of them is too entirely fickle to trust.

Here ends the Legend of Lucrece of Rome, Martyr.

---

[7] Livy. See note at the beginning of the tale of Lucrece.

[8] Faith as in a woman. Likely refers to Matthew 15.28 in which a woman whose daughter is tormented by a demon persists in asking Christ's aid, to the effect that he heals her.

VI. THE LEGEND OF ARIADNE

ॐ

Here begins the Legend of Ariadne of Athens.

Y ou Judge in Hell, Minos,[1] lord of Crete,[2] now your turn comes; now you come into the ring! Not for your sake alone do I write this history, but to call to mind once more the great untruth in your love, Theseus, for which the gods of high heaven are angered and have taken vengeance for your guilt; may you grow red with shame! Now I begin your life.

Minos, great king of Crete, who had a hundred great and strong cities, sent his son Androgeus to school at Athens, where it happened that while he was learning philosophy he was slain in that very city, for no reason but envy. The great Minos, of whom I speak, came to avenge his son's death. Long and hotly he laid siege to Alcathoe.[3] Nevertheless, the walls were so strong, and Nisus, king of that city, was so knightly, that he feared little; he took no heed of Minos or his army until one day the chance arose that the daughter of Nisus stood on the wall and saw the entire workings of the siege. It so happened that, watching a skirmish, she set her heart so sorely upon Minos the king for his beauty and his chivalry that she thought she would die. And, to hasten over this long story, she enabled Minos to win that place and to have the city all at his will, to save or destroy whom he wished. But he repaid her wickedly for her kindness and would have left her drowning in sorrow and woe, had not the

---

[1] Minos. In Canto V of Dante's *Inferno*, Minos is depicted as the judge of the underworld.

[2] Crete. Island kingdom south of Greece.

[3] Alcathoe. The citadel of Megara, near Athens, named after Alcathous, founder of Megara.

gods had pity upon her. But that story would be too long for me now.[4]

This King Minos also won Athens, Alcathoe, and other towns. And this was the outcome: that Minos so harshly oppressed the people of Athens that from year to year they had to give him their own beloved children to be slain, as you shall hear. This Minos had a monster, an evil beast, so cruel that, when a man was brought to him, without pause he would devour him; no defense could help. And truly every third year they cast lots, and as the lot fell, on the rich or the poor, they had to give up their son and present him to Minos to be saved or destroyed, or let his beast devour him at his will. And Minos did this out of hatred; all his pleasure was set to avenge his son and to make the people of Athens his slaves from year to year as long as he should live. And when this town was won he sailed home.

This evil custom continued a long time, until Aegeus, king of Athens, had to send his own son Theseus, since the lot fell upon him, to be devoured, for there was no reprieve. And this woeful young knight was led forth straight to the court of King Minos and was cast fettered into a prison, until the time when he would be devoured.

Well may you weep, woeful Theseus, who is the king's son, thus condemned! It seems to me you were deeply indebted to any who should save you from cold troubles. And now if any woman should help you well ought you to be her slave and true lover year by year. But now to return to my tale.

The tower where this Theseus was cast, down in the dark and extremely deep bottom, adjoined the wall of an outer chamber belonging to the two daughters of King Minos, who

---

[4] Too long for me now. Nisus' daughter Scylla helped Minos by cutting off the purple lock of hair that made her father invincible. After her father was defeated and Minos, disgusted by her treason, set sail, she swam to meet him, but, though she almost caught Minos' ship, she was attacked and drowned by her father who had been transformed into an eagle.

in much mirth and joy and comfort dwelt in their great chambers above, facing the chief street. By chance, I know not how, it happened that, as Theseus was making his complaint one night, the king's daughter, named Ariadne, and her sister Phaedra as well, heard all his complaint, as they stood upon the wall and looked upon the bright moon. (They cared not to go to bed early.) They had compassion for his woe; for a king's son to be in such a prison and be devoured seemed to them a great pity.

Then Ariadne spoke to her noble sister and said, "Phaedra, dear sweet sister, can you not hear how woeful this lord's son is, how piteously he laments his kindred, and the wretched plight he is in, although he is entirely guiltless? Now surely, it is a pity. And if you will assent, by my faith he should be helped, however we can!"

Phaedra answered, "I am certainly as sorry for him as ever I was for any man; and for his assistance the best counsel I know is that we cause the jailer to come secretly speak with us directly, and bring this woeful man with him. For if he could overcome this monster, then he would be free; there is no other remedy. Let us test him well to his heart's root, whether, if it may be so that he has a weapon, he might dare to fight this fiend and defend himself, to keep and save his life. For you well know that in the prison where he must descend, the beast is in a place that is not dark, and this man has room to wield an axe or a sword or staff or knife; so it seems to me he ought to save himself. If he is a man he will do so. And we shall also make him balls of wax and flax, that when the beast fiercely opens his mouth, he shall cast them into his throat, to encumber his teeth and satisfy his hunger. And as soon as Theseus shall see the beast choke, he shall leap on him to slay him before they would ever meet together. This weapon the jailer shall hide, before that time, secretly within the prison. And because the beast's dwelling-place winds much in and out, and has such intricate paths – for it is shaped like a maze, and for this I have in mind a remedy – that by means of a ball of twine he may directly return the way he went, following the thread continually. And when he has overcome the beast, then he may flee away from this horror and can take the jailer with him, and advance him at home in his country, since he is the son of so great a lord. This is my advice, if he should dare to take it."

Why should I make a longer story? The jailer came, and Theseus with him; and when all was thus agreed, down fell Theseus upon his knee before Ariadne: "True lady of my life," he said, "I, a sorrowful man, condemned to die, will not part from you, after this stroke of fortune, so long as I have life or breath, but I will thus remain in your service, so that as an unknown outcast I will serve you forevermore, until my heart shall die. I will forsake my own heritage, and, as I said, be a page of your court, if you stoop to grant me so great a grace to have my meat and drink here; and for my sustenance I will still labor just as you shall wish it, so that not Minos, who never saw me with the sight of his eyes, nor any other man, shall be able to recognize me, so cunningly and well shall I bear myself and so skillfully and wretchedly disguise myself, so that I shall be detected by no man in this world.

"This I will do to preserve my life and to remain in the presence of you, who do me this excellent kindness. And I will send this worthy man here, now the jailer, to my father, and for reward he shall be one of the greatest men of my country. And if I yet dare say it, my fair lady, I am a king's son, and a knight. Would to God, if it could be, that you were in my land, all three of you, and I with you to bear you company, then you would see if I lie about this. And if I offer you humbly to be your page and serve you here, and if I should not serve you as humbly there I pray to Mars to grant me such favor that a shameful death may there fall upon me, and death and poverty upon all my friends; and that after my death my spirit may roam by night and walk to and fro; and that I may have the shameful name of traitor. May my spirit walk for this reason! And if I ever claim any higher station, unless you stoop to give it to me, may I die a shameful death, as I have said! Have mercy, lady! I can say nothing else!"

Theseus was a handsome knight to behold, and young, only twenty-three years old. Whosoever had seen his countenance would have wept for pity of his woe. Therefore this Ariadne in this way answered to his offer and his appealing look: "For a king's son," she said, "and a knight as well to serve me in such a low degree, may God forbid it, for the shame of all women; and may God grant me that such a thing may never happen, but send you grace and cunning of heart to defend yourself and slay your foe in knightly fashion; and may God grant hereafter that I may find you so kind to me and to my sister here that I regret not to have saved you from death! Yet it would be better if I were your wife, since you are as gently born as I and have a kingdom not far from here, than that I should allow you to die guiltless or let you serve as a page. It is not a reasonable offer for one of your kindred, but what is it that a man will not do for fear? As for my sister, since it is so that she must go with me if I depart, or else suffer death, and I too, arrange for her to be faithfully wedded to your son[5] at your home-coming. This is the final end of this thing. Swear to it here, by all that may be sworn on."

"Yes, my lady," he said, "or else may I be entirely torn to pieces by the Minotaur tomorrow! And here take my heart's blood in pledge, if you will; if I had a knife or spear, I would bear it and vow upon it, for I know only then will you believe me. By Mars, who is chief in my creed, if I should live and not fail tomorrow to win my battle, I would never flee from this place until you should see the very proof of my words. For now if I am to tell the truth to you, in my own

---

[5] Your son. In one version of his story, Theseus and the Amazonian woman Antiope had a son, Hyppolotus. Theseus was not one of the youths selected to be devoured by the Minotaur, but, though older than the rest, volunteered to take the place of one of them.

country I have loved you for many days, though you knew it not, and most desired to see you of any earthly creature living. By my faith I swear and assure you that for these seven years I have been your servant. Now I have you, and you also have me, my dear heart, Duchess of Athens!"

This lady smiled at his steadfastness, and at his earnest words and his look, and spoke all softly to her sister in this way. "Now my sister," she said, "now we are duchesses, both you and I, and assured of royal rank in Athens, and both likely to be queens afterwards; and we have saved from his death a king's son, as it is ever the custom of well-born women to save a man of gentle blood if they can, in an honest cause, and most of all if he is in the right. It seems to me that no person ought to blame us for this, nor give us an evil name."

And to explain this matter briefly, Theseus took leave of her, and every point in this covenant was carried out as you have heard me relate. His weapon, his ball of flax, all the things that I have named, were laid by the jailer right in the house where this Minotaur had his dwelling, near the door where Theseus should enter. And Theseus was led to his death, and he came forth to this Minotaur, and following the instruction of Ariadne he overcame the beast and slew him; and by the ball of flax he came out again secretly when he had slain the beast.

Through the jailer he got a barge and loaded it with his wife's treasure, and he took his wife and her fair sister, and the jailer as well, and with all three of them stole away from the land by night, and turned toward the land of *Oenopia*,[6] where he had a close friend. There they feasted and danced and sang. And he had in his arms this Ariadne who had preserved him from the beast. Soon he got himself another ship there, and a great number of his countrymen as well, took his leave, and sailed homeward.

And he brought his ship ashore on an island amid the wild sea, where there dwelt no creature except wild beasts,

---

[6] Oenopia. The modern island of Aegina, about fifteen miles southwest of Athens.

and many of them. And he remained on that island half a day and said he must rest himself on land, and his mariners did as they desired. And, to tell the matter briefly, while his wife Ariadne his wife lay sleeping, because her sister was fairer than she, Theseus took Phaedra by the hand and went forth to the ship, and like a traitor stole off, while this Ariadne still slept. And toward his country he swiftly sailed – may the wind drive him to twenty devils! – and found his father drowned in the sea.[7]

I wish to speak no more of him, in faith. These false lovers, may poison be their destruction! But I will return to Ariadne, who for weariness was overtaken with sleep. So sorrowfully her heart may awaken! Alas! Now my heart has

---

[7] Father...sea. Upon his departure from Athens, Theseus promised his father Aegeus that, if his voyage were successful, he would hoist white sails on his return (black would be hoisted if he were unsuccessful). Theseus forgot to hoist the white sails on his return; when his father saw this, he cast himself from a cliff and drowned in the sea, which came to be known as the Aegean.

pity for you! Right at dawn she awoke and groped in the bed and found nothing. "Alas!" she said, "that ever I was created! I am betrayed!" And she rent her hair, and hastened barefoot to the shore, and cried, "Theseus! My sweet heart! Where are you, now that you are not here with me, and may be slain thus by beasts?"

The hollow rocks answered her; she saw no man. And the moon still shone, and high upon a rock she climbed speedily, and saw his barge sailing in the sea. Her heart grew cold, and she said, "Milder than you I find the wild beasts!" Had he who thus betrayed her not sinned? "O, return," she cried, "for the pity and sin of it! Your ship does not have all its crew!" She stuck her kerchief up on a pole, in case he should indeed see it and remember that she was left and return and find her on the shore. But she did this all for nothing at all; he had gone his way. And down she fell swooning on a stone; and she arose, and in all her sorrow she kissed the prints of his feet where he had passed.

And then she spoke in this way to her bed: "You bed," she said, "which has received two, you shall answer for two, and not for one only! Where has your greater part gone? Alas, what will become of me, wretched creature! Even if a ship or a boat should come here, I dare not for fear go home to my country. I cannot counsel myself in this situation!"

Why should I tell more of her lament? It was so long, it would be a heavy thing to tell; Ovid records everything in Ariadne's epistle.[8] But I shall tell it quickly to the end. The gods helped her, out of pity; and in the sign of Taurus people may see the gems of her crown shining brightly.[9] I will speak no more of this tale; but this is how this false lover could

---

[8] Ovid…epistle. Ariadne's letter in Ovid's *Heroides*.

[9] Taurus…brightly. Chaucer's version of the tale is different than the more popular one in which Ariadne is received by Bacchus and his followers. In sympathy Bacchus turns Ariadne into the Corona Borealis (Northern Crown) constellation. As it is opposite Taurus, it shows brightly when the sun is in Taurus.

beguile his true love. May the devil repay him for his trouble!

Here ends the Legend of Ariadne of Athens.

VII. The Legend of Philomela

Here begins the Legend of Philomela.

God is the giver of forms.[1]

Y ou giver of its forms to matter, who has created the beautiful world, and eternally bore it in your mind before you did begin your work, why did you make to the shame of man – or even if it were not your doing to create such a thing for that end – why did you allow Tereus to be born, who was so false and deceitful in love that when people mention his name, all things from this world up to the highest heaven are corrupted? So grisly was his act that, as for me, when I read his foul story, my eyes grow foul and sore. Even now the venom of so long ago lasts and infects any who will behold the story of Tereus of whom I tell.

He was lord of Thrace,[2] and kin to the cruel god Mars, who stands with bloody spear. And with blissful cheer he had wedded King Pandion's fair sweet daughter, who was named Procne, the flower of her country.[3] Juno, however, cared not to be at the festival, nor Hymen, who is the god of marriage; but ready at the feast, in truth, were the three Furies with their deadly torch; and the owl, prophet of woe and misfortune, all night fluttered among the roof-beams. The revels, with much singing and dancing, lasted a fortnight or a little less.

But to pass soon over this history, for I am weary to tell of him, five years he and his wife lived together, until one

---

[1] God…forms. Attributed to Plato, Greek Philosopher (428 BC – 347 BC).
[2] Thrace. The southeast tip of the Balkan Peninsula, including northeastern Greece, Bulgaria, and Turkey.
[3] Her country. I.e., Greece: she is from Athens.

day she began to yearn so sorely to see her sister, whom she
had not seen for a long while, that for her desire she did not
know what to say. But she begged her husband for God's
love that she might once go to see her sister and return
directly; or else, if she could not go to her sister, Procne
asked him to send after her. And this was continually her
petition day by day, with all wifely meekness in word and
expression.

This Tereus had his ships made ready, and fared forth
himself to Greece to his father-in-law, and prayed him to
grant that Philomela, his wife's sister, might just this one
time have a sight of Procne, his wife, for a month or two:
"And she shall directly return to you; I myself will both
come and go with her, and I will guard her as my heart's
life."

This aged Pandion, this king, began to weep for
tenderness of feeling when he thought to give his daughter
permission to go; in this entire world he loved nothing as
much. But at last she got permission, for with salty tears she

sought from her father the gift to see her sister, whom she longed after so; and she embraced him with her two arms. And she was so young and beautiful as well that when Tereus beheld her beauty, how she had no peer in attire, and how she was yet twice as rich in goodness, he so set his fiery heart upon her that he wished to have her, howsoever it should happen. And with his wiles he kneeled and prayed until at last Pandion spoke thus: "Now, son," he said, "so dear to me, I commit to you my young daughter here, who bears the key of all my heart. Greet well my daughter and your spouse, and give her leave to follow her pleasure now, so that she may see me once before I die."

And in truth Pandion made splendid entertainment for Tereus and for his people, great and small, who had come with him; he gave him costly gifts, conveyed him through the chief street of Athens, and escorted him to the sea. Tereus returned home, and Pandion suspected no evil.

The oars speedily pulled the vessel on, and at last it arrived in Thrace. And up into a forest he led her and secretly hastened into a dark cave, and there, whether she wished to remain there or not, he ordered her to remain. At this her heart shuddered, and she said, "Where is my sister, brother Tereus?"

And at that she wept tenderly, and trembled with fear, pale and piteous just like the lamb that is bitten by the wolf; or like the dove stricken by the eagle, that escapes from his claws, yet is dazed and afraid lest it be seized again, even so she sat. But it could not be otherwise, this was all: by force this betrayer did his deed, all in spite of her. Lo! Here was a manly deed, and a righteous one! She cried, "Sister!" with a loud voice, and "Father dear!" and "God in heaven, help me!" All of these cries did not avail her. And this false thief did this lady still more harm, out of fear lest she should cry out his shame and openly disgrace him, and he cut off her tongue with his sword; and in a castle he put her secretly in prison for evermore and kept her in his possession, so that she could never escape him.

Ah, hapless Philomela, woeful is your heart! May God avenge you and grant you your prayer! Now it is time I made a brief end.

This Tereus came to his wife and took her in his arms and wept piteously and shook his head, and swore to her he found that her sister was no more. At this, the luckless Procne was so woeful that her sorrowful heart nearly broke in two. And thus I leave Procne in her tears, and will tell more about her sister.

This woeful lady had learned in her youth to make embroidery, and to weave tapestry in her frame, as women have long been accustomed to do. And, to tell it briefly, she had her fill of food and drink, and clothing at her desire, and could both read and compose rather well, but truly she could not write with a pen. She knew, however, how to weave letters back and forth, so that by the time the year was all gone, she had woven on a large woolen cloth how she had been brought in a ship from Athens and taken into a cave; and well she wove all that Tereus had done and composed on the top the story of how she had been treated because she loved her sister. And then she gave a ring to a page, and by signs asked him to go to the queen and take to her that tapestry, and by signs she swore many oaths to him that she would give him whatever she could obtain.

This page directly went to the queen and gave it to her, and told her everything about it. And when Procne beheld this thing, for sorrow and frenzy she spoke no word, but pretended to go on a pilgrimage to the temple of Bacchus.[4] And in a little while she found her mute sister sitting weeping all by herself in the castle. Alas, for the woe, lament, and waling that Procne voiced over her mute sister! Each took the other in her arms; and thus I leave them in their sorrow.

---

[4] Bacchus. Roman god of wine and revelry: Dionysus in Greek tradition.

The rest of the story it matters not to tell,[5] for this is the sum of it, that she who never merited the wickedness of this cruel man, nor caused him any harm that she knew of, was treated this way. You must beware of man, if you please. For though he may not wish to act shamefully as Tereus did, lest he lose his fair reputation, or may not be a villain or murderer, yet you shall find him true for only a short time – unless it should happen that he can find no new love. I would say this, even if he were my own brother

Here ends the Legend of Philomela.

---

[5] Rest of the story. Chaucer omits the meal of the flesh of Tereus' son Itys that the two sisters serve to Tereus. Upon the revelation that he is eating his own son, Tereus attacks the sisters in his rage, and the three of them are transformed into birds (Philomela into the nightingale, Procne into the swallow, and Tereus into the hoopoe).

VIII. The Legend of Phyllis

❧

Here begins the Legend of Phyllis.

By experience as well as authority you may find, if you are willing, that wicked fruit comes from a wicked tree. But I say this now for this end: to tell you of false Demophon; never have I heard of anyone falser in love, unless it were his father Theseus. May God in His mercy keep us from such a one! Thus may those women pray who hear of Demophon. Now I turn to the substance of my tale.

The city of Troy was destroyed. This Demophon came sailing over the sea to Athens, to his huge palace; with him came many ships and barges full of his people, of whom many were sorely wounded and sick and woebegone. And they had lain long at the siege. Behind him came a rain and a wind, and drove him so fiercely that his sails could not withstand it; more than all the world he wished he were ashore, as the tempest hunted him back and forth. It was so dark he could go nowhere, and his steering-gear had been broken by a wave. His ship was destroyed so far below and in such a way that no carpenter could mend it. By night the sea glowed wildly, as if it were a torch, and rolled him up and down, until Neptune had compassion on him, as well as Thetis, Thorus, Triton,[1] and all the deities of the sea, and let him come upon a shore of which Phyllis was lady and queen, the daughter of Lycurgus, fairer to see than the flower in the bright sunshine.

Scarcely could Demophon make it to shore, weak and weary, and his company wasted by weariness and famine; he was nearly driven to his death. His wise men counseled him to seek help and aid from the queen, to see what grace he might obtain, and to make a purchase of provisions in that land to keep him from woe and misfortune. For he was sick and nearly dead; scarcely could he speak or draw breath, and he lay near Rhodopeya[2] to rest himself. When he could walk, he thought it would be best to seek aid at the court.

People knew him well and paid him honor, for he was the duke and lord of Athens, as Theseus his father had been, who in his day was of great renown – no man so great in that entire region. And he was like his father in face and form, and false in love; it came to him by nature. Like Reynard the fox, the fox's son by nature knows his old father's ways without teaching; and a drake can swim when it is caught and carried to the water's edge.[3] This honorable Phyllis, well

---

[1] Neptune...Triton. Neptune: god of the sea (Poseidon). Thetis: a goddess of the sea; leader of the Nereides (sea nymphs). Thorus: not identified; possibly a mistake. Triton: messenger of the sea; son of Poseidon and Amphitrite.

[2] Rhodopeya. The country near the Rhodope mountain range near Thrace, which is the southeast tip of the Balkan Peninsula.

[3] Drake...edge. I.e., it will remember its true nature, like Demophon,

pleased with his bearing and demeanor, treated him in a friendly manner. But because I am already oversupplied with writing about men false in love, and so that I may also hasten myself in my legend (may God grant me grace to finish it), therefore I pass on quickly this way. You have fully heard the scheme of Theseus in betraying fair Ariadne, who in pity had preserved him from death. In a few words, in exactly the same way Demophon trod the same path of his false father Theseus. For he swore to Phyllis to wed her, and pledged her his word, and picked from her all the goods he could, when he was whole and sound and had rested himself, and he did with Phyllis as he wished. And well could I, if I wished, describe all his doings back and forth.

He said he must sail to his own country, for there he desired to prepare for her wedding, as fitted her honor and his also. And openly then he took his leave, and swore to her that he would not delay, but in a month would return. And in that land he ordered matters as if he were a true lord, received people's obedience well and familiarly, ordered his ships to be made ready, and went home as soon as he could. And he did not come again to Phyllis. So cruelly and sorely she suffered for that – alas as the stories remind us – that she caused her own death directly with a rope, when she saw that Demophon had betrayed her.

But first she wrote to him[4] and earnestly begged him to come and deliver her from her pains, as I shall retell in a word or two. I will not stoop to toil over him or spend a penful of ink on him, for he was false in love, just as his father. May the Devil burn up both their souls! But I will write a word or two from the letter of Phyllis, though it may be but a small part.

"O Demophon," she said, "your hostess of Rhodopeya, your Phyllis, so encompassed with woe, must complain upon you, that you are not keeping the covenant that you made,

---

[4] Wrote to him. As noted in other tales, Chaucer is drawing from Ovid's *Heroides*, letters from women left by their male lovers.

but are delaying over the length of time set between us. Your anchor which you did drop in our haven gave promise that you would truly come again before the moon once completed her circuit; but the moon has hid her face four times since that day you left from this land, and four times she has lighted the world again. But for all that, in very truth, the Thracian[5] waves have not yet brought the ship from Athens; and still it does not come. And if you would only calculate the appointed time, as I or other true lovers should, you would see I am not making my complaint, God knows, before the appointed day."

But I cannot write all her letter, point by point, for it would be a burden to me; her letter was very long and broad. But here and there I have set it in rhyme, where it seems to me she has spoken well.

She said, "Your sails do not return, nor truly is there any good faith in your words. But I know why you are not coming; it is because I was so generous in my love to you. And if the vengeance of the gods to whom you are forsworn should fall on you for that, you are not sufficient to bear the penalty. Too much I trusted, well may I complain, in your lineage, your fair tongue, and your tears that were falsely wrung out. How could you weep thus by deceitfulness?" she said. "Can such tears be feigned?

"Now surely, if you would only remember it, this ought to be but a small glory to you, to have betrayed thus a simple maiden! I pray to God, and often have prayed, that this may be the greatest praise of all and the highest honor that ever shall come to you! And when your ancestors of old shall be depicted, so that men may see their worthiness, then I pray to God that you also may be depicted, so that people may read as they pass by, 'Lo, this is he who betrayed with his flattery and basely wronged her who was his true love in thought and deed.' And truly, one point more may they see, that in this you are like your father; for he deceived Ariadne, in truth,

---

[5] Thracian. From the southeast tip of the Balkan Peninsula.

with such treachery and duplicity as you have in beguiling me. And in that point, and not a worthy one, you follow him and are his heir in very truth. But since you have beguiled me so sinfully, though you are harder than any stone, within a while, you may see my body floating in the very harbor of Athens without burial place and burial."

And when this letter was sent forth, she, knowing how fickle and false he was, soon destroyed herself in despair,[6] alas! Such sorrow she had, because she had so used herself up. Beware of your subtle foe, you women, since even this day examples may be seen; and in the matters of love trust no man but me!

Here Ends the Legend of Phyllis.

---

[6] Destroyed herself. In some versions of the story, she hangs herself from a tree. The tree then sprouts from her burial spot the *nux Phyllidos*, or the Filbert tree. Some versions name it as an almond tree. Demophon, upon opening a box that she gave him, finds the contents so horrifying (though these contents are not identified) that he rode off madly on his horse and, when the horse tumbled, fell on his sword and died.

IX. The Legend of Hypermnestra

Here begins the Legend of Hypermnestra.

In Greece there once were two brothers, of whom one was named Danaus, and he had many sons from his body, as such false lovers often know how to do. Among all his sons there was one he loved best of all; and when this child was born, this Danaus crafted him a name and called him Lynceus. The second brother was named Aegyptus, and in love he was false as ever he pleased, and in his days he begat many daughters, among whom he begot by his own wife a dear daughter, the youngest of them all, and let her be named Hypermnestra. This child, by arrangement of the heavenly bodies at her birth, was born to all good virtues, as it pleased the gods before her birth that she should be the wheat of the sheaf.[1]

The Fates,[2] whom we call Destiny, ordained for her that she should be compassionate, steadfast, wise, and true as steel, as these women[3] well agreed. For though Venus gave her great beauty, she was so compounded by the influence of Jupiter that tenderness, fidelity, fear of disgrace, and preservation of the good name of her wifehood – these all seemed to her to yield happiness on earth. And at that time of year red Mars was so feeble that he was bereft of his power for malice; Venus repressed his cruel activity. What with her power and other oppression by celestial houses,

---

[1] Wheat of the sheaf. She would be the best part of the entire stalk of wheat, i.e., of all his children.

[2] Fates. Chaucer uses the word "Wirdes," just as Shakespeare uses the term "Weird Sisters" for the witches in *Macbeth*.

[3] Women. I.e., the Fates.

Mars' venom was kept down, so that Hypermnestra dared not handle a knife with evil intent, even if it were to save herself. But as the heavens then revolved, she came under the evil aspects of Saturn, which made her to die in prison, as I shall afterwards tell.

To Danaus and to Aegyptus as well, though they were two brothers, it seemed good to make a marriage between Hypermnestra and Lynceus (for at that time consanguinity was no hindrance to marriage), and appointed that it should be on an appointed day. Thus the full agreement was made. The preparation was completed, and the time was near at hand. And thus Lynceus wedded the daughter of his uncle, and each had the other. The torches and the bright lamps burned, the sacrifices were fully prepared, and the incense emanated sweetly from the fire; flower and leaf were plucked up by the roots to make garlands and high crowns. The place was full of the sound of minstrelsy of the amorous songs of marriage, as was he custom at that time. And this was in the palace of Aegyptus, who ruled in his house as he wished. And thus they wore the day to an end, and friends took their leave and went home.

The night had come, and the bride had to go to bed. Aegyptus hastened to his chamber and secretly summoned his daughter. When the house was emptied of all people, he looked on his daughter with a joyful expression and spoke to her as you shall hear: "My own true daughter, my heart's treasure, since the day when my first shirt was made,[4] or when I received my lot at the hands of the Sisters of Fate, never has a thing come so near my heart as you, my Hypermnestra, beloved daughter! Take heed what I, your father, say here to you, and always follow the will of one who is wiser than you. For, first of all, daughter, I love you so that the entire world is not half so dear to me! And I would not advise you to your harm for all the wealth under the cold moon. And what is in my mind shall be said

---

[4] First…made. An old saying, i.e., when he was born.

directly, with this protestation, that unless you do as I shall tell, you shall die, by Him who created all! In a few words, you will not escape from my palace before you die, unless you consent and work according to my counsel. Take this as my full resolution."

Hypermnestra cast down her eyes and quaked like the leaf of the green aspen; her hue grew deathly and like ashes, and she said, "Lord and father, God knows I will do all your will, according to my power, so it may be no dishonor to me."

"I will not," he said, "have any exception." And he brought forth a knife, sharp as a razor. "Hide this," he said, "so that it may not be seen. And when your husband has gone to bed, cut his throat in two while he sleeps. For in my dreams I am warned that my nephew shall be my slayer, but which nephew I know not; therefore I wish to be safe. If you say no, by Him to whom I have sworn, we two shall have a quarrel, as I have said."

Hypermnestra nearly lost her wits, and, to pass from there unharmed, she consented to him; there was no other way to behave graciously. And with that he took up a flask and said, "Give him a glass of this, or two or three, to drink when he goes to rest, and he shall sleep as long as ever you would like him to sleep, as the narcotics and opiates are so strong. And go on your way, lest he grow impatient."

Out came the bride; and with a grave countenance, as is often the manner with maidens, was brought to the chamber with revel and song. And in brief, lest this tale be too long, this Lynceus and she were soon brought to bed, and every person hastened out the door.

The night wore on and he fell into slumber. She began to weep full tenderly, and she arose and quaked with fear, like a branch that Zephyrus[5] buffets; and all in that city of Argos was hushed. Now she grew cold as frost; for pity so constrained her heart and fear of death so pained her that three times she fell down in distress. She arose and staggered here and there, and looked hard at her hands.

"Alas! And shall my hands be bloody? I am a maiden, and, by my nature and my appearance and my clothes, my hands are not created to tear any man from his life with a knife. What the Devil do I have to do with this knife? And shall I have my throat cut in two? Then I shall bleed, alas, and perish. This thing must necessarily have an end: either he or I must die. Now surely," she said, "since I am his wife, and he has my vow, it is better for me to die with wifely honor than to be a traitor living in shame. Be as it may, for earnest or game, he shall awake and arise, and go on his way by this rain-gutter, before it is light."

And she wept tenderly on his face, and embraced him in her arms, shook him, and gently awoke him. And when she had warned him and provided his escape, he leaped out at

---

[5] Zephyrus. The west wind, the warmth of which usually signifies the arrival of spring.

the window from the upper room. This Lynceus was swift and light of foot, and ran swiftly before his wife.

This hapless woman, alas, was so weak and helpless that before she had gone far, her cruel father had her seized. Alas, Lynceus, why so unkind? Why did you not remember to take her and lead her forth with you? For when she saw that he was gone and that she could not go so fast or follow him, she sat herself down at that moment, until she was caught and fettered in prison.[6]

This tale is told for this end—[7]

[Unfinished.]

---

[6] She...prison. If Chaucer were to follow Ovid's version of the tale, Hypermnestra would be abandoned by Lynceus and die of a broken heart. In another version, Hypermnestra is soon saved by Aphrodite. Lynceus, the only husband among the fifty sons of Aegyptus to be spared, kills Danaus in revenge. Lynceus and Hypermnestra then have a son, Abas; thus the beginning of the Argive kings (the Danaid Dynasty).

[7] This end. Chaucer is nearly finished with this tale. There is much speculation as to why he ends this tale, and the work as a whole, at this point. Some point to the narrator's frustration or lack of interest in the tales; others believe that he had discovered a better framework for tale-telling, specifically, a group of tales told by a group of pilgrims on their way to Canterbury.

THE HOUSE OF FAME

ॐ

INTRODUCTORY NOTES

Chaucer's *The House of Fame* is a sort of puzzle. Though it is similar to his other early works in its form as a dream vision and its presentation of a narrator who is somewhat incompetent at understanding the world around him, *The House of Fame* presents some new twists.

The plot and style of *The House of Fame* is rambling, including elements of narration, bibliography, history, mythology, philosophy, ethics, and social commentary. It begins as a meditation on the logic and value of dreams (discussed more extensively than elsewhere in his works) and moves to the narrator's dream of a temple of glass, the most memorable part of which is a tablet of brass containing the story of Aeneas and Dido. After the retelling of this tale from *The Aeneid* the narrator is seized by an eagle, which takes him, after a lengthy discussion about fame and the inadequacies of the narrator (presumably Chaucer himself), to the House of Fame, where he sees, among other things, one group of plaintiffs after another pleading for Fame herself to bestow the best of fame on them. (Fame is not only the modern concept of fame, but reputation as well.) As we might expect, Fame is entirely inconsistent in her awarding of that fame. The many vignettes of groups of people being judged in an unearthly setting is often seen as Chaucer's version of Dante's *Inferno*; in fact John Lydgate, a contemporary of Chaucer, called this work "Dante in Englyssh."

After pages of shifting action, the poem ends suddenly with the introduction of "a man of great authority" in the last line of the poem. This has led many scholars to believe that this is an attempt by Chaucer to begin the telling of a number of tales, just as he does in *Legend of Good Women* and *The Canterbury Tales* (both of which were also left incomplete). One might anticipate that a man of authority such as this might speak at length, tell a story, and, as in Chaucer's other collections of stories, bid others to tell stories.

Regardless of the peculiarities of the poem, Chaucer's *House of Fame* remains a dazzling work of fiction and a compelling discussion of the nature of fame.

THE HOUSE OF FAME

Book I

The Proem

May God turn every dream to good for us! For to my mind it is a wonder, by the Cross, what causes dreams by night or by morning; and why some are fulfilled and some not; why this one is a vision and that a revelation; why this is one kind of dream and that one is another, and not the same to everyone; why this one is an illusion and that one is an oracle.

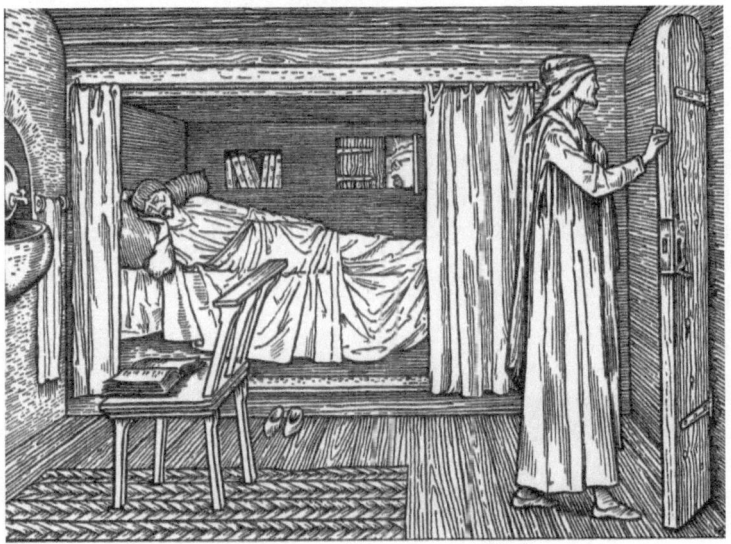

I know not, but whosoever knows the causes of these miracles better than I, let him explain them; for I certainly know nothing about that, and never think to work my wit too busily to understand the kinds of their significance, or the length of time to their fulfillment, or why this is the cause of dreams rather than that: whether people's temperaments make them dream of what they have been thinking about; or whether, as others say, over-enfeeblement of brain from sickness or abstinence, imprisonment, or great distress, disorder of the natural routine (as when a person is too zealous in study), melancholy, or so much inward fear that nobody may offer one relief; or whether the devoutness and meditation of some people often causes such dreams; or whether it may be that the cruel, hard life that these lovers lead, who hope or fear too much, so that their mere fancies cause visions; or whether spirits have the power to make people dream at night; or whether the soul from its proper nature might be so perfect, as men judge, that it foreknows what is to be, and warns one and all of each of their risks to come, by means of visions or prefigurings, though our flesh cannot understand these correctly, because the warnings are too mysterious – I know not what the cause is.

Good luck in this to great scholars, who comment on this matter and others! For I will now make note of no opinion, but only pray that the holy cross will turn every dream to good for us. For never have I since I was born, nor anyone else before me, I firmly believe, dreamed so wonderful a dream as I did the tenth day of December;[1] which, as I can now recall it, I will tell you in full.

---

[1] Tenth day of December. Early readings of the poem tried to link this date with some important historical event such as a royal marriage, but none have been convincing. The most valid approaches have noted the fact that December 10 is one of the shortest days of the year and the least suggestive of spring and love. In this sense, the opening of the poem is much different than the opening of the *General Prologue* to *The Canterbury Tales*.

The Invocation

But trust well, at my beginning I will make an invocation without delay, with special devoutness, to the god of sleep,[2] who dwells in a cave of rock by a stream which comes from Lethe,[3] which is a bitter river of hell; near a people called the Cimmerians this mirthless god always sleeps with his thousand sleepy sons, whose custom is always to sleep. And I pray to this god I speak of to grant me success to tell my dream properly, if every dream should be within his power. And may He who is the Mover of all that is and was and ever shall be give them that listen to it joy from all they dream this year; and to stand all in the favor of their loves or in whatever place they would be glad to stand in, and shield them from poverty and shame and mishap and every trouble, and send all their desire to them that receive it well and scorn it not or misjudge it in their minds through malicious intent.

And whosoever through presumption or hate or scorn or envy, through spite or mockery or wickedness, may misjudge it – whether one dreams with stockings on or stockings off – I pray to Jesus Christ that every ill that anyone has had since the beginning of the world may happen to that person therefore before death, deserving it all, yes, with such a fulfillment as Croesus, King of Lydia,[4] had of his vision, who died upon the high gallows! This prayer shall that one have from me; I have no more charity than this!

---

[2] The god of sleep. Probably Morpheus, as mentioned in *Book of the Duchess*.

[3] Lethe. The river in the underworld that causes one to forget.

[4] Croesus. Wealthy king of Lydia (in the west of present day Turkey) in the sixth century BC. He dreamed that he was on a tree, where Jupiter washed him and Phoebus dried him, a dream which his daughter correctly interpreted as: he would hang on the gallows, after which the rain would soak him and the sun would dry him. Chaucer also tells the story of Croesus in *The Monk's Tale*.

Now, as I have told you, listen to what I dreamed before I awoke.

The Story

The tenth day of December, when it was night, I lay down to sleep just where I was accustomed, and fell asleep very soon, like one who was weary from walking a pilgrimage of two miles to the shrine of Saint Leonard,[5] to make soft what had been hard.[6]

But as I slept I dreamed I was within a temple of glass, in which were more golden images standing on various stands, more rich decorative niches, more pinnacles of gemmed work, and more skilful portraits and curious types of figures in ancient styles than ever I had seen. For truly I did not know where I was, but well I knew that this was truly the temple of Venus;[7] for immediately I saw her figure pictured, floating naked in a sea, with her white and red rose garland, by God, about her brows, her comb to comb her hair, her doves, as well as Sir Cupid, her blind son, and Vulcan, with his brown face.

But as I roamed about, I found a tablet of brass on a wall, where was written: "I will now sing, if I am able, of the arms and the man, who, fugitive from Troy, first came by his fate into Italy to the Lavinian shore with great suffering."[8] And then after this the story began, as I shall tell you all.

---

[5] St. Leonard. Sixth-century French saint, patron both against robbers and for prisoners. *The Golden Legend* of Jacobus de Voragine (c. 1230 – 1298) notes that his name is a combination of "leos" (people) and "nardus" (sweet-smelling herb), "for by the odour of good fame he drew the people to him."

[6] To make soft…hard. Presumably one's heart would be made soft by such a pilgrimage.

[7] Venus, Cupid, and Vulcan. Venus is the goddess of love, born of the foam of the sea; Cupid, the god of love, her son (not blind, but blindfolded); Vulcan, the smith of the gods, her husband.

[8] I will now sing…suffering. These are the first lines of Vergil's *Aeneid*. What follows is a summary of much of the Roman epic poem.

First I saw the destruction of Troy, because of the Greek Sinon, who with his false oaths and his feigned expression and his lies arranged for the horse[9] to be brought into the city, through which the Trojans lost all their joy. And after this, alas, there was depicted how Ilum[10] was assaulted and won, and King Priam and his son Polites were pitilessly slain by Sir Pyrrhus.[11]

And next to that I beheld how Venus, when she saw the castle burning, descended from heaven and bade her son Aeneas to flee; and how he fled and escaped from the entire crowd, and took Anchises his father and bore him away on his back, crying, "Alas and Alack!" Anchises carried in his hands the images of those gods[12] of the country, which were not burned in the fire.

And next in all this company I saw how Creusa, the wife of Sir Aeneas, whom he loved as his soul, and her young son Iulius, and Ascanius also,[13] fled with such heavy looks that it was pitiful to see. And I saw how at a turning of a path as they went through the forest Creusa was lost and died, alas, but I know not in what fashion. And I saw how he sought her, and how her spirit told him to flee the army of the Greeks, and said he must go to Italy without fail, as was his destiny; so that it was piteous to listen to her words when her spirit appeared to him, and how she prayed him to guard her

[9] Horse. The Trojan Horse, designed by the Greek leader Odysseus to be wheeled to the gates of Troy and left as a peace offering, while the Greek ships left the shores of Troy. Greek warriors inside the horse waited until the Trojans celebrated victory, exited the horse, and, combined with the returning forces, set Troy on fire and defeated the Trojans.

[10] Ilium. The city or fortress of Troy; specifically, the royal residence.

[11] Pyrrhus. Also known as Neoptolemus.

[12] Images...gods. The sacred image of Athena carved in wood, the palladium, brought safety to Troy. At once stolen by Odysseus and Diomedes, it was later recovered and taken by Aeneas and Anchises on their voyage when they left the burning city of Troy.

[13] Iulius...Ascanius. These are two names for the same person. Either Chaucer or his source (a translation or retelling of *The Aeneid*) has made a mistake here.

son. There I saw also depicted how he and his father and his household sailed forth with his ships towards the land of Italy, as directly as they could go.

There, cruel Juno, you who are Lord Jupiter's[14] wife, and have hated always all the Trojan blood, I saw you run like a mad woman and call on Aeolus, the god of winds, to blow out from all directions so wildly that he should drown lord and lady, serving-man and serving-woman, of the whole Trojan nation without any rescue.

There I saw arise such a tempest that every heart might shudder just to see it painted on the wall.

There, Venus, I saw also depicted how you, my lady dear, weeping with woeful countenance, prayed to Jupiter on high, because the Trojan Aeneas was your son, to save and guard his fleet.

There I saw Jove kiss Venus and grant abatement of the tempest. There I saw how it ceased, and how Aeneas proceeded with great toil and secretly arrived in the country of Carthage;[15] and in the morning, how he and a knight called Achates met with Venus walking in an unusual disguise, as if she had been a huntress, with the wind blowing through her hair. And I saw how Aeneas, when he recognized her, began to bewail his sufferings, and the fact that his ships were sunk, or else lost, he knew not where; and how she began to comfort him and told him go to Carthage. There he would find his people who had been left behind on the sea.

And, to pass over this thing shortly, Venus put Aeneas in such grace with Dido,[16] queen of that land, that, to tell it briefly, Dido became his love in heart and body. Why should I speak more artfully or strive to paint my words in speaking

---

[14] Jupiter. Supreme god in Roman mythology, also called Jove. In Greek, known as Zeus. Juno, also known as Hera.

[15] Carthage. Coastal city in northern Africa, in what is now Tunisia.

[16] Dido. Chaucer also tells the story of the love of Dido and Aeneas in *The Legend of Good Women*.

of love? It will not be; I know nothing of that craft. And to tell the manner also in which they became acquainted, it would be a long story to tell, and would delay you too long.

There I saw depicted how Aeneas told Dido every adventure that had happened to him on the sea.

And after that was depicted how she made of him, in brief and in a word, her life, her love, her joy, her master, and showed him every reverence, and lavished on him all the wealth that any woman could, believing all had been as he had sworn to her, and by this judging that he was good, for so he seemed.

Alas! What evil is forged by appearance when it is false to the truth of the case! For he was a traitor to her, therefore, alas, she slew herself. Lo! How a woman makes a mistake to love one who is unknown. For indeed, by heaven, all that glitters is not gold!

For, on my life, many cursed faults may be covered under righteousness; therefore, let there be no creature so foolish as to take a lover only because of their looks, speech, or friendly manner. For every woman shall find this, namely, that sometimes a man by his nature will appear outwardly the fairest until he has gained what he desires, and then he will invent excuses and swear that she is unkind or false or sly or two-faced. All this I say on account of Aeneas and Dido, and her foolish desire, who loved her guest all too soon. Therefore I will say a proverb, "He who knows the herb perfectly may safely lay it on his eye." Without a doubt, this is true.

But let us speak of Aeneas, how he betrayed her and left her unkindly, alas! So when she utterly perceived that he would fail in his pledge to her and would turn from her to Italy, she began to wring her two hands. "Alas!" she said, "alas, woe is me! Is this the pledge of every person, that he will have a new lover every year (if it will last that long), or else three, perhaps? He would have them thus: from one he would have fame[17] in magnifying his reputation; another, he says, for friendship; and there shall be yet the third, that shall be taken, indeed, for delight or personal pleasure."

In such words Dido bemoaned her great pain. So I dreamed; I cite no other author. "Alas!" she said, "my sweet heart, have pity on my bitter sorrows, and slay me not! Don't go away! Ah, woeful Dido, alas!" Then she said to herself, "O Aeneas, what will you do? Ah, that neither your love, nor your pledge that you have sworn with your right hand, nor my cruel death, may keep you here with me still! Ah, have pity on my death! Surely, my dear heart, you know full well that never yet, as far as my wit could stretch, have I wronged you in thought or deed. Ah, how do you men have such excellence in speech, and never a bit of truth?

"Alas, that ever any woman had pity on any man! Now I see well and can tell others that we wretched women can recognize no deception; for certainly we are treated so, every one, for the most part. However sorely you men can groan, as soon as we have accepted you, in truth we are deceived! For though your love may last for a while, watch for the conclusion, how for the most part you will end.

"Alack that I was born! For through you my good name is lost, and all my deeds are read and sung over all this land, in every mouth. O Wicked Fame! For indeed there is nothing as swift as she is. Ah, it is true, everything is known, even if it is wrapped deep in mist. And, even if I should live forever, I can never so retrieve what I have done, so that, alas, I shall not be said to have been shamed through Aeneas, and that it shall not be judged of me thus: 'Lo, just as she has done, she will surely do again.' Thus the people say secretly." But what is done is not yet to do; truly, all her lament and moan helped her not one straw.

And when in truth she knew that he had gone forth to his ships, she went without delay into her chamber and called

---

[17] Fame. In the context of this poem, fame is not only fame, but reputation, renown, and gossip as well.

her sister Anna and lamented to her. She told Anna that she was the reason that she first loved Aeneas, as she had counseled her to do so. But what! When this was said and done, she stabbed herself to the heart and died of the bitter wound. But whoever would like to know all the details of her death and the words she said, let them read Vergil[18] in the book of the *Aeneid*, or in her epistle in Ovid,[19] which she wrote before she died. And if it would not be too long to compose, by heaven, I would put it here.

But, alack, for the harm and pity that have come about from such faithlessness, as people may often read in books, and see it still in deed every day, so that it is an affliction to think about!

Witness Demophon, duke of Athens, how he falsely perjured himself, wickedly betrayed Phyllis,[20] who was the king's daughter of Thrace,[21] and falsely delayed past his appointed time; and when she knew he was false, she hanged herself by the neck because he had been so faithless to her. Lo! Was not this a woe and a pity?

And see how false and heedless was Achilles to Breseyda,[22] and Paris to Oenone,[23] and Jason to Hypsipyle,[24]

---

[18] Vergil. Publius Vergilius Maro (70 BC – 9 BC), author of the Roman epic *The Aeneid*, the complete story of Aeneas's adventures from the fall of Troy to his victory over Turnus and the Rutuli, and the ultimate source of the narrative Chaucer has just concluded.

[19] Ovid. Publius Ovidius Naso (43 BC – 18 AD), author of *The Heroides* is a collection of letters, among them Dido's written by women who have been left by men. Several of the other women in the collection are named in the following paragraphs, including Phyllis, Hypsipyle, Medea, and Ariadne. Chaucer also used the *Heroides* to compose his *Legend of Good Women*.

[20] Demophon...Phyllis. Demophon married Phyllis on his return from the Trojan War. He soon departed: he promised to return, but did not. See her story in *The Legend of Good Women*.

[21] Thrace. The southeast tip of the Balkan Peninsula, including northeastern Greece, Bulgaria, and Turkey.

[22] Achilles to Breseyda. Breseyde (or Briseyde, or Briseis), a princess of Lyrnessus (in Troy) surrendered to Achilles after he had sacked her city and killed all her family. References to any the unfaithfulness of Achilles

and again Jason to Medea,[25] and Hercules to Dyanira[26] (for he left her for Iole, who brought him his death, God!).

Also, how false was Theseus, who betrayed Ariadne,[27] as the story tells us – may the Devil be his soul's destruction! For he would have been entirely devoured, whether he liked it or not, if it had not been for Ariadne. And because she pitied him, she helped him to escape from his death. And he played her a very false trick; for some time after this he left her sleeping alone on a desert island in the sea, and stole away and left her alone; and took her sister Phaedra with him and went to his ship. And yet he had sworn to her by all that ever he could swear upon that, if she saved his life, he would wed her; for, as the book says, in truth she desired nothing else.

But to excuse Aeneas fully for his great trespass, the book says in truth that Mercury[28] told him to go into Italy and leave the region of Africa and Dido and her fair town.

---

to his concubine are difficult to find, unless one would consider his affection toward Patrocles infidelity.

[23] Paris to Oenone. Paris, a Trojan prince, abandoned his wife Oenone for Helen of Sparta, wife of Menelaus, thus beginning the Trojan War. Mortally wounded by Philoctetes, Paris died, as Oenone refused to heal him.

[24] Jason to Hypsipyle. Hypsipyle, Queen of Lemnos and leader of a mortal attack on all the men of the island (except her father, Thoas), fell in love with Jason, who was en route to Colchis to gain the Golden Fleece. After he impregnated her, he abandoned her.

[25] Jason to Medea. After Medea, princess of Colchis, helped Jason to gain the Golden Fleece and gave him five children, he abandoned her for Glauce, princess of Corinth. This tale and the tale of Hypsipyle are told in *The Legend of Good Women*.

[26] Hercules to Dyanira. Dyanira, having been attacked by the centaur Nessus and rescued by Hercules, who shot Nessus with an arrow, added, on the revenging Nessus' advice, the centaur's blood as a love potion in a cloak she had made for Hercules. She had hoped that this would stop his philandering. This blood caused what would have been his death, had he not been rescued by Hera, who took him to Olympus.

[27] Theseus...Ariadne. Theseus, an Athenian prince, was able to slay the Minotaur of Crete with the aid of Ariadne. The story is told more completely in *The Legend of Good Women*.

[28] Mercury. The messenger god. In Greek, known as Hermes.

Then I saw depicted how Sir Aeneas set sail for Italy; and how there arose a great tempest, and how he lost his helmsman, whom the rudder, before he noticed, struck overboard, indeed, as he slept.

And also I saw how the Sibyl and Aeneas, near an island, went down into Hell to see his father, the noble Anchises, and how he found there Palinurus,[29] and Dido, and Deiphobus;[30] and how he saw every torment of hell, which would take too long to relate. Whoever wishes to know this must read many lines in Vergil[31] or Claudian[32] or Dante,[33] who know how to tell it.

Then I saw depicted entirely the arrival of Aeneas in Italy, and his treaty with King Latinus,[34] and all the battles that he and his knights were in, before he gained what he wished to have; and how he took Turnus' life and won Lavinia[35] in marriage. And I saw all the marvelous signs of the celestial gods; how, despite Juno and all her arts and snares, Aeneas succeeded in his entire enterprise, for Jupiter took care of him at the petition of Venus – to whom I pray

---

[29] Palinurus. Aeneas' beloved helmsman who drowned when he fell asleep and fell overboard (noted above).

[30] Deiphobus. Son of Priam and probably the third finest of the Trojan warriors, after Hector and Troilus. He takes Helen as his lover after the death of Paris, but is killed by Menelaus in the siege of Troy.

[31] Vergil. As noted above, Roman poet, author of the *Aeneid*, source of much of Book I of *House of Fame*. Book VI of *The Aeneid* describes the underworld. Vergil does not use the word "Hell" for the underworld. Rather, he names specific sections of the underworld such as Dis, Elysium, and Tartarus.

[32] Claudian. The reputed last classical Roman poet, author of *The Rape of Proserpine*, which also describes the underworld.

[33] Dante. Dante Alighieri (1265-1321), Italian poet and philosopher, whose works, especially his *Divine Comedy*, influenced Chaucer greatly. As noted above, *The House of Fame* is sometimes referred to as "Chaucer's Dante." His Inferno is the most famous description of Hell.

[34] King Latinus. King of the Rutuli, whom Aeneas defeats in order to establish the relative peace that will lead to the founding of Rome.

[35] Turnus...Lavinia. Until Aeneas' arrival, Turnus was the primary suitor to Lavinia, the daughter of King Latinus.

always to save us and forever ease us of our sorrows.

When I had seen all these sights thus in this noble temple, I thought, "Ah, Lord who made us! Never have I seen such magnificence of figures and such wealth as I have seen depicted in this church. But I know not who had them created, nor where I am, nor in what land. But now I will go out directly to the gate and see if I can detect anyone stirring anywhere who can tell me where I am."

When I came out at the doors I gazed around me carefully. Then I saw only a large field as far as I could see, without town or house or tree or bush or grass or plowed ground; for all the field was sand, as fine as people may see yet lying in the desert of Libya. Nor did I see any type of being that is formed by Nature, to instruct or direct me. "O Christ, Who reigns in blessedness," I thought, "save me from hallucination and illusion!"

And devoutly I cast my eyes to the heavens. There at last I noticed then how, near the sun, as far up as I could discern with my eye, it seemed to me I beheld an eagle soaring, only it seemed much greater than any eagle that I had ever seen.[36] But for certain – this is as true as death – it was golden, and it shone so brilliantly that never had anyone seen such a sight, unless the heaven had gained another sun all new and of gold; so brightly shone the eagle's feathers. And then it began to descend.

Here ends the first book.

---

[36] Eagle. Dante in *Purgatorio* 9.19-20 dreams that he is taken up by an eagle.

Book II

Here begins the second book.

Proem[37]

Now listen, every type of person who can understand English and wishes to learn about my dream; for now or never you shall hear of so wondrous a vision that Isaiah,[38] Scipio,[39] King Nebuchadnezzar,[40] Pharaoh,[41] Turnus,[42] or Elcanor[43] never dreamed such a dream as this. Now, fair

---

[37] Proem. A preface.

[38] Isaiah. Old Testament prophet (eighth century BC). In Isaiah 6.1-8, the prophet sees a vision of heaven and the angels worshipping God. One of the angels takes a burning coal and, burning Isaiah's mouth with it, tells him that he is thus purified.

[39] Scipio. The conclusion of *The Republic* of Cicero (107 BC – 43 BC) contains a memorable passage that is known as *The Dream of Scipio*, which was preserved with a long commentary by Macrobius (fifth century AD), the version Chaucer most likely knew. In the dream, the Roman general Scipio the Younger (185 BC – 129 BC) meets his grandfather, Scipio the Elder (Africanus; 236 BC – 183 BC) in a dream in which the younger is shown the entire universe. For a short summary of the dream, see the beginning of Chaucer's *Parliament of Fowls*.

[40] King Nebuchadnezzar. Old Testament king of Babylon (c. 605 – 562 BC). His vision in Daniel 2:1-45 of a large statue composed of various materials from head to toe was interpreted by Daniel as the declining generations that would succeed the king

[41] Pharaoh. In Genesis 41:1-36, the Pharaoh's dream of seven fatted cows followed by seven emaciated cows is interpreted by Joseph to be seven years of good harvest followed by seven years of famine. Pharaoh was much pleased with Joseph for his help.

[42] Turnus. The enemy of Aeneas who in *The Aeneid* (VII.413-59) has a dream in which the Fury Alecto appears to him. He is visited by Iris in another dream in IX.1-13.

[43] Elcanor. The identity of this person is uncertain, but it may be an indirect reference to Elkanah, father of the prophet Samuel, who receives a vision or revelation from God (1 Samuel 3:11-14) that the family of the tribal leader or priest Eli will no longer be honored because of their crimes.

blessed Cyprian woman,[44] be my helper in this task! And you who dwell on Parnassus,[45] by the pure fount of Helicon,[46] help me to compose and rhyme! O Thought, that recorded all that I dreamed and locked it in the treasury of my brain, now shall people see if there is any power in you to tell my entire dream properly. Now make known your power and craft!

The Dream

This eagle that I have spoken of, that soared so far on high and shone as with feathers of gold, I began to behold more and more, and to see its beauty and the marvel of it all.

But never was a lightning stroke, or that thing that is

---

[44] Cyprian woman. I.e., Venus.

[45] Parnassus. Mountain in central Greece, sacred to the Muses.

[46] Helicon. Another mountain near Parnassus. The springs of Helicon, namely, Hippocrene and Aganippe, were also believed to be the home of the Muses.

called the thunderbolt (which sometimes has smitten a tower to powder and burned it by its swift onslaught) so swift in its descent as this bird, when it beheld me in the open in the field.

And with his grim and mighty feet, within his long sharp claws, he caught me at a swoop as I fled, and soared up again, carrying me in his strong claws as easily as if I were a lark – how high I cannot tell you, for I did not know not how I rose up. For every faculty in my head was so stunned and dazed, for, with his swift ascent and my own dread, all my sense of feeling died away, so great was my fear.

Thus I remained long in his claws until at last he spoke to me in human voice and said, "Awake, and don't be so afraid. Fie upon you!" And then he called me by name, and, to arouse me better, so I dreamed, he said "Awake!" to me, in the very same voice and tone that one whom I could mention uses.[47] And at that voice, to tell the truth, my mind returned to me, for it was spoken to me kindly, as it never was.

And at this I began to stir, and he bore me further in his talons until he felt my heart beating and that I grew warm as well. Then he began to be mirthful with me and to comfort me with words, and said twice, "By blessed Mary, you are troublesome to carry, and more than you need be, by God! For, so God help me, you shall have no harm from this.

"This thing that has happened to you is for your instruction and your profit. Let's see! Do you dare to look yet? Be fully assured, I tell you plainly, I am your friend." And with that I began to marvel within my mind.

"O God Who made nature," I thought, "am I to die in no other way? Will Jove transform me into a star? Or what may this entire business mean? I am neither Enoch[48] nor Elijah[49]

---

[47] One...uses. This is typically thought to refer to Chaucer's wife.

[48] Enoch. Old Testament Patriarch and ancestor of Noah; he was believed to have ascended directly to heaven. See Genesis 5:24.

[49] Elijah. Like Enoch, Elijah (ninth century BC) was also believed to have ascended directly to heaven.

nor Romulus,[50] nor Ganymede,[51] who, as books tell, was borne up to heaven by Lord Jupiter and made the gods' butler."[52]

Indeed, this was my delusion then! But he who carried me discerned what I was thinking and said, "You think incorrectly in your own mind; for Jove is not intending – I dare well put you fully out of doubt – to make a star of you as yet. But before I bear you much farther I will tell you what I am, where you shall go, and why I came to do this, so that you will take good heart and tremble not for fear."

"Gladly," I said.

"Now that is well," he said. "First, I who have you in my feet and whom you fear and marvel, dwell with the god of thunder, known as Jupiter, who sends me often flying far to do all his commands.[53] And for this cause he has sent me to you. Now listen, by your word! He has pity for you, truly, because you have served his blind grandson Cupid,[54] and the fair Venus as well, so long and attentively, always without reward. And nevertheless you have set your mind – as small as it may be – to making books, songs, and ditties, in rhyme or in cadence, as you best know how, in worship of Love, and of his servants also, who seek and have sought his service. And you strive to praise his art, although you have never had a portion of it.

"For these reasons, so God bless me, Jove deems it great

---

[50] Romulus. The founder of Rome who was carried to heaven by Mars, the god of war. See Ovid's *Metamorphoses* XIV. 816-28.

[51] Ganymede. The servant or butler to Jupiter who was abducted by the god's eagle. Many have noted that Chaucer's father was butler to the king. For her story, see Vergil's *Aeneid* V.252-57 and Ovid's *Metamorphoses* X.155-61.

[52] I am neither Enoch...butler. Dante, when he is taken up by the eagle, remarks the same thing in *Inferno* 2.32: "I am not Aeneas, neither am I Paul; neither I nor others think that I deserve it."

[53] Jupiter...commands. Here the eagle is implicitly compared to Mercury, the messenger god.

[54] Blind...Cupid. Cupid is often depicted blindfolded, though the term "blind" is typically used, and understood to mean blindfolded.

humility and great virtue, that you will often set your head to aching by night, so diligently composing, and always about Love, in honor and praise of him and to the benefit of his followers;[55] and you have set forth all of their concerns, and despise neither him nor his followers, though you must go into the dance with those he cares little to promote.

"As I said, for these reasons, in truth, Jupiter considers this and other things also, fair sir; that is, that you gain no tidings of Love's followers, whether or not they are glad tidings, nor of anything else that God made. It is not only so that no tidings come to you from far lands, but you hear neither this nor that from your very neighbors who dwell almost at your door. For when your labor is ended and you have made all your calculations, instead of rest and recreation you go home without delay to your house, and as dumb as any stone you sit at another book until your eyes are entirely dazed. Thus, though your abstinence is rather little, you live like a hermit![56]

"And therefore Jove by his kind favor wills that I should bear you to a place that is called the House of Fame, to give you some amusement and diversion, as some compensation for your labor and devotion (lo, you who are ever without reward!) to Cupid the reckless. And thus this god will by his grace requite you with some type of thing, if you will be of good heart. For trust well, when we have arrived where I have noted, you shall hear of more wondrous things, I dare wager: more tidings of Love's followers, both truthful words and lies; and more loves newly started; more love's long labors won; more loves that happen by chance (nobody knows why, except that such things happen, just as when a blind man startles a hare); more jolliness and goings-on (while they find love true as steel, as they think, and see joy and well-being

---

[55] Love...followers. The followers of Cupid, i.e., lovers.

[56] Hermit, abstinence. A hermit would be expected to abstain from all worldly pleasures, but presumably the narrator, though he lives in solitude, does not abstain from such pleasures.

everywhere); more discords, more jealousies, more murmurs, more changes, more deceptions and feigned makings-up, and more beards[57] – not the kind with razor or scissors – in two hours than there are grains of sand; more lovers falsely led on; more renewals of old abandoned acquaintances; more love days and reconciliations than there are strings played on instruments of music; and more exchanges of loves also than ever were grains of wheat in barns. Can you scarcely believe all this?" he said.

"No, so surely may God help me!" I said.

"No? Why?" he said.

"Because to my thinking it seems impossible – even if Fame had all the magpies and all the spies in a whole kingdom – that she should yet hear all this, or they discover it."

"Ah, yes, yes!" he said to me. "I can prove that by reason worthy of believing, so you may pay attention to understand my words. First you shall hear where she dwells, as your own book relates it. As I shall tell you, her palace stands in the very midst of the way between heaven, earth, and sea; so that, whatever is spoken secretly or openly in all three of these domains, every sound must pass to it, or whatever comes from any mouth, be it read or sung or whispered, or spoken in security or fear, certainly it must go there, since that palace stands in so exact a spot, and the road to it is so open.

"Now listen well, for I will show you a very proper argument and a noble demonstration from my own imagining.

"Geoffrey, you know well that everything that is in nature has a natural place where it is best conserved; toward this place everything is naturally inclined and moves to come to that place when it is far away from it. As such you may

---

[57] Beards. There is a pun here that can not be translated. A beard in Middle English can be either a type of deception or something that grows on a man's face.

indeed see at all times with respect to any heavy thing, such as stone or lead or something of weight, if you carry it to any height and let it drop from your hand, it will fall down. Likewise, I say the same for fire or sound or smoke or other light things: they always seek to go upward on high. While each is free, light things go up and heavy things down. And for this reason you perceive that every river, by its nature, tends to go to the sea, fish have their dwelling in the river and sea, as I read, and trees are also in the earth. And hence each thing has its proper dwelling place, to which it seeks to go and where it is ever at its best. Doubtless, this opinion is well known from the mouth of every philosopher, including Aristotle, Lord Plato,[58] and many other scholars. And, to confirm my interpretation, you know this well: that speech is sound, or nobody could hear it. Now listen to what I shall teach you.

"Sound is nothing but broken air; and every speech that is uttered, aloud or silently, good or bad, is in substance nothing but air. For as flame is but lighted smoke, sound is broken air. But this may be so in many ways, of which I will tell you two: with sound that comes from a pipe, or from a harp. When a pipe is blown strongly, the air is twisted and rent with violence; indeed, this is my interpretation. And when people strike harp-strings, heavily or lightly, witness, the air breaks apart with the stroke. Likewise, it breaks when people speak; thus you have learned what speech is.

"Next, I will now teach you how every word or noise or sound, even if it were piped by a mouse, must through its multiplication come to the House of Fame. I prove it thus, by experiment. Pay attention, now. For if now you throw a stone into water, you know well that immediately it will make a little round spot, like a circle, perhaps as broad as a

---

[58] Aristotle, Plato. The Greek philosopher Plato (428 BC – 347 BC), who was the student of Socrates (470 BC – 399 BC) and the teacher of Aristotle (384 BC – 322 BC), who was the teacher of Alexander the Great (356 BC – 323 BC).

pot-lid; and right away you shall see how that wheel will cause another wheel, and that one, a third, and so forth, friend, every circle causing another wider than itself was. And thus from small circle to great, each circumscribing the other, each caused by the other's motion, but ever increasing until they go so far that they both are at their brinks. Although you cannot see it from above, these circles spread beneath the water as well, though you may think it a great marvel. And whoever says that I vary from the truth, make that person try to prove the reverse. And even so, certainly, every word that is spoken, loud or quietly, first moves a circle of air around it, and from this motion directly another circle is stirred. As I have proven about the water, that every circle causes a second, even so is it with air, my dear brother; each circle passes into another greater and greater, and bears up speech or voice or noise, word or sound, through constant increase, until it comes to the House of Fame – take this in earnest or game.

"Now I have told, if you can bear it in mind, how speech or sound by its very nature is inclined to draw upward; this I have well proven, as you can perceive; and that the abode to which each thing is inclined has in truth its particular location. Then it is plainly clear that the natural abode of every speech and sound, fair or foul, has its natural position in the firmament. And since everything that is out of its natural place, for certain, tends to go there, as I have before proven to you, it follows, by God, that every sound naturally tends to go right up to its natural place.

"And this place I tell of, where Fame is pleased to live, is set in the midst of these three, the sea, the sky, and the earth, as the place where sound is most readily received. Then this is the conclusion: every speech of every creature, as I began first to tell you, moves up on high to pass to Fame's place, by its very nature.

"Tell me this faithfully, have I not thus simply made a proof without any deception in speech or great prolixity of philosophical terms or poetical figurative language or rhetorical colors?[59] By God, it ought to please you, for difficult language and difficult matter together are annoying to hear: do you not know this well?"

And I answered and said, "Yes!"

"Aha!" he said. "Lo! Thus I can speak simply to a simple man, and show him such arguments that he can shake them by the beaks, they shall be so palpable. But tell me this, I pray you, what do you think of my conclusion?"

I said, "It is a good argument, and likely to be just as you have proven to me."

"By God," he said, "and as I believe, you shall yet, before it is evening, have proof of every word of this argument by experience. And with your ears you will hear well that every word that is spoken, top and tail and every bit, certainly comes into Fame's house, as I have said. What more would you want?" And with this word he began to soar higher, and he said, "By Saint James, now we will speak entirely of amusement."

Then he said to me, "How are you doing?"

"Well," I said.

"Now by your faith," he said, "see down yonder whether you know any town or house or any other thing. And when you recognize anything, be sure to tell me, and I shall tell you directly how far you now are from it."

And then I looked down and beheld fields and plains, and now hills, now mountains, now valleys, now forests, and now (but I scarcely saw them) great beasts, now rivers, now cities, now towns, now great trees, now ships sailing on the sea. But soon, after a while, he had flown so high from the ground that the entire world seemed no more than a point to my eyes; or else the air was so thick that I could discern nothing. With that he spoke to me then and said, "Do you see any town or anything that you know down yonder?"

I said, "No."

---

[59] Rhetorical colors. Ornaments of speech, like figurative language.

"No wonder is it," he said, "for Alexander of Macedon[60] was not half as high as this, nor the king Sir Scipio,[61] who in a dream saw every point of hell and earth and paradise; nor luckless Daedalus, nor foolish Icarus his child,[62] who flew so high that the heat melted his wings and he fell wet amid the sea and there drowned; for him there was made great lamentation.

"Now," he said, "turn your face upward. And behold this large region, this air. But see that you are not afraid of those that you shall see; for in this region, in truth, dwell many citizens, of whom Sir Plato speaks. Surely, these are the aerial beasts."

And so I saw that entire multitude both walk and fly abroad.

"Now," he said then, "lift up your eyes; look and see yonder the Galaxy, which is called the Milky Way, because it is white; and some, in faith, call it Watling Street.[63] It was once burned with fire, when the red sun's son,[64] called Phaethon, wished at all odds to drive and guide his father's chariot. The chariot horses knew well that he did not know how to govern them, and began to leap and plunge and to bear him now up, now down, until he saw the Scorpion,[65] which is still a sign in heaven. And for fear of that he lost his wits and let go of the reins of his horses; and immediately

---

[60] Alexander of Macedon. Alexander the Great (356 BC – 323 BC), ruler of much of the Eastern Mediterranean in the fourth century BC.

[61] Sir Scipio. Scipio Aemilianus (Scipio the Younger, 185 BC – 129 BC), grandson of Scipio Africanus (236 BC – 183 BC), victor of the Second Punic War, was shown a vision of the universe in Cicero's *The Dream of Scipio* (Book Six, *On the Commonwealth*). Scipio appears in *Parliament of Fowls*.

[62] Daedalus, Icarus. Daedalus, archetypal engineer, who constructed wings for his son Daedalus and adhered them to his body with wax, only to see his son fall to earth after the wax melted when he flew too close to the sun, See Ovid's *Metamorphoses* VIII.183-235.

[63] Watling Street. Probably a road leading from London to some other location; no clear identification has yet been made.

[64] Red sun's son. Phoebus Apollo's son, Phaeton.

[65] Scorpion. Sign of the Zodiac.

they mounted and descended until both air and earth burned; until in fact Jupiter at last slew him and hurled him from the chariot. Is it not indeed great harm to let a fool have the management of a thing that he cannot control?"

And with this word, to tell the truth, he began to soar steadily upward; and gladdened me more and more, as he spoke to me with such friendly wisdom. Then I looked below me and beheld the aerial beasts, clouds, winds, mists, tempests, snows, hails, rains and their generation according to their natures, and all the way over which I had come. "O God that made Adam," I said, "great is your power and your splendor!"

And then I thought of Boethius,[66] who writes, "A thought may fly so high on the wings of Philosophy as to mount above every element; and when it has gone so far, then the clouds may be seen behind its back," and all of which I have spoken.

Then I began to grow confused and said, "I know well that I am here, but whether in body or in spirit truly I know not; but You, God, know!" For not as yet had He sent me clear understanding. Then I thought of Martian,[67] and on the *Anticlaudianus*[68] as well, and that their description of the entire heavenly region was true, so far as I had experience of it. Therefore I can now believe them.

And at this the eagle cried out and said, "Set aside your fancies. Do you wish to learn anything about stars?"

---

[66] Boethius. Boethius. Ancius Manlius Severinus (c. 475 – 525 AD), Roman philosopher, consul and minister to Theodoric, accused of treason. While awaiting execution he wrote *De Consolatione Philosphiae* (*The Consolation of Philosophy*), one of the most important books for the Middle Ages, which Chaucer translated into English (*Boece*).

[67] Martian. Martianus Capella (Early fifth century AD), whose work, *The Marriage of Mercury and Philology*, is an extended discussion on astronomy in relationship to philosophy.

[68] *Anticlaudianus*. This work, by Alain of Lille (Alanus de Insulis, c. 1128 – 1202), contains an extended discussion on the configuration of the heavens.

"No, in truth," I said, "nothing. And why? Because I am too old now."

"Otherwise," he said, "I would have told you the names of the stars, and all the signs of the heavens, too, and what they are."

"No matter," I said.

"Yes, it does matter, truly," he said; "and do you know why? For you read in the poets how the gods have made stars of birds, fish, beasts, man, and woman, such as the Raven, Bear, Arionis' fine harp,[69] Castor and Pollux, the Dolphin, or the seven daughters of Atlas,[70] and how all these are set in the sky. For though you often hear of them, yet you know not where they are."

"No matter," I said. "There's no need; so God help me, I believe those who write of this matter just as much as if I knew their places here; and they shine so radiantly here, it would ruin all my sight to look on them."

"That may well be," he said. And so he carried me on a while, and then cried out so that I had never heard a thing so loud. "Now up with your head, for all is now well over. By Saint Julian![71] Here is a good lodging! Behold, here is the House of Fame! Can you not hear what I hear?"

"What?" I asked.

"The great sound," he said, "that rumbles up and down in Fame's House, full of rumors, both of kind words and chidings and composed of both lies and truth. Listen well, it is not whispered, in faith! Do you not hear the great murmur?"

"Yes," I said, "well enough, by God."

"And what sound is it like?"

---

[69] Raven...harp. Raven: the constellation of Corvus. Either Bear: Ursa Major or Ursa Minor. Arionis' fine harp: the constellation of Lyra.

[70] Castor...Atlas. Castor and Pollux: the constellation of Gemini. Dolphin: the constellation of Delphinus. Daughters of Atlas: the Pleiades, whose mother was the sea-nymph Pleione.

[71] St. Julian. Julian the Hospitaller (as early as the seventh century or as late as the thirteenth), patron saint of travelers and hospitality.

"By Peter!"[72] I said, "Like the beating of the sea against hollow rocks, when a tempest engulfs the ships, to a person who stands a mile from there and hears the roar. Or else it is like the last mutter after a thunder-clap, when Jove has struck the air. But it makes me sweat for fear."

"No," he said, "don't fear about that: it is nothing that will bite you! Truly you shall have no harm."

And at this word we had come as close to the place as someone might hurl a spear. I knew not how, but he set me squarely on my feet on a street, and said, "Walk on at your ease and take your chance or lot, whatever you shall find in Fame's place."

"Now," I said, "while we have time to speak, before I depart from you, for the love of God, tell me – in truth, I wish to learn it from you – whether this noise that I hear is, as I have heard you tell, from people who live down upon the earth and comes here in the manner that I heard you describe just now; and whether there is not in all that house yonder a living creature that makes all this loud clamor."

"No," he said, "by Saint Claire,[73] and so surely may God help me! But I will warn you of one thing at which you will marvel. Indeed, you know how every speech comes to the House of Fame yonder; there is no need to tell you again. But now understand this very well: when any speech has come up to the palace, soon it becomes like the same person who spoke those words on earth, whether it is clothed in red or black. And it has so much the very likeness of him who spoke the words that you would believe it is the same body, man or woman, he or she. And is this not marvelous?"

"Yes, by the heavenly King!" I said.

---

[72] Peter. St. Peter, one of Christ's apostles and the first head of the Christian Church.

[73] Saint Claire. Claire of Assisi (1194 – 1253), a disciple of St. Francis; the order of the Poor Claires is named after her.

And at this word he said, "Farewell, and here I will await you. And may the God of heaven send you grace to learn some good here."

And then I took leave of him and walked on to the palace.

Here ends the second book.

ě

Book III

Here begins the third book.

Invocation

A pollo, god of knowledge and light, through your great power please guide this last little book! Not that I desire that poetical art be shown here as a sign of skill, but, even if the rhyme is simple and unsophisticated and some verses may be lacking a syllable, please make it somewhat pleasing; and in this I seek not to display art, but only my meaning. And if, divine power, you will help me to show now what is noted in my mind, that is, to describe the House of Fame, you shall see me go swiftly to the nearest laurel that I can find and kiss it, because it is your tree.[74] Now enter directly into my breast!

The Dream

W hen I had departed from this eagle, I began to look about. And truly, before I proceed further, I will

---

[74] Laurel...tree. Apollo was at one time attracted to Daphne; when he pursued her, she ran and called for aid to her father Peneus, the river god, who turned her into the laurel tree, from which Apollo created a wreath to crown his head. The laurel came to signify glory in poetry and other fields.

describe to you the overall aspect of house and site; and the manner in which I approached the place, which stood upon so lofty a rock that there stands none higher in Spain. But I climbed up with great labor, yet I was still attentive to see and to observe below at my feet, to find out if I could in any way what type of stone this rock was; for it was like crystallized alum,[75] except that it shone much more brightly. But of what solidified matter it was, I could not readily tell, in truth. But at last I detected that it was every bit a rock of ice, and not of steel. I thought, "By Saint Thomas of Kent,[76] this would be a feeble foundation on which to build so lofty a place! Whoever builds on it should not boast much, may God save me!"

---

[75] Crystallized alum. A cloudy white crystal.

[76] St. Thomas of Kent. St. Thomas of Canterbury or Thomas à Becket (1119 – 1170), Archbishop of Canterbury whose struggles with his lifetime friend Henry II over the relationship between church and state ended in Becket's assassination; the pilgrims in Chaucer's *Canterbury Tales* are to visit his shrine in Canterbury Cathedral.

Then I saw the whole side depicted with many names of famous people, who had lived in much happiness and had their renown blown afar. But scarcely could I make out any letters to read their names; for in truth they were so nearly thawed away that one or two letters of every name were melted away, so unfamous had their fame grown. But as people say, "what can endure forever?"

Then I pondered in my heart how they were melted away by heat, and not worn away by storms. For on the opposite side of this hill, which lay to the north, I saw how it was written full of names of people who had great renown in ancient times, and still they were as fresh as if people had written them there that very day or the very hour when I looked upon them. And well I knew the reason; all this writing that I saw was preserved by the shadow of a castle which stood on high; and the writing lay on so cold a spot that heat could not deface it.

Then I went up the hill and found on top an abode so beautiful that all the people alive would not have enough skill to describe it, nor could they devise a plan to make another such place that would be its match in beauty and so wondrously created. It still astonishes my mind and makes all my brain labor to think on this castle. The great art and beauty, the plan and curious workmanship, I cannot describe to you; my brain does not suffice.

Nevertheless all the substance of it I have yet in my memory. For it seemed to me, by Saint Giles,[77] all was made of beryl,[78] without piecing or joints, including castle and tower and hall and every chamber. I saw many clever architectural features, gargoyles and pinnacles, statues and finely ornamented recesses for them; and it was as full of windows as flakes that fall in great snow-storms. And in each of the pinnacles were also various niches, in which

---

[77] St. Giles. Giles the Hermit (650 – 710), patron saint of cripples, because he was injured when a hunter's arrow missed a deer and struck Giles.

[78] Beryl. A type of crystal that is formed in different colors.

throughout the castle stood all types of minstrels and tellers of tales, both tearful and merry, of all those who minister to Fame.

There I heard Orpheus[79] playing so skillfully upon a harp which sounded clear and beautiful; and by his side sat the harper Arion, Eacides Chiron, the Welsh bard Glascurion,[80] and many other harpers; and in seats below them sat small harpers with their musical instruments, and stared up at them and counterfeited them like apes, or as art counterfeits nature.

Then I saw standing behind them, far away and all by themselves, many scores of thousands, who made loud music with bagpipes and reed-pipes and many other kinds of pipes, and skillfully played both wind and reed instruments, such as are played at feasts with the roast-meat, and many a flute and lilting-horn and pipes made of green stalks, such as these little shepherd boys have who watch over beasts in the broom bushes.

Then I saw there Atiteris,[81] Sir Pseustis of Athens,[82] and that Marsyas[83] who lost her skin, face, body, and skin, because she wished to vie with Apollo, to pipe better than him.

---

[79] Orpheus. Quintessential musician whose love for his wife Euridyce was so great that he descended to the underworld to seek her. The Middle English *Sir Orfeo* takes this as its subject

[80] Arion...Glascurion. All famed musicians. Arion: Dionysiac Greek poet, perhaps the inventor of the dithyramb. Eacides Chiron the Centaur, was important as the teacher of Asclepius, Achilles, Patroclus, and Jason. (Eacides refers to his grandfather Aeacus.) Glascurion may refer to the story-teller and magician Gwydion son of Don.

[81] Atiteris. Little is known of Atiteris. Perhaps a reference to Tityrus, the idle shepherd poet who appears in Vergil's *Eclogues*.

[82] Sir Pseustis of Athens. In the tenth-century *Ecloga Theoduli*, as a representative pagan musician he debates Alethia, a descendent of the Biblical David who plays a harp.

[83] Marsyas. Usually described as masculine, Marsyas challenged Apollo to a music contest on the double-flute, or aulos. The Muses judged in favor of Apollo, who then flayed his competitor.

There I saw famous pipers of the German speech, both young and old, learning love-dances, springs, rounds and these foreign capers. In another part I saw standing in a large space certain ones that make bloody sounds with trumpet, clarion, and horn; for those who fight and shed blood are glad to have clarion playing.

There I heard Misenus,[84] of whom Vergil speaks; also I heard Joab[85] trump there, Thiodamas,[86] and others besides. And I saw trumpeting there all those in Aragon and Catalonia[87] that were acquainted with the clarion, who were famous in their time.

On other seats I saw sitting there, playing upon various instruments that I cannot name, more people than there are stars in heaven; of these I will not now rhyme, considering your pleasure and the time that would be lost. For this you know: time lost can in no way be recovered. There I saw jugglers playing, magicians, wizards and pythonesses,[88] enchantresses, old witches, and sorceresses, who use exorcisms and these mystic fumigations as well; and scholars who well know all this natural magic and who give their minds and their craft, in certain aspects of the ascendant, to making images, through which magic they may make a person sick or well.

There I saw you, queen Medea, and Circe and Calypso.[89] There I saw Hermes Ballenus, Limote, and Simon Magus[90]

---

[84] Misenus. Trumpeter for Hector and Aeneas, as noted in Vergil's *Aeneid*.

[85] Joab. Trumpeter for David, as noted in Samuel 2.18 and 2.20.

[86] Thiodamas. Named in *The Thebiad* of Statius (45 – 96 AD) as an augur (interpreter of divine and natural signs) succeeding Amphiaraus, he incited the Argive forces to attack Thebes.

[87] Aragon and Catalonia. Regions in northwestern Spain.

[88] Pythonesses. Women who call up spirits.

[89] Medea...Calypso. All three, magicians and seductresses. The story of Medea's betrayal by Jason is told in *Legend of Good Women*. Circe and Calypso were seducers of Odysseus, keeping him at length in their thrall and preventing him from returning to his homeland in Ithaca.

[90] Hermes...Magus. Hermes Ballenus: disciple of Hermes Trismegistus, mythical figure who found the secrets to the universe in a book buried

as well. There I saw, and knew by name, those who by such arts gained renown. There I saw the magician Colle[91] perform upon a table of sycamore a thing strange to describe. I saw him carry a windmill under a walnut shell.

Why should I make a longer story, from now to doomsday, of all the people that I saw? When I had beheld this entire company and found myself free and not a bit restrained, and had again mused a long while upon these walls of beryl, which shone more brightly than glass, and made all things, in truth, to seem greater than they were, as is natural to Fame, I roamed on until I found on my right the castle-gate, which was so well carved that there was never another such as it; and yet the workmanship was done by chance as often as by pains. There is no need to make you tarry too long, to tell you of the flourishes on this gate, nor of the images, nor of the sculptures, nor how they are termed in the art of masonry, such as corbels[92] full of sculptures. But Lord, how beautiful it was to the eye, all pointed with beaten gold!

But I went in, and did so without delay. And there I met many people crying, "A gift! Give us a gift! Hold your hands out! God save our own noble lady Fame, the lady of this castle; and all those who desire to have renown through us!" Thus I heard them cry, and they came quickly out of the hall and threw down sterling coins, nobles and others. And some were crowned like kings in arms, with crowns sculpted full of diamond-shaped figures, and on their garments many ribbons and fringes. Then at last I discovered that they were

---

under a statue of Hermes (Mercury). Limote: the identity is unclear, but it may refer to the sorcerer named as Elymas in Acts 13.8. Simon Magus: another sorcerer named in Acts (8.9-24) who, seeing the apostles Peter and John healing the sick, offered money for them to give him such powers; Peter cursed him for this. The sin of simony (buying or selling ecclesiastical privileges) is named for him

[91] Colle. An English magician, probably fourteenth-century, who practiced his arts in France.

[92] Corbels. Stones extending from a wall as support of the structure above.

all heralds and their assistants, who announce the praises of rich people; and every one of them, I can tell you, had thrown upon him a vestment that is called a surcoat,[93] richly embroidered, although they were not alike. But, on my life, I will not go about to describe all the coats-of-arms that they thus wore on their surcoats, for it could not be done; people might make a book about it twenty feet thick, I believe. For truly whoever knew them might have seen there all the coats-of-arms of famous people that have lived in Africa, Europe, and Asia since knighthood first began.

How should I tell all this now? And, likewise, what need is there to tell you of the great room of the castle, that every wall of it and floor and ceiling and everything else was plated half a foot thick with gold? And this gold was not at all alloyed, but to every test as fine as a ducat[94] of Venice (of which all too few are in my pouch)! And all was set with jeweled clasps of the finest fair stones, of which people read in the Lapidary,[95] as thick as grasses growing in a meadow. But it would be entirely too tedious to recite the names; therefore I pass on.

But in this rich, lusty place, which was called Fame's hall, there was not a very large gathering of people, nor any crowding of too great a throng. But on high, on a dais, sitting on an imperial throne made entirely of one ruby, which is called a carbuncle, I saw eternally enthroned a being in woman's form; and never was seen such another formed by Nature. For, to tell the truth, at the first it seemed to me she was so little that the length of a cubit was longer; but before long she stretched out so wondrously that she reached to earth with her feet and with her head touched the sky, where the seven planets shine. And, to my mind, I saw a still greater wonder, looking upon her eyes; but truly I never

---

[93] Surcoat. A long and loose outer garment.

[94] Ducat. Gold coin currency.

[95] Lapidary. Work of Marbode of Rennes (c. 1035 – 1123) treating the various types, qualities, and uses of stones.

counted them; for she had as many eyes as there are feathers upon birds, or as were on the four beasts that did honor God's throne, as John writes in the Apocalypse.[96] Her hair, which lay in waves and curls, shone before my eyes like burnished gold. And, to tell the truth, she also had as many projecting ears and tongues as there are hairs on beasts. And on her feet truly I saw partridge's wings growing.

But Lord, the gems and riches that I saw adorning this goddess! And Lord, the heavenly melody of songs full of concord that I heard sung about her throne, so that all the palace walls rang! So sang the mighty Muse, she who is called Calliope,[97] and her eight sisters as well, so gracious in their visages. And evermore and eternally the people sang of Fame, as I heard then,

"Blessed are you and your name,
Goddess of renown and Fame!

Then at last I noticed, as I turned my eyes upward, that this noble queen bore on her shoulders both the coat-of-arms and the name of those who had wide glory, Alexander, and Hercules, who lost his life because of a shirt! Thus I found this goddess sitting in dignity, honor, and splendor, all of which I will leave a while, to tell you of other things.

Then I saw standing on either side, straight down from the dais to the broad doors, many metal pillars, which shone not very brightly. Though they were of no great splendor, they were nevertheless made for noble use and great significance; and I saw honorable and reverend people standing upon the columns, of whom I will try to tell you

---

[96] Apocalypse. The last book of the Bible, also named Revelation. The four beasts were a lion, a calf, a man, and an eagle. Each had six wings and were full of eyes.

[97] Calliope. The ancient Greek Muse of (inspiration for) epic poetry. The nine Muses include: Clio (history), Euterpe (lyric poetry), Thalia (comedy and pastoral poetry), Melpomene (tragedy), Terpsichore (dance), Erato (love poetry), Polyhymnia (sacred poetry), and Urania (astronomy).

First of all I saw standing on high, upon a column of lead and fine iron, him of the school of Saturn, the Hebrew, the ancient Josephus,[98] who told of Jewish history; and upon his lofty shoulders he bore up the fame of the Jewish people. And by him stood seven others, wise and worthy to be named, helping him to bear the burden so great and so heavy. And because they wrote of battles as well as other ancient wonders, this column of which I tell you was therefore made of both lead and iron. For iron is the metal of Mars, god of battle; and the lead, in truth, is the metal of Saturn, that turns in so large an orbit.

Then in every row stood forth some whom I could recognize, though I tell them not in order, lest I make you wait too long. These of whom I shall speak I truly saw standing there. Upon a strong iron pillar, stained all over with tiger's blood, was one from Toulouse who is named Statius,[99] who bore the renown of Thebes upon his shoulders, and the name of cruel Achilles[100] also.

And in truth there stood beside him, so high on an iron pillar, the great Homer;[101] and in front of him were Dares and Dictys[102] as well as Lollius,[103] Guido delle Colonne,[104]

---

[98] Josephus. Flavius Josephus (37 – 95 AD), Romanized Jew, author of *History of the Jews*; source for Roman-Jewish history in the time of Christ.

[99] Statius. Publius Papinius Statius (c. 45 – c. 96 AD), Roman poet and author of the *Thebiad*, indirectly one of Chaucer's primary sources for *Troilus and Criseyde*. Also Dante's second guide through the *Purgatorio*.

[100] Achilles. Greek champion, invulnerable except his heel, who defeated the otherwise invincible Hector after the latter had killed Achilles' beloved Patroclus in battle.

[101] Homer. Author of the *Iliad* and *Odyssey*, which tell the stories of the Trojan War and of Odysseus' long journey home to Ithaca after the war.

[102] Dares and Dictys. Historians of the Trojan War, supposedly eye-witness sources for Homer; both are now believed to be forgeries: Dares Frygius (or Phrygius), *Daretis Phrygii de excidio Trojae historia*; Dictys Cretensis, *Ephemeris de Historia Belli Trojani*.

[103] Lollius. Also named as one of the sources of *Troilus and Criseyde*, Lollius seems to be a fictitious invention by Chaucer or perhaps a designation for Boccaccio and/or Petrarch (both relevant sources for Chaucer's works), or some other lesser-known author.

and the English Geoffrey[105] also. And each of these was busy to bear up the fame of Troy, and so heavy was it that to bear it was no sport. But still I fully discerned that there was a little ill-will among them. One held that Homer's story was just a fable, and that he spoke lies, and composed lies in his poems, and that he favored the Greeks.[106]

Then I saw standing on a pillar of bright tinned iron that Latin poet Vergil, who for many years has borne up the fame of pious Aeneas.[107] And next to him on a pillar of copper was the scholar of Venus, Ovid,[108] who sowed so broadly the name of the great god of Love. And there he well bore his renown upon this pillar, as high as I could see; for this hall of which I speak had grown in height, length, and breadth, far greater, a thousand times, than it had first been; that I saw well.

Then I saw close by on a column made of stern iron the great poet Sir Lucan;[109] and he bore upon his shoulders, as high as I could see, the fame of Julius and Pompey.[110] And by him stood all these scholars who wrote of the mighty

---

[104] Guido delle Colonne. Thirteenth-century author of *Historia Destructionis Troiae*, which sets out to correct Homer's account of the Trojan War.

[105] English Geoffrey. Geoffrey of Monmouth (c. 1100 – 1154), author of *Historiae regum Brittanniae*, a major source of Arthurian legend.

[106] One…Greeks. This most likely refers to Guido delle Colonne.

[107] Aeneas. Trojan prince whose story is told above.

[108] Ovid. Publius Ovidius Naso (43 BC – 18 AD) Roman poet most famous for his *Metamorphoses*; he also wrote *The Art of Love* (*Ars Amatoria*) and *The Heroides*, one of the primary sources for Chaucer's *Legend of Good Women*.

[109] Lucan. Marcus Annaeus Lucanus (39 AD – 65 AD), Roman poet and author of *Bellum Civile*, also known as *Pharsalia*, on the civil war between Caesar and Pompey.

[110] Julius and Pompey. Gaius Julius Caesar (100 BC – 44 BC) and Gnaeus Pompeius Magnus (106 BC – 48 BC), two of the three members of the First Triumvirate of Rome. They broke alliance after Pompey's fourth wife, Julia, daughter of Caesar, died. Caesar's troops pursued Pompey to Egypt, where he was assassinated by Roman and Egyptian soldiers. Julius Caesar was later famously assassinated by some twenty-two conspirators, many of whom were allied to Pompey, in front of the statue of Pompey.

deeds of Rome; if I should tell their names, I would need to delay too long.

And on a pillar of sulfur next to him stood Sir Claudian,[111] as if he were in a gloomy frenzy, to tell the truth; he bore up all the renown of Pluto's hell, and of Proserpine,[112] queen of the dark torments. Why should I tell more? The hall was as full of those who wrote old histories as trees are of rooks' nests. But it would be confusing to hear all the exploits that they wrote of, and what their books were named.

But while I beheld this sight, I heard a noise swiftly approaching, as if it were of bees in a hive toward the time of their swarming out; it seemed to me, I declare, such a murmuring. Then I looked about and saw that there came entering the hall a great company, and from various lands, of all sorts and conditions, poor and rich, that dwell on earth under the moon. And as soon as they had come into the hall, they fell on their knees before this noble queen and said, "Of your grace, bright lady, grant each of us a request!" And to some of them she granted it at once, and some she refused flatly, and to some she granted the very contrary of their request. But truly I tell you I knew not what her reason was, for I knew full well that each one of this company had deserved good fame, although they were treated differently; just as her sister, lady Fortune, is ever accustomed to treat people.

Now listen to how she requited those who prayed her grace; and yet all this company spoke truth and nothing false.

---

[111] Claudian. Claudius Claudianus (c. 370 – c. 404 AD), classical Roman poet, author of *The Rape of Proserpine*.

[112] Pluto, and of Proserpine. Ruler of the underworld (also known as Hades) and his wife (also known as Persephone), whom he abducted. Her mother Demeter (or Ceres) pleaded for her release, but, because she had eaten six pomegranate seeds in the underworld, she had to spend half of the year in the underworld.

"Madame," they said, "we are people that here beseech you to grant us now fair renown and let our achievements have that name; in full recompense for good works, give us good reputation."

"I deny it to you," she said without delay. "You get no good fame from me, by heaven, and therefore go your ways."

"Alas and alack!" they cried. "Tell us, what may be your reason?"

"Because I wish not," she said. "No person shall speak good or ill of you, in truth, neither this nor that." And at that she summoned her messenger who was in the hall, and ordered him, on pain of blinding, to go speedily and summon Aeolus, the god of winds: "You shall find him in Thrace,[113] and tell him to bring his clarion that is diverse in its tone, the one that is called Clear Laud,[114] with which he is accustomed to herald those whom I please to have praised; and bid him also to bring his other clarion, which everywhere is called Slander, with which he is accustomed to dishonor and to shame those whom I wish."

The messenger went speedily and found where, in a rocky cave in a country called Thrace, this Aeolus held the winds in harsh constraint and oppressed them under him until they roared like bears, so sorely did he bind and press them.

This messenger cried on high, "Rise up," he said, "and rush quickly until you come to my lady; and take your clarions with you, and hurry forth." And at once he delivered his clarions to a man called Triton[115] to carry, and let go a certain wind, that blew so high and hideously that it left not a cloud in the entire high and wide sky. This Aeolus delayed

---

[113] Thrace. The southeast tip of the Balkan Peninsula, including northeastern Greece, Bulgaria, and Turkey.

[114] Clear Laud. Pure praise.

[115] Triton. Sea god famous for blowing his conch, controlling sea winds.

nowhere until he had come to Fame's feet, and with him the man named Triton; and there he stood, still as a stone.

And there came directly another huge company of good people and cried, "Lady, grant us good fame, and let our deeds be known so, in the honor of nobility, and so may God bless your soul! For since we have well deserved it, it is right that we should be requited accordingly."

"On my life," she said, "it shall not be; good works shall not help you to get good fame from me. But do you know what? I grant you that you shall have a cursed fame, a bad reputation, and a worse name, even if you have deserved fair praise. Now go your ways, you are finished. And you, Lord Aeolus," she said, "let us see now. Take now your trumpet that is called Quick Slander, and blow their renown so that every creature shall speak evil and cursedness of them, instead of what is good and worthy. For you shall trumpet the contrary of what they have done fairly or well."

"Alas," I thought, "what bad fortune these sorry creatures have! For among the entire crowd shall they thus be shamed, though they are guiltless. But so it goes! It must be."

What did this Aeolus do but take out his black trumpet of brass, fouler than the Devil; and he blew this trumpet as if he would overthrow all the world, so that this foul trumpet's noise went throughout every land as swift as a cannonball from a cannon when fire is touched to the powder. And such a smoke came out of the end of his foul trumpet: black, blue, dark red, greenish, as comes on high from a chimney where lead is melted.

And one thing more I saw well, that the farther it went the greater it grew, as a river from its source; and it stunk like the pit of hell. Alas, thus guiltless was their shame sounded on every tongue!

Then came the third company and hastened to the dais, and immediately fell on their knees and said, "We are all people that have rightfully deserved fame, and we pray you that it may be proclaimed just as it is and blown forth."

She said, "I grant it, because it pleases me now that your good works should be known; and, in spite of all your foes, you shall have yet better praise than you merit, and soon. Aeolus," she cried, "set aside your trumpet that is so black, and take out your other trumpet that is called Laud, and blow it so that their fame may spread nimbly throughout the world, but not too speedily, only so that it may finally be known."

"Gladly, my lady," he said, and immediately drew out his trumpet of gold and set it to his lips, and blew it east, west, north, and south, as loud as any thunder, so that every person marveled at it, so widely ran the sound before it ceased. And for certain all the breath that issued from his trumpet's mouth smelled as if a potful of balm were placed amid a basket full of roses. This favor he did for their renown.

And upon that I detected that the fourth band was coming, but certainly they were amazingly few, and they stood in a row and said, "In truth, bright lady, we have done well with all our power, but we care not for glory. For God's love, hide our works and our name; for surely we have done them out of goodness and for no other type of thing."

"I grant your request," she said; "let your works die!"

With that I turned my head and soon saw the fifth band, who bowed down to this lady and fell on their knees immediately, and then all implored her to hide their good works and said they gave not a leek for fame or such renown; for they had labored out of piety and love of God, and wished nothing of fame.

"What!" she said. "Are you mad? And do you think of doing good and having no glory for it? Do you have contempt for my name? No! Then you shall live,[116] every one of you! Aeolus," she said, "blow your trumpet, I command, and do so immediately, and ring out in music the deeds of this company so that all the world may hear of them." And he blew their praise so clearly in his golden clarion that the sound went throughout the world sharply and softly; but at last it mounted to the sky.

Then came the sixth band and began to cry earnestly to Fame in this manner: "Mercy, dear lady! To tell the very truth, we have done neither this nor that, but have been idle all our life. But nevertheless we pray to have as fair a fame and great renown and glory as they that have done noble deeds and achieved all their will in love as in other matters; albeit never was brooch or ring or anything else sent to us from women, nor once did they think in their hearts to make us friendly company, but would have liked to see us in our graves. Yet let us seem so to the people that all may judge of us that women loved us madly.

"It shall do us as much good, and help our hearts to balance ease and travail, as if we had won it with labor. That would have been expensive honor, at the cost of all our ease. And you must do for us yet more; let us be held also as

---

[116] You...live. I.e., your fame shall continue to live.

worthy, wise, good, rich, and lucky in love, for the love of God who sits above. Though we may not have the bodies of women, yet, may God save you, please allow people to fasten on us the credit![117] It shall suffice us to have the fame!

She said, "By my word, I grant it! Now Aeolus, let us see. Delay not. Take out your trumpet of gold and blow as they have asked, so that everybody may think them at ease, though they may find themselves in a bad situation." This Aeolus blew it so loud that it was known throughout the world.

Then soon came the seventh assembly, and all fell on their knees and said, "Lady, grant us without delay the same thing, the same favor that you have granted for this last company."

"Fie on every one of you!" she said. "You gluttonous swine, idle wretches full of the rotten vice of sloth! What, false thieves, do you wish to be famed as good, while deserving and caring nothing about it? You ought rather to be hanged!

"You are like the tired cat that would gladly have fish; but what do you suppose? He would not wet his paws! Bad luck on your pates and on mine as well, if I should grant it, give you favor, or extol you!

"Aeolus, king of Thrace," she said, "go and blow this company directly a sorry bit of grace. And do you know what? Just as I shall tell you without delay. Say, 'These are those who wish to have honor and do nothing to work for it; and do no good, and yet have praise. And they desire that men should think that the beautiful Isolt[113] herself could not

---

[117] Though…credit. Though we may not have the bodies of the women we claim to have served as witnesses of our honor, still we ask that people will think that we had such honor.

[118] Isolt. Lover of Tristram, though she was married to King Mark of Cornwall. Part of the Arthurian tradition.

refuse them love, and yet she that grinds at a hand-mill[119] is entirely too good to ease their hearts.'"

This Aeolus started up immediately, and with his black clarion blew out a sound as loud as winds bellowing in hell, and in truth the sound was as full of mockery as ever apes were full of grimaces.

And that went around the entire world, so that every person began to shout at them and to laugh as if they were mad, as they found them so ridiculous!

Then came another group, which had done treachery, harm, the greatest wickedness any heart could imagine, and they prayed her to grant them fair fame, and not to disgrace them, but blow them glory and good name by the clarion. "No, certainly," she said; "that would be a mistake. Though there may be no justice in me, I care not to do it now; I will not grant you this."

Then a crowd came leaping in, rapping every person about on the pate until the entire hall resounded, and they said, "Sweet and dear lady, we are such people as we shall tell you. In good truth we are rogues, every one of us, and delight in wickedness, just as good people delight in goodness. And we rejoice to be known as rogues and full of vice and sins. Here in a row therefore we pray that our fame be known in all things just as it really is."

"Truly, I grant it you," she said. "But who are you who say this, and wear a stripe on your hose and such a bell on your tippet?"[120]

Madame," he said, "to tell the truth, I am that very rogue that burned the temple of Isis in the city of Athens!"[121]

"Why," she said, "did you do that?"

---

[119] She...hand-mill. A woman of the working class, as opposed to the aristocratic audience of the poem.

[120] Tippet. A scarf or shawl.

[121] Isis...Athens. Probably Herostratus, who burned the temple of Artemis (Diana) in Ephesus (one of the Seven Wonders of the Ancient World, in ancient Greece, modern Turkey) to win fame.

"By my thrift, Madame," he said, "I would gladly have had glory just as other people in the town had, though they were famous for their excellence and their moral virtue. I thought, rogues have as great a fame, though it may be only for roguery, as good people for goodness. And since I cannot have the one, I will not forgo the other. And to get the payment from Fame I set the temple afire. Now let our renown be blown quickly, as ever you hope for joy!"

"Gladly," she said. "Aeolus, do you not hear their prayer?"

"Yes, Madame," he said, "I hear well. And I will trumpet it, by God!" And he quickly took his black trumpet and puffed and blew until the sound was at the world's end.

With that I turned around; for one who stood right at my back spoke to me kindly, it seemed to me, and said, "Friend, what is your name? Have you come here to ask for renown?"

"No, in truth, friend!" I said. "Mercy! I did not come here for any such cause, by my life! It suffices me that no person may have my name on his lips, even if I were dead. I myself best know how I stand; for whatsoever I think or suffer I myself will swallow it all – or certainly the greater part, so far as I am able."

"But what are you doing here then?" he said.

I said, "That I will tell, the reason why I stand here: to learn some new tidings, some new things, I know not what; tidings of this or that, of love, or such glad things. For certainly he who caused me to come here told me that I should both see and hear wondrous things in this place. But these are no such tidings as I speak of."

"No?" he said.

And I answered, "No, in truth! For since I first had understanding, I always knew that people have desired fame and glory and renown diversely. But truly until now I knew not how or where Fame dwelt; nor yet what kind of creature she is, in appearance or quality, nor the manner of her judgments, until the time I came here."

"Lo, what is this that you have heard, which you just now spoke of?" he asked me. "But now it does not matter, for I see well what you wish to hear. Come forth, stand here no longer, and without doubt I will lead you into another place where you shall hear many things."

Then I went forth with him out of the castle, and saw in a valley below the castle close by such a house that the House of Daedalus, which is called the Labyrinth, was not half so wondrously and curiously fashioned. And always swift as thought this wondrous house whirled around, so that it never stood still. And there came out from it such a roar that if the house had stood upon the Oise,[122] I believe truly that it might easily have been heard it as far as Rome. And the noise that I heard there went on for the entire world like the roar of the stone which is shot from the catapult. This whole house was made of twigs, yellow, green, red, and some white, such as people whittle for these cages, or make into these wicker baskets for carrying bread or to be carried on the back or by a horse; so that with the gusts and the whirring of the twigs, this house was full of squeaks and creakings and much commotion. And this house also had as many entries as there are leaves on trees in the summer when they are green; and in the roof one could also see a thousand holes, and more yet, to let out the sound easily.

And the doors were open wide the entire day and night. There is no porter there to hinder any kind of tidings from passing in; and there is never quiet in that place, never without tidings, either aloud or whispered. And all the corners of the house are full of whisperings and prattlings of war, peace, marriages, rest, labor, journeys, and abidings; of death, life, love, hate, accord, and enmity; of praise, learning, gains, health, and sickness; of buildings, fair winds, tempests, and pestilence; of humans and beasts; of various changes of estate for people and nations; of trust, fear, jealousy, wit, profit, and folly; of plenty, and of great

---

[122] Oise. River in France, a tributary of the Seine.

famine, ruin, and times of scarcity and prosperity; of good or ill government; of fire, and of various events.

And rest assured it was not small, this house of which I write; for it was sixty miles in length. Though the timber was not strong, the house was still founded to last while it should please Chance, which is the mother of tidings, just as the sea is the mother of springs and founts. And it was shaped like a cage.

"Surely," I said, "in all the years of my life I never saw such a house." And as I marveled at it, I noticed that my eagle was perched high upon a rock nearby; and I went straight to him and said, "I pray you, for God's love, wait for me a while, and let me see what wonders are in this place. For perhaps I may yet learn some good from it or hear something that would be pleasant to me, before I go."

"By Peter,[123] that is my intention!" he said to me. "Therefore I am waiting. But certainly I tell you one thing: unless I take you in there, without doubt you shall never know the trick to enter it, so rapidly it whirls around. But since Jove through his grace, as I have said, wishes to give you solace with such matters, strange sights and tidings, to drive away your heaviness, such pity he has on your troubles, which you endure meekly. And know yourself quite hopeless of all joy, since Fortune has unjustly made the fruition of all your heart's ease to languish and be on the point of bursting, since he[124] of his great kindness will do you pleasure, though it may be but little, and gave express command, to which I am obedient, to assist you all I can, and guide and direct you properly to where you may hear most tidings, therefore you shall directly learn many here."

With this word and without delay, he caught me up between his toes and brought me in through a window of this house, it seemed to me; and at that the house seemed to stop,

---

[123] By Peter. An oath, presumably to Peter the Apostle, though such a reference here seems to have little significance.
[124] He. I.e., Jove, or God.

and revolved not at all; and he set me down on the floor. But never was seen, and never again shall be, such a congregation of people as I saw roaming around, some within, some without; surely there are not left in the world so many formed by Nature, nor so many creatures dead, so that scarcely had I one foot's breadth of room in that place. And every person whom I saw was whispering secretly in another's ear a fresh piece of news, or else openly spoke thus and said, "Do you not know what has happened lately or now?"

"No," said the other, "tell me." And then he told him this and that, and swore it was true. "Thus has he said," "Thus he does," "Thus it shall be," "Thus I heard tell," "That shall be found," and "That I dare wager," so that all the people alive have not the skill to relate the things I heard, some aloud, some in the ear. But the most wondrous was this; when one had heard a thing, he came forth to another and immediately told him the same thing that he had heard before it was a moment older, but in the telling he made the tidings somewhat greater than ever they had been.

And as soon as he had departed from him, the second met a third; and before he was done, he told him everything; whether the tidings were true or false, he would tell them nevertheless, and with more additions still than at first. Thus every word went from mouth to mouth in all directions, always increasing, just as a fire will kindle and spread from a spark thrown amiss, until a whole city is burned up.

And when that story was fully spread, and had grown greater on every tongue than it ever had been, soon it went up to a window to go out; but before it could pass out there, it crept out at some crevice and flew forth directly and quickly. And sometimes then I saw a lie and a sober truth at the same time by chance draw near to pass out of a window. And when they met there, they were both checked and neither could go out, each so crowded the other, until each cried shrilly, "Let me go first!"

"No, but let me! And so you will do so, I here assure you that I shall never part from you, but be your own sworn brother. We will both so mingle together that no person, no matter how angry, can get only one of us, but both at once, all without his permission, whether we come by morning or night, or summoned loudly or quietly whispered." Thus I saw falsehood and truth compounded fly abroad as one piece of news.

Thus all the tidings squeezed out of holes and straight to the goddess, and she named each according to its nature, and allotted to each its duration, some to grow and diminish quickly, as does the fair white moon, and let them go. There I could see winged wonders fly fast, twenty thousand in a company, as Aeolus blew them about.

And, Lord, at all times this house was full of shipmen and pilgrims, with bags brimful of lies, mingled with true tidings or alone by themselves. And I saw, ah, many thousand scores of these pardoners, couriers and messengers, with boxes crammed as full of lies as any vessel ever was with dregs. And I went about as fast as I could go, and gave all my mind to entertain myself and to learn, as well as to hear news which I had heard of some country (which for my part shall not now be told, for truly there is no need; other people can sing it better than I can, for all must come out, sooner or later, all the sheaves in the barn).

Then I heard a great noise in a corner of the hall where people were telling tidings of love, and I began to look there; for I saw every creature running as fast as he could, and each cried, "What is it?" And some said I know not what. And when they were all in a mass, those behind began to leap up, and crowded and climbed up on the others, and lifted up their noses and eyes, and trod hard on others' feet, and stamped, as people do after eels.

At last I saw a man whose name I know not, but he seemed to be a man of great authority.

[Unfinished.][125]

---

[125] Unfinished. Please see the introduction for a brief discussion of the unfinished nature of the poem.

MINOR POEMS

INTRODUCTORY NOTES

In addition to the more ambitious poems that fill the pages of this volume, Chaucer also composed dozens of shorter poems, some for specific purposes or occasions, mostly in the courtly style that was popular in France. In this type of poetry, we may find the gentle complaint of an unrequited lover, as in "To Rosamonde," or a complaint about the changeable ways of the world, as in "Lack of Steadfastness," which is, as many poems were in Chaucer's day, directed to the King.

Chaucer also created poems from other impulses as well. For example, his "A.B.C." is a poem in praise of Mary, the mother of Jesus. His "Complaint of Chaucer to His Purse" is a sort of begging poem, of which there are several other examples in England and the Continent. One of the shortest poems in this collection, "Chaucer's Words to Adam, His Scribe," can only have been written by Chaucer. Though the sentiment echoes what we might find in other texts, the poem is written from Chaucer's unique position to his actual scribe, Adam. Chaucer was unable to write with his right hand (since he was missing his thumb and forefinger: such was the punishment for archers who were prisoners of war) or his left (as he had developed a palsy).

Please note that eight of the poems end with an "envoy." This is a common feature of occasional or lyric poetry of Chaucer's day. In a poetical context, an envoy is a postscript addressed either to a specific individual or to the poem itself (a bidding for the poem to go to a specific individual).

AN ABC

Here begins the song
according to the order of the letters of the alphabet.

Almighty, all-merciful Queen, to whom all this world flees for succor, to have release from sin, sorrow and trouble, glorious Virgin, flower of all flowers, to you I flee, confounded in error! You mighty, gracious lady, help and relieve me, pity my perilous malady! My cruel adversary has vanquished me.

Bounty has so fixed his tent in your heart that well I know you will be my succor; you can not reject him who with pious mind asks your aid. Your heart is ever so bounteous; you are the liberal giver of full felicity, haven of refuge, of quiet and rest. Lo, how the seven thieves pursue me! Help, bright lady, before my ship goes to pieces!

Comfort is there none, save in you dear lady, for lo! my sin and confusion, which ought not to come into your presence, have brought against me a grievous suit, founded on strict justice and my despair. And in justice they might well maintain that I would be worthy of condemnation, were it not for your mercy, blessed queen of heaven.

Doubt is there none that you, queen of mercy, are the source of grace and mercy on earth. Through you God vowed to be reconciled with us. For surely, dear, blessed mother of Christ, were the bow of justice and wrath bent now in such wise as it was at first, the righteous God would hear of no mercy; but through you we have favor, as we desire.

Ever has my hope of refuge been in you, for in various manners you have to this day received me into mercy so often. But grant me favor, lady, at the Great Court,[1] when we shall come before the high Judge! So little fruit shall be found in me at that time that, unless you well chasten me before that day, by strict justice my work will destroy me.

Fleeing, I flee to your tent for aid, to hide me from the terrible tempest, beseeching you that, though I may be wicked, you will not withdraw yourself from me. Ah, help me in this need! Though I have been a beast in will and in act, lady, clothe me with your grace. Take heed, lady, your enemy and mine is determined to pursue me unto my death.

Glorious maid and mother, who never in earth or heaven was bitter, but ever full of sweetness and mercy, in order that my Father may not be angry with me, help me. Please speak, for I dare not behold Him! Alas the time! I have done such things on earth that surely, unless you will be my relief, He will exile my spirit to eternal stench.

---

[1] Great Court. I.e., Judgment Day

He promised, tell Him, to become a man, to have kinship with us, as was His will; and with His precious blood He drew up the contract upon the cross as general release for every penitent that believes in Him. And therefore, bright lady, pray for us! Then you shall both put to rest all His displeasure, and snatch the prey from our foe.

I know it well, you will truly be our comfort, as you are so full of bounty. For when a soul falls into sin, your pity goes and hails him back again. Then you make his peace with his Lord and draw him away from the crooked path. Whoever loves you shall find, as he leaves this life, he loves not in vain.

Kalendars and illuminated texts2 are those in this world that are lighted with your name; and whosoever takes to you by the straight path need not fear to be maimed in soul. Now, queen of comfort, since you are she from whom I seek my medicine, let my foe no more re-open my wound; I commit my health entirely into your hand.

Lady, I cannot portray the sorrow you had beneath the cross, nor His grievous suffering. But by the pains of both I pray you, let not the foe of us all make his boast that he has vanquished in his fatal battles what You both have ransomed for such a great price. As I first said, you, the foundation of our being, please keep your merciful bright eyes upon us.

Moses, who saw the bush burning with red flames, of which was never a stick consumed, saw the sign of your unspotted maidenhood. You are the bush which Moses deemed had been afire, on which descended the Holy Spirit; and this was a symbol. Now, lady, defend us from the fire which shall last eternally in hell.

---

2 Illuminated texts. Calendars were illuminated on feast days.

Noble princess, who never had any peer, surely, if there may be any comfort for us, it comes from you, you beloved mother of Christ. No other melody or song do we have to make us rejoice in our adversity, no other advocate who will and dare so pray for us; and you do so for such small payment, and help us for an Ave-Mar a[3] or two.

O true light for blind eyes, O true delight of them in labor and trouble, O treasurer of grace to mankind, you who for your humility God chose as mother! From His handmaiden He made you mistress of heaven and earth, to whom we offer up our petitions. This world ever waits upon your goodness, for you never fail any creature in need.

Purpose I have at times to seek out why the Holy Ghost sought you, when Gabriel's voice came to your ear. He did not work such a marvel to make war upon us, but to save us whom afterwards He redeemed. Then we need no weapon to save us; but only required penance, when we have not done it, and to ask and receive mercy.

Queen of comfort, yet when I consider that I have sinned toward both Him and you, and that my soul is worthy to sink, alas, where can I, a churl, go? Who shall be my mediator to your Son? Who but yourself, who are the fountain of pity? More pity do you have on our adversity than any tongue in this world can tell.

Reform me, mother, and chasten me, for truly my Father's chastening I dare in no way to endure, so hideous is His just reckoning. Mother, from whom all mercy to humankind has ever sprung, may you be you my judge and my soul's healer as well. For pity in you always abounds for all who will beg you for pity.

---

[3] Ave Maria. The Hail Mary prayer.

Sooth[4] is it that God grants no mercy without you; for God of His goodness forgives none unless it should please you. He has made you vicar and mistress of all the world and empress of heaven as well; and He restrains His justice according to your will, and in token of that He has crowned you in such a royal fashion.

Temple of devotion, where God has His abode from which infidels are forbidden, to you I bring my penitent soul. Receive me; I can flee no further! O queen of heaven, with those venomous thorns for which the earth was accursed so long ago I am so wounded, as you may well see, that I am almost lost; it pains me so grievously.

Virgin so splendid in apparel, who leads us unto the high tower of Paradise, counsel and guide me, how I may obtain your grace and your succor, although I have been in filth and error. Lady, please summon me to that court that is called your bench, O fresh flower, where mercy shall ever remain!

Xristus[5] your Son descended into this world to suffer His passion upon the cross, and that Longinus[6] also should pierce His heart and let His heart's blood run down; and all this was to save me. I am false and unkind to Him, and yet He desires not my damnation. For this I thank you, comfort of all humankind.

---

[4] Sooth. True.

[5] Xristus. The name of Christ was often abbreviated with an X, which stood for the cross on which he died. The form Xristus is rare.

[6] Longinus. The Roman soldier who pierced the side of Jesus when he had died upon the cross. Many legends grew up around him, including the notion that he was blind and that the blood that poured out from Christ's side cured his blindness.

Young Isaac was truly the prefiguration of His death; he so obeyed his father that it troubled him not to be slain; even so your Son wished to die as a lamb. Now lady full of mercy, since He measured out His mercy so liberally, I entreat you, please do not be scant; for we all sing and say that you are ever our shield against vengeance.

Zachariah[7] calls you the open spring to wash the sinful soul from its guilt. Therefore I ought well to read this lesson, which teaches us that, were it not for your tender heart, we would be lost. Now, lady bright, since you can and will be merciful to the seed of Adam, bring us to that palace that is built for penitents who are deserving of mercy. Amen.

---

[7] Zachariah. Old Testament prophet who foretold of the coming of Christ.

THE COMPLAINT UNTO PITY

ಶ

P ity,[1] whom I have sought so long with a sore heart and gnawing pain that there was never in this world a creature so woeful who did not die! To speak the truth, my purpose was to complain unto Pity of the cruelty and tyranny of Love, who slays me for my faithfulness.

And when through the length of certain years I had continually sought a time to speak, I ran to Pity, all wet with weeping, to pray her to avenge me on Cruelty. But, before I could break out with a word, or tell any of my bitter pains, I found Pity dead, and buried in a heart.

When I saw the funeral bier I fell down, dead as a stone while the swoon lasted. I arose with color all changed, and piteously turned my eyes on her, and pushed my way nearer to the corpse and began to pray for the soul. I was a lost man; there was no more to say.

Thus I am slain, since Pity has died. Alas, that ever that day should come! What manner of man would dare hold up his head now, on whom shall any heart call in sorrow? Now Cruelty has prepared to slay each one of us, folk with vain hopes, without counsel in our pains; to whom shall we complain, now that she is dead?

Yet this fresh wonder increases in me, so that no creature but I knows that she is dead, out of all the pople who have

---

[1] Pity. In modern usage the word "mercy" is closer to the meaning of Chaucer's "pite" than the modern "pity."

known her in her time. And yet she died not so suddenly. I have ever full diligently sought her since I first had wit or man's mind; but she was dead, before I could ever come upon her.

About her bier there stood cheerily, without any woe, as it seemed to me, perfect Bounty, well and richly armed, and fresh Beauty, Jollity, and Pleasure, Assured Manner, Youth, Honor, Wisdom, High Estate, Dignity, and Fair Demeanor, confederated both by bond and by kinship.

I had a written complaint in my hand, to be given to Pity as a petition, but when I found all this company there, who would rather ruin all my cause than give me help, I held my complaint quiet; for surely without Pity no petition can succeed with those people.

Then I left all these virtues, except Pity, watching over the corpse, as you have heard me say; all confederate by the bond drawn by Cruelty, and all of one consent that I should be slain. And I put away my complaint, for I dared not show to my foes my petition, the import of which in few words runs thus:

The Petition

Humblest of heart, most worthy of reverence, benign flower, crown of all virtues, your servant, if I dare so call myself, shows you the mortal hurt into which he is fallen; and not only for his evil plight, but for your renown, as he shall declare.

It stands thus: your foe Cruelty, under guise of womanly Beauty, that men should not know her tyranny, is allied against your royal estate with Generosity, Nobility and Courtesy, and has now deprived you of your station, which is called "Beauty Belonging to Grace."

For by nature and by your true inheritance you are ever allied unto Generosity; and truly you ought to use your power to help Truth in his adversity. You are also the crown of Beauty. And surely, if you are lacking in these two, the world is lost; and there is no more to say.

Also, what avails Demeanor and Nobility without you, gracious creature? Shall Cruelty be your mistress? Alas, what heart may long suffer it? Therefore, unless you soon take care to break that perilous alliance, you slay those who are obedient to you.

And further, if you allow this, your renown is destroyed in an instant; no person shall know well what Pity is. Alas that your renown should ever sink so low! You are then cast down from your heritage by Cruelty, which occupies your station, and we are in despair who seek after your favor.

Queen of the Furies, have mercy on me who have sought you so tenderly and long; let some beam of your light shine on me, who ever more and more love and fear you. For in truth the sorrow is mine; and, though I am not cunning in my lament, for God's love have mercy on my pains!

My pain is this, that whatever I wish, I do not have, nor anything like it; and Desire at all times sets my heart on fire. Also, wherever else I may go, I have everywhere nearby, ready at hand, whatever sort of thing that can increase my pains. Nothing is lacking, save my death, and then my bier.

What need to show any part of my pain, since I suffer every woe that heart can think, and yet I dare not lament to you? For well I know, though I wake or sleep, that you care not whether I float or sink. But nevertheless, as shall be seen, I will maintain my faithfulness until my death.

This is to say, I will be yours forever; though you slay me through Cruelty, your foe, still my spirit shall never part from your service, for any pain or grief. Since you are dead – alas, that ever it should be! – I may well weep thus for your death and make lament, with heart sore and full of gnawing pain.

Here ends the Exclamation on the Death of Pity.

A COMPLAINT TO HIS LADY

I

In the long night, when every creature should naturally have some rest, or else his life cannot long endure, it falls most into my woeful mind how I have dropped so low that, save death, nothing can comfort me, so despair I of all happiness.

This thought abides with me until morning, and forth from the morning until evening. I need borrow no grief, for I have both leisure and leave to mourn. There is no creature who will take my woe or forbid me to weep enough and wail my fill; the sore spark of pain destroys me.

II

This love has set me in such a place that he will never fulfill my desire; for neither pity, mercy, nor grace can I find. Yet even for fear of death can I not root out love from my sorrowful heart. The more I love, the more my lady pains me; through this I see that, without remedy, I may in no way escape death.

III

Now in truth I will tell you what she is called. Her name is Goodness-Set-in-Womanhood, Constancy-in-Youth, Beauty-without-Pride, and Pleasure-under-Control-and-Fear. Her surname is Fair-Ruthless-The-Wise as well as Good-Fortune. Because I love her she innocently slays me.

Her I love best, and shall, as long as I may live, a hundred thousand times better than myself, better than all the riches and created beings of this world. Now has not Love bestowed me well, to love where I never shall have any part? Alas, so is Fortune's wheel turned for me, so am I slain with Love's fiery arrow! I can only love her best, my sweet foe. Love has taught me no more of his art than to serve always and to cease for no sorrow.

IV

Within my true, care-worn heart there is so much woe, and so little joy as well, that woe is me that ever I was born. For all that I desire I lack, and all that I would never want I find available to me at all times. And I know not to whom to complain of all this, for she who might bring me out of this cares not whether I weep or sing, so little pities she my pain.

Alas! In sleeping-time I wake; when I should dance I tremble with fear. This heavy life I lead for your sake, though you pay no heed to it, my heart's lady, the queen of my entire life! For truly I dare say it, as I feel it: it seems to me that your sweet heart of steel is now whetted against me too sharply.

My dear heart and best-beloved foe, why do you wish to cause me all this sorrow? What have I done or said to grieve you, except that I serve and love you and nobody else. And as long as I live will ever do so, and therefore, sweet, be not displeased. You are so good and fair as you are, it would be a very great wonder if you did not have suitors of all kinds, both good and bad; and the least worthy of all, I am he.

Nevertheless, my own sweet lady, though I may be unskillful and unfit ever to serve your highness, even as best I knew how, yet this I swear, there is nobody more glad than I to do your pleasure or to cure whatever I know to distress you. And had I as much power as will, then should you feel whether it were so or not; for in this world is no living being who would more gladly fulfill your heart's desire.

For I both love and fear you so sorely, and ever must and have done so for a long time, that none is better loved, and never shall be. And yet I would only beg you to believe me well, and be not angry, and let me continue to serve you. Lo, this is all! For I am not so bold or mad as to desire that you should love me, for well I know – alas! – that may not be; I have so little worth, and you so much.

For you are one of the most excellent of the living, and I the most unlikely to prosper. Yet, for all this, you know very well that you shall not so drive me from your service that I shall not ever serve you faithfully, with all my five senses, whatever woe I feel. For I am so set upon you that, though you may never pity me, I must love you and ever be as true as any man living can, or may, be.

The more I love you, gracious and noble one, the less I find you love me. Alas! When will that cruel spirit soften? Where now is all your womanly pity, your noble gentleness, your graciousness? Will you spend nothing of it on me? And as wholly as I am yours, sweet one, and as great will I have to serve you, if thus you let me die, you have gained but little from it.

For to my knowledge I have given no cause. And this I will beseech you heartily, that if ever you find, so long as you live, a servant more true to you than I, then leave me and boldly slay me, and I will forgive you all my death. And if you find no truer man, why will you allow me to perish thus, and for no type of guilt except my good desire? As good would then be as untrue as to be true.

But to your will I submit my life and death, and with a very obedient heart I wholly pray, do with me as is your pleasure.

Much rather had I please you and die than to think or say anything to offend you at any time. Therefore, pity my bitter pains, sweet, and of your grace grant me some drop; for else neither hope nor happiness may remain with me, nor linger in my troubled and careworn heart.

THE COMPLAINT OF MARS

❧

Rejoice, you birds, at the gray dawn; lo, Venus, arisen among yonder ruddy streaks! And you fresh flowers, honor this day, for you will open when the sun rises. But you lovers that are in fear, flee, lest wicked tongues discover you. Behold the sun yonder, the candle of Jealousy!

Stained with tears and with wounded heart, take your leave; and, with Saint John as your guarantee, take comfort somewhat in your bitter sorrows; the time will come again when your woes shall cease. A heavy morning is not too great a price for a joyous night. Thus, Saint Valentine, I heard a bird sing upon your day, [1] before the sun rose.

And yet sang this bird: "Waken all, I counsel you. And you who have not humbly chosen your mates in good time, make your faithful choice now. And you who have chosen as I prescribe, renew your homage at least; confirm it, to last perpetually, and patiently accept what befalls you.

"For the honor of this high festival yet will I sing, in my bird's fashion at least the contents of the complaint which woeful Mars[2] made at parting from fair Venus,[3] upon a morning when Phoebus[4] with his fiery red torches, came searching out every fearful lover."

---

[1] Saint Valentine . . . day. As mentioned also below in the "Complaynt D'Amours," this is the subject of Chaucer's *Parliament of Fowls*.

[2] Mars. The god of war.

[3] Venus. The goddess of love.

[4] Phoebus. The god of the sun.

Long ago, Mars, the lord of the third heaven above, as well by the heavenly revolutions as by his merit, had won Venus his love, and she took him as her subject, and as a mistress taught him his lesson, commanding him he should never, as long as he served her, be so bold as to despise any lover.

She forbade him all jealousy and tyranny, cruelty and arrogance. She made him so humble and docile to her pleasure that, when she deigned to look upon him, he patiently accepted her will, whether it were to live or die. And thus she bridled him according to her custom, with no scourge but of her look.

Who reigns now in joy but Venus, with this worthy knight under her rule? Who sings now but Mars, that serves thus the fair Venus, giver of pleasure? He binds himself to obey her perpetually, and she binds herself to love him always, unless his trespass should sever the bond.

Thus were they knit, and reigned in the skies, gazing upon each other, until it fell upon a day that they set a time when Mars should glide as rapidly as he might into her nearest palace, to tarry there, walking slowly upon his course, until she should overtake him; and he prayed her to hurry.

Then he said, "Sweet lady of my heart, you well know my misfortune in that place; for truly until I meet with you my life remains entirely subject to chance and grace. But when I see the beauty of your face, no fear of death can hurt me, for all your desire is a joy to my heart.'

She had such great compassion upon her knight, dwelling in solitude until she should come, that very nearly her mind was overcome with woe; for it so was that there was nobody at that time to counsel him or make him welcome. Therefore she sped on her way almost as much in one day as he in two.

And no tongue can tell the great joy between the two of them when they met once more. Without more ado they went to bed, and thus I leave them in joy and bliss. This valiant Mars, fount of knighthood, folded the flower of beauty in his arms, and Venus kissed Mars, the god of war.

Now this Mars of whom I read travelled secretly into a chamber in the midst of the palace for a certain time, until fear came upon him because of Phoebus, who had come quickly and boldly within the palace gates, with torch in hand, of which the bright rays struck the chamber of Venus brilliantly.

The chamber where laid this blooming queen, Venus, was painted over with great white bulls.[5] Venus knew, by the light which shone so brightly, that Phoebus came so that he might burn them with his heat. This hapless Venus, drowned in wet tears, embraced Mars, and said, "Alas, I am dying! The torch has come that will reveal all this world."

Up started Mars. He wished not for sleep when he heard his lady so lament. But because tears were not in his nature, instead of tears fiery sparks burst for woe out from his two eyes. And he seized his hauberk which lay by him; he would not flee, nor could he hide himself.

He threw on his helmet of huge weight, and girt himself with his sword; and in his hand he so shook his mighty spear, as he was accustomed in battle, that very nearly it snapped. He was very heavy to walk over the land. No longer could he remain with Venus, but he bade her to flee lest Phoebus spy her.

---

[5] Bulls. The symbol of the zodiacal sign of Taurus. The entire poem is cast in terms of celestial imagery.

O woeful Mars, what can you say, you who are left behind in this perturbed palace, in peril to be slain, alas? And your penance is also double, for she who has governance of your heart is passed half beyond the beams of your eyes. Well may you weep and lament because you are not swift.

In fear of Phoebus' light Venus now fled on her lonely course into the tower of Mercury. Alas, she had no assistance there, for she neither found nor saw any type of creature, and there had but little power. Therefore she fled into a cave within the gate, to hide and remain safe.

Dark was this cave and as smoky as hell, and she stood but two paces within the gate, and there I leave her in the dark for the space of one natural day. Now I will speak of Mars, that for mad and furious sorrow would gladly have seen his own heart's blood; since he must lose her company, he cared not a farthing for his life.

So feeble he grew because of passion and woe, that he nearly died. He could scarcely endure. He climbed only one stair in two days; but nevertheless, and for all his heavy armor, he followed after her who was his life's cure, for whose departing he had more wrath and woe than for all his burning in the sun's fire.

Slowly after her he walked, lamenting until it was piteous to hear. "Oh, lady bright, Venus," he said, "alas that my course ever had so wide a compass! When shall I meet you, dear heart, alack! This twelfth day of April[6] I endure this misfortune, through Phoebus' malice."

God help luckless solitary Venus! But as God willed, it

---

[6] Twelfth day of April. The beginning of the period when the sun, Phoebus, is in Taurus. There may be some significance beyond this, but it is not clear.

happened that while Venus wept and made lament, Mercury,[7] riding on his course, could see his palace-tower across from Venus, and he saluted her, made her welcome, and received her as his very dear friend.

Mars lived still in his adversity, ever lamenting her departure, and now I remember me of his lament. And therefore, on this lusty morning, I will say and sing it as best I can; and then I will take my leave. God give every creature joy of his mate!

Mars's Lament

The law of laments requires in reason that if a person shall make a piteous complaint there must be a cause for it; or others may deem that this person complains foolishly and causelessly. Alas, that is not my case! For this reason, as well as my troubled wit can reach, I will rehearse the ground and cause of my pain; not to gain a remedy, but to make known the ground of my heaviness.

I

When I was first created, alas, and brought here for certain ends by Him who rules over each intelligence, I gave my loyal service and my thought forevermore (how dearly I have paid for it!) to her who is of such excellent power that, if any creature should come into her presence when she is angry and will take no heed of him, he cannot long remain rejoicing in his love.

This is no false matter that I relate. My lady is the very source and spring of beauty, pleasure, generosity, and nobility; of rich array (how precious it is!), of all friendly amusements, of love and merriment, of benign humility, of

---

[7] Mercury. The messenger god; god of commerce and speed. Chaucer uses the alternative name for him here, Cilinius.

the melody of all sweet instruments; and she is also so well endowed by fortune and virtue that her goodness is made manifest through the whole world.

What wonder is it then, though I have knit my service to such a one, who may devote me to joy or woe, since it lies in her power? Therefore I have promised my heart to her forever; nor, truly, though I die, shall I cease to be her most loyal servant and her knight. I flatter not, as all may know. For this day I shall die in her service. Unless I am in her grace, I shall never again set eyes upon her.

II

To whom then shall I lament my distress? Who can help me? Who can cure my hurt? Shall I complain to my bountiful lady? Nay, for certain! For she is in such heaviness from fear and sorrow that it will soon be her slayer, I believe. If only she were safe, it would not matter to me. Alas that ever lovers must endure so many perilous chances for love!

For though lovers may be as faithful as any metal newly forged, misfortune often comes to them. Sometimes their ladies will have no pity; sometimes, when they know jealousy, they would lightly devote themselves to death; sometimes envious people with foul tongues slander them. Alas, whom can they please? Only the false lover has comfort.

But what use is so long a sermon about the fortunes of love? I will return, and speak of my pain. What destroys my peace is this: my true lady, my salvation, is in terror, and knows not to whom to make lament. O dear heart! O sovereign lady! I have good cause to swoon and die away for your distress, though I feel no other hurt or fear.

III

To what end has God, enthroned on high, created love or companionship beneath him, and constrained people to love in spite of themselves? And then, it seems to me, their joy lasts not for the twinkling of an eye; and some never gain joy to the day of their death. What does this signify? What does this mean? To what end does he constrain his people to desire a thing so eagerly, unless it should endure?

Though he may cause a lover to love a thing, and make it seem steadfast and lasting, yet he subjects it to such mishap that there is no rest that comes with the giving. And that is a wonder, that so just a king would do such cruelty unto his creation. Thus, whether love should break or endure, in any way he who has to do with love has sorrow more often than the moon changes.

It seems that God has enmity toward lovers, and, like a fisherman, as people may see any day, he so baits his hook with such delightful bait that many a fish is crazed until he has taken the bait; and then for the first time he has all his desire, and at the same time all misfortune; and though the line may break, yet he has suffering, for he is wounded so sorely by the hook that he has his wages forevermore.

IV

The brooch of Thebes,[8] so full of rubies and precious stones of India, was of such nature that every creature who set eye on it would soon go out of his mind; so sorely would the beauty of it bind his heart, until he had it, that he thought he should die. And as long as it was his, he should endure such distress of fear that he very nearly would go mad.

---

[8] Brooch of Thebes. A brooch made by Vulcan, Venus' smith husband, for Harmonia, the daughter of Venus and Mars, in revenge for their adulterous relationship: it was to bring bad luck to all associated with it.

And when it went from his possession, then he had double the woe and passion because he had foregone so fair a treasure. Yet, after all, this brooch was not the cause of this destruction; but he who created it gave it the power that every creature who possessed it should have sorrow. And therefore the fault was in the craftsman as well as in the foolish coveter.

So it goes with all lovers and with me. For though my lady may have had such beauty that I was mad until I had won her favor, she did not cause my adversity, but he who created her, so help me God, who set such beauty in her face that it made me covet and to win my own death. I blame him that I die, and my own folly that ever I climbed so high.

V

But you bold knights of renown, since you are of my division[9] (although I am unworthy of so great a name, yet these scholars say I am your patron), therefore you ought to have some compassion upon my distress, and take it not as a game. The proudest of you may yet be well tamed; for this reason I pray you by your noble kindness that you will lament my sorrow.

And you my ladies, made by nature true and steadfast, you ought to have pity upon people in pain. Now you have cause to wear sable,[10] since your glorious empress is desolate; well ought you to lament. Now should your holy tears fall as rain. Alas, your honor and your empress, nearly dead with fear, fails to reach her goal.

Likewise you lovers, all together, lament for her who with sincere and meek demeanor was at all times ready to come to your assistance. Bewail her who always held you dear;

---

[9] Division. I.e., ruled by the planet of Mars.
[10] Sable. Black, i.e., in mourning.

bewail Beauty, Bounty, and Courtesy; bewail her who ends your toil; bewail that paragon of all honor, who never did anything but gentle deeds; show to her, therefore, some kindness.

THE COMPLAINT OF VENUS

I

When I am in such a heavy state, there is in my mind no solace that allows me the leisure to remember the manhood and worth, the fidelity and steadfastness, of him whose I am entirely as long as I live. No creature should blame me, for every creature praises his nobility.

In him is goodly kindness, wisdom, self-control, far more than any wit can devise; for good fortune has willed to advance him so far that he is the perfect treasure of knighthood. Honor itself honors him for his nobility, and Nature has also formed him so well that I assure him I am his forever; for every creature praises his nobility.

And notwithstanding his excellency, his noble heart is so humble toward me in word, deed, and expression, and he is so diligent in his service to me that I am entirely secure. Thus I ought indeed to bless my fair fortune, since it pleases him to serve and honor me; for every creature praises his nobility.

II

Now surely, Love, it is very fitting that a creature should buy your noble gift so dearly with lying awake at nights, fasting at the table, weeping in laughter, lamenting in song, casting face and glances down, often changing color and look, lamenting in sleep, and daydreaming in the dance – all the reverse of heart's content.

Jealousy be hanged by a rope! She would gladly know all things by spying! A creature may do nothing, no matter how reasonable, without her imagining it all to be evil. Thus we pay dearly for love and his gifts, which often he gives inordinately, as enough of sorrow and little delight – all the reverse of heart's content.

A little time is his gift joyous, but very burdensome is the use of it; for crafty Jealousy, the deceitful one, brings oftentimes disquietude. Thus we are ever in dread and pain, in uncertainty we languish and suffer, and very often have many hard misfortune – all the reverse of heart's content.

III

But surely, Love, I speak not in this way because I intend to escape from your net; for I have served you so long that I am glad never to cease. No matter if Jealousy should torment me; it suffices to see him when I can, and therefore, surely, to my ending-day I shall never repent of loving him best.

And surely, Love, when I consider all the estates of people, I feel that through your noble generosity you have made me choose the best that ever walked on earth. Now, heart, love well; see that you never leave it. Let the jealous learn by trial that for no pains will I ever say no; I shall never repent of loving him best.

Heart, it ought to satisfy you that Love has sent you so high a grace, to choose the worthiest of all, the closest to my own soul. Seek no further, on road or path, since I have found my heart's satisfaction. Thus I end this my complaint or lay;[1] I shall never repent of loving him best.

---

[1] Lay. A lyrical poem, often narrative.

The Envoy[2]

Princess, receive in good part this complaint, addressed unto your excellent benignity according to my little wit. For age has dulled my spirit, and very nearly bereft my mind of all its craft in composing; and it is also a great penance to me, since rhymes are so scarce in English, to follow word by word the curious art of Grandson,[3] the flower of poets in France.

---

[2] Envoy. An envoy is a post-script which is directly addressed to the audience or patron.

[3] Grandson. The works of Chaucer's contemporary Oton de Grandson (or Granson; 1340-97) are the models for this poem. Granson, a knight in service to John of Gaunt, also wrote seven Valentine poems.

TO ROSAMONDE

❧

Madame, you are the shrine of all beauty, as far as the map of the world extends, for you shine as glorious as crystal, and your round cheeks are like ruby. Furthermore, you are so carefree and joyful that when I see you dance at a merry-making, it is an ointment to my wound, even if you do not dally with me.

For though I weep a tub full of tears, yet that woe cannot put a stop to my heart; your lovely voice, which flows out so softly, fills my thought with joy and bliss. So courteously I move, so bound by love, that I say to myself in my pains, "it suffices for me to love you, Rosamonde, even if you do not dally with me."

Never was a pike so wallowed in spicy sauce as I am wallowed and immersed in love; and for this reason so often I imagine myself to be the true second Tristram.[1] My love can never grow cold or numb. I will always burn in amorous pleasure. Do as you wish, I will always be your lowly servant, even if you do not dally with me.

The Very Genteel Chaucer.

---

[1] Tristram. Famous lover of Isolt, in the Arthurian tradition. Isolt, though married to King Mark of Cornwall, loves Tristram, who is Mark's most able and dedicated knight.

WOMANLY NOBILITY

ও

A BALLAD THAT CHAUCER MADE

My heart has so caught in its memory your complete beauty and steadfast self-control, all your virtues, and your high nobility, that all my pleasure is set in serving you. So do I delight in your womanly bearing, your fresh features, and your loveliness, that my heart has fully chosen you as mistress so long as I live, in true constancy, never to change for any manner of grief.

And since I shall pay you this homage all my life without grudging, serving you with all diligence, keep me somewhat in your memory. My woeful heart is in great hardship. See how humbly, with all simplicity, I conform my will to your ordinance, so that, as it pleases you, you may heal my pains.

Considering also how I hang in the balance in your service, lo, such is my fortune! I await your grace, when your nobleness may be pleased to alleviate my woe, and through your pity may promote me somewhat, fully abate my heavy spirit, and deem it to be within reason that womanly nobility should not seek to inflict extremities where it finds no disobedience.

The Envoy

Source of gentle breeding, lady of delights, sovereign of beauty, flower of womanhood, regard not my ignorance, but receive this through your kindness, keeping in mind that I have caught in my memory your complete beauty and your steadfast self-control.

CHAUCER'S WORDS TO ADAM, HIS SCRIBE

Adam my scribe, if it should ever happen that you write my *Boece*[1] or *Troilus*[2] in some new way, may you have scales and scabs under your long locks, unless you copy in true fashion in accord with my lines. So often I must revise your work and correct it and erase it and scrape it; and all is on account of your negligence and haste.

---

[1] Boece. Chaucer's translation of *The Consolation of Philosophy* by the late Roman philosopher Boethius (Anicius Manlius Severinus Boëthius; c. 480 – 524 AD).

[2] Troilus. Chaucer's *Troilus and Criseyde*, his epic tale of two star-crossed Trojan lovers in the age of the Trojan War

THE FORMER AGE

Ablissful life, peaceful and sweet, people led in the former age. They remained content with the fruits they ate, which the fields naturally gave them. They were not pampered with excess. Unknown were the quern[1] and the mill; they fed on acorns, hawthorn berries, and similar food, and drank water from the cold spring.

As yet the ground was not wounded by the plough, but wheat sprang up not sown by man's hand; this they ground into meal, and ate not half what they do now. No man had yet seen the soil turned in furrows, nor found the fire in the flint; the vine lay unpruned and uncultivated, and no man as yet ground spices in a mortar to put in wine or sharp sauces.

No dyer knew madder, weld or woad,[2] the fleece remained in its original hue; no flesh knew the attack of knife or spear; man knew no coin, true or counterfeit; no ship yet cut the green and blue waves; no merchant yet fetched foreign wares. People knew no trumpets for the wars, no high towers and walls square or round.

Of what purpose is there to make war? There lay no profit, there was no booty. But cursed was the time, I dare well say, when people first did their sweaty business to grub up metal, lurking in the dark, and first sought gems in the rivers. Alas, then sprang up all of the accursed covetousness that first

---

[1] Quern. Handmill.

[2] Madder, weld or woad. European plants yielding red, yellow, and blue dyes respectively.

brought about our sorrow!

These tyrants are not glad to put them in the press of battle, as Diogenes[3] says, to win a wilderness or a few bushes where poverty dwells, where food is so scarce and thin that there is nothing but acorns or apples. But where money-bags and fat meats are, there they will go and spare for no sin to assail the city with all their armies.

As yet were no palace halls or chambers. In caves and woods sweet and soft slept these blessed people in perfect peace, with no walls, on grass or leaves. Neither down of feathers nor whitened sheets were not known to them, but in security they slept. Their hearts were as one, with no spot of envy, and each kept his faith to others.

The hauberk and the plate-mail were yet unforged. The lamb-like people, void of all sin, had no wild idea to contend against each other, but each cherished the other tenderly. No pride, no envy, no avarice, no lordship, no tyrannical taxation, but only humility, peace and good faith, the empress of all virtues.

The lecherous Jupiter, the first father of voluptuous living, had not yet come into the world; nor had Nimrod, with lust to rule, built his lofty towers. Alas, alas! Well may people now weep and lament! For in our days there is nothing but covetousness, duplicity, treason, envy, poisoning, manslaughter, and many kinds of murder.

Here Ends The Former Age of Chaucer.

---

[3] Diogenes. Diogenes of Sinope or Diogenes the Cynic (412 BC – 323 BC), controversial ancient Greek Philosopher.

FORTUNE

☙

BALADES DE VISAGE SANZ PEINTURE.[1]

I

The Complaint Against Fortune.

This wretched world's mutability, from well-being to woe, from poverty to honor, is governed by wayward Fortune, without order or wise discernment. Nevertheless, though I die, the lack of her favor shall not make me sing, "*J'ay tout perdu mon temps et mon labour;*"[2] For at last, Fortune, I defy you!

Yet there is left in me the light of reason, by which I may know friend from foe in your mirror; your whirling up and down has taught me to know so much in little time. But, in truth, no matter for your rigor to him who has the mastery over himself. My self-sufficiency shall be my aid: for at last, Fortune, I defy you!

O Socrates, steadfast champion, she could never be your tormentor! You never dreaded her tyranny, nor found pleasure in her expression. You knew well the deceit of her colors, and that she prides herself most in lying. I too know her to be a false dissembler: for at last, Fortune, I defy you!

---

[1] *Balades de visage sanz peinture.* Ballads of faces (countenances) without depiction.

[2] *J'ay tout perdu mon temps et mon labour.* I have lost my time and my labor.

II

The Response of Fortune Against the Plaintive

No man is wretched, unless he should deem himself so; and
he who has himself has sufficiency. Why then do you say I
am so harsh to you, who is free from my control? Say thus,
"Grant mercy for the abundance which you have lent before
this." Why will you strive against me? What do you know of
how I may yet advance you? And you have also your best
friend yet living!

I have taught you to know a friend in deed from a friend in
appearance. You need no gall of the hyena, which cures dim
eyes of their pains; already you see clearly, who were in
darkness. Still your anchor holds, and still you may come to
that port where bounty carries the key to my riches: and you
have also your best friend yet living

How many have I refused sustenance while I have cherished
you in your pleasant life! Will you then enact a statute
against me, your queen, that I shall ever be at your
command? You are born under my realm of variability, and
you with others must whirl around the wheel. In my teaching
is more good than there is evil in your affliction. And you
have also your best friend yet living

III

The Response of the Plaintive Against Fortune.

I condemn your teaching; it is but bitterness. You may not
rob me of my friends, blind goddess; I know my fair-weather
friends, and for that I thank you. Take them back, let them be
packed away in a closet; their miserly wealth is a sign that
you will assail their tower. A corrupt appetite always comes

before sickness. Everywhere this rule shall hold.

The Response of Fortune Against the Plaintive

You chide my mutability, because I lent you a drop of my riches and now am pleased to withdraw myself. Why should you reproach my royal power? The sea may ebb and flow, more or less; the sky has the power to shine, rain, or hail; even so may I reveal my instability. Everywhere this rule shall hold.

Lo, the execution of that majesty[3] which oversees all things in righteousness, that same thing you, you blind ignorant beasts, call "Fortune"! Heaven by nature is stable, this world is ever in restless travail. Your last day is the end of my interest in you. Everywhere this rule shall hold.

The Envoy of Fortune

Princes, I pray you of your noble courtesy, let not this man scold this way and cry out upon me, and I will reward the three or two of you for your trouble, and, unless you wish to relieve him, pray his best friend by his nobleness to help him to some better estate.

Explicit.

---

[3] Majesty. Generally taken to mean God or Providence.

TRUTH

BALLAD OF GOOD COUNSEL

Flee from the crowd and dwell with truth. Let your goods suffice you, small though they may be, for a hoard of goods brings hatred and climbing insecurity, crowds bring envy, and prosperity brings blindness in all cases. Desire no more than is necessary for you to have. You who can advise other people, conduct yourself well; and truth shall make you free, doubt it not.

Be not in a tempest to make straight all that is crooked, trusting Fortune that turns her wheel like a ball. Little anxiety means great repose, and beware also of kicking an awl; strive not like the crock against the wall.[1] You who control the deeds of others, control yourself; and truth shall make you free, doubt it not.

Receive submissively what is sent you; wrestling to win the world invites an overthrow. Here is no home; here is only wilderness. Forth, pilgrim, forth! Forth, beast, out of your stall! Know your country, look up, thank God for all things; stay on the safe road and let your spirit lead you; and truth shall make you free, doubt it not.

Envoy

Therefore, Sir Philip,[2] leave to the world your old sorry

---

[1] Kicking an awl…Crock against the wall. I.e., you will hurt yourself or be broken. (Awl: tool used for piercing holes, especially in leather.)

[2] Sir Philip. Sir Philip de la Vache, Chaucer uses only the word "vache" (cow) here, but the consensus is now that he is referring to the nobleman.

ways; cease now to be a slave. Cry mercy to Him Who of His own great goodness made you from nothing, and most of all draw yourself to Him; pray for a common heavenly payment for you and for others as well. And truth shall make you free, doubt it not.

Here ends The Ballad of Good Counsel of Geoffrey Chaucer.

GENTILESSE

ề

MORAL BALLAD OF CHAUCER.

Whatever man claims to be noble must tread in the steps of Him Who was the first stock and father of nobility, and set all his wit to follow virtue and to flee from vices. For dignity belongs to virtue and not, I dare safely hold, to iniquity, even if one may wear a miter, crown, or diadem.

This first stock of nobility was full of righteousness, true of His word, calm, pitiful, generous, clean in spirit, and loved honorable diligence and not the vice of sloth; and unless, like Him, His heir will love virtue, though he may seem rich, he is not noble, even if one may wear a miter, crown, or diadem.

Vice may well be the heir to ancient wealth, but, as all may well perceive, nobody can bequeath to an heir virtuous nobleness (which is appropriated to no station, except to the Father, foremost in majesty, who makes that person who can best please him His heir) even if one may wear a miter, crown, or diadem.

LACK OF STEADFASTNESS

❧

A Ballad

At one time this world was so steadfast and stable that a man's word was a sufficient bond; now it is so false and deceitful that, in effect, word and deed are in no way alike, for the whole world is so turned upside-down by willfulness and corruption that all is lost for the lack of steadfastness.

Why is this world so variable, except the desire that people have in dissension? Among us now a man is believed to be powerless unless by some conspiracy he can wrong or oppress his neighbor. What except willful wretchedness causes all to be lost for the lack of steadfastness?

Truth is put down, reason is judged to be a fable, virtue has now no dominion, pity is exiled, no man is merciful, and through covetousness discretion is blinded. The world has made a transmutation from right to wrong, from fidelity to instability, so that all is lost for the lack of steadfastness.

The Envoy to King Richard
O prince, desire to be honorable, cherish your people and hate extortion! Allow nothing to be done in your domains that may be a reproach to your office. Show forth your sword of chastisement, fear God, execute the law, love fidelity and worthiness, and wed your people again to steadfastness.

Here ends the Poem.

THE ENVOY OF CHAUCER TO SCOGAN

Shattered are the high statutes of heaven, which were created to endure eternally; for I see that the seven shining gods[1] can wail and weep and endure suffering, even as a mortal creature on earth. Alas! Where can this come from, of which I die almost with fear at this confusion?

By the eternal word it was decreed long ago that not a drop of tears should escape down from the fifth circle;[2] but now Venus so weeps in that her sphere that she will drown us on earth. Alas! Scogan, this is for your offence; you are the cause of this pestilential deluge.

Have you not said, blaspheming this goddess, through pride or extreme rashness, such things as are forbidden in love's law? That, because your lady looked not upon your pain, you gave her up therefore at Michaelmas?[3] Alas, Scogan! Never before, by man or woman, was Scogan blamed for his tongue!

Also in scorn you called Cupid to witness for those rebellious words you spoke, for which reason he will no longer be your lord. And, Scogan, though his bow be not broken, he will not be avenged with his arrows on you, or me, or any of our figure; by him we shall have neither hurt nor cure.

---

[1] Gods. I.e., planets.

[2] Fifth circle. The sphere of Venus.

[3] Michaelmas. The feast of St. Michael the Archangel, celebrated on September 29.

Yet now surely, friend, I fear ill-fortune for you, lest for your guilt the outcasts of Love go forth upon all those who are gray and round of shape, those who are not so likely to succeed in love! Then we shall have no reward for our labor. But I well know that you will answer and say, "Lo, old Grisel[4] is pleased to run[5] and be merry!"

Nay, Scogan, say not so, for I beg your pardon. God help me so! Without a doubt, I would never intend to wake from sleep my muse into verse, which rusts in my sheath quietly in peace! While I was young I put her forth in the public. But all shall pass away that people write in prose or rhyme; let every man take his turn in his day.

Envoy.

Scogan, who kneels at the source of the stream of grace, of all honor and excellence, at the end of this stream[6] am I, dull as if dead, forgotten in solitary wilderness. Yet, Scogan, think on the kindness of Tully,[7] make mention of your friend where it may bear fruit! Farewell! And see that you never again defy Love!

---

[4] Old Grisel. Perhaps an old horse.

[5] Run. Though the word that is usually used here is "ryme" (rhyme), two of the earliest editors, Caxton and Thynne, read "renne" (run). Since the previous sentence refers to going about upon others (presumably on the backs of them) and Grisel was a French term used for an old horse, the image is made complete with the horse running.

[6] End of this stream. At the head of the Thames is Windsor Castle, where Chaucer was probably living at this late point in his career.

[7] Tully. Marcus Tullius Cicero (106 BC – 43 BC), Roman statesman and the author of *De Amicitia* (*On Friendship*).

THE ENVOY OF CHAUCER TO BUKTON

Here follows the Counsel of Chaucer concerning Marriage,
which was sent to Bukton.

My master Bukton,[1] when it was demanded of Christ our Lord, what is truth or truthfulness, he answered not a word to that question; just as one might say, "No man is entirely true," I believe. Therefore, though I promised to describe the sorrow and woe that is in wedlock, I dare not write no evil of it, lest I fall myself into such folly again.

I will not say how it is Satan's chain, on which he always gnaws, but I dare to say that, were he out of his torment, he would never again willingly be bound. But that feeble-minded fool who had rather be chained again than crawl out of prison, may God let him never part from his woe, and may no man bewail his case, even though he may weep!

But still, lest you do worse, take a wife. It is better to wed than to burn in a worse manner. But all your days you shall have sorrow upon your flesh and be your wife's slave, as wise ones say. And if the Holy Bible is not enough proof, perhaps experience shall teach you that it would be better to be taken prisoner in Frisia[2] than again to fall into that trap of marriage.

---

[1] Bukton. The identity of Bukton (or Buckton, or Boughton) is still unclear. It may be Sir Peter Bukton of Yorkshire (1350 – 1414), steward to the future Henry IV, or Sir Robert Bukton (dates uncertain), who was a squire to Queen Anne and later to Richard II.

[2] Frisia. In the southeastern North sea, north of the Netherlands and Germany. Also called Friesland.

Envoy

This little writing, proverb, or allegory, I send you; heed it, I counsel you. He is unwise who cannot bear prosperity. If you are safe, put not yourself in jeopardy. I pray you read the Wife of Bath[3] on this matter that we have in hand. May God grant you your life to lead in freedom, for it is so hard to be enslaved.

Explicit

---

[3] Wife of Bath. One of the pilgrims in *The Canterbury Tales*: she is an advocate for worldly love and marriage. Her tale is layered with irony, as is this poem to Bukton.

THE COMPLAINT OF CHAUCER TO HIS PURSE

A SUPPLICATION TO KING HENRY

To you, my purse, and to no other creature I lament, for you are my lady dear! I am so sorry now that you are light;[1] for surely, unless you appear to me to be heavier, I may as well be laid upon my bier. Therefore unto your mercy thus I cry – be heavy again, or else surely I will die.

Promise this day, before night arrives, that I may hear the blessed sound of you, or see, like the bright sunshine, your color, whose yellowness none may match. You are my life, you are the rudder of my heart, the queen of comfort and of good company; please be heavy again, or else surely I will die.

Now, purse, who are to me my life's one light and savior in this world down here, help me out of this city[2] through your might, since you refuse to be my treasurer. For I am clipped like priest or an austere monk. But yet I pray you of your courtesy, be heavy again, or else surely I will die.

L'Envoy[3] de Chaucer.

O conqueror of the isle of Brut's Albion,[4] through whose

---

[1] Light. Though he does mean this in a physical way, the word "light" here also means cheerful or fickle; likewise "heavy" can mean serious.

[2] City. The reference may be to his residence in Greenwich, where he may have been pursued by his creditors, from whom he might get relief if he could gain asylum among the monks at Westminster.

[3] *L'Envoy.* An envoy is typically a post-script addressed directly to the audience or patron.

lineage and our free choice you are King of it, this song to you I send; set your mind, you who can all our woes amend, upon my supplication.[5]

---

[4] Brut's Albion. Brutus, Thirteenth-Century conqueror of England, thus Brutain or Britain, from whose line came Henry IV, to whom the poem is addressed.

[5] Supplication. This plea may have been successful, as it appears that on October 13, 1399, Henry IV granted Chaucer forty marks a year, which would have been rather generous.

PROVERBS OF CHAUCER

I

What shall be done with these many garments on this hot summer's day! After great heat comes the cold; may no man cast his furs away!

II

The span of all this world will not go in my two short arms; one who will embrace too much shall retain little of it.

Against Women Inconstant[1]

A Ballad

Madame, in your love of novelty[2] you have banished many a servant[3] from grace. I take my leave of your lack of steadfastness, for well I know that as long as you live you cannot love for a full half-year in one place. Ever sharp is your appetite for new things; thus instead of blue you may wear nothing but green.[4]

Just as no image can be fixed upon a mirror, but it passes as lightly as it comes, so too is your love, as your deeds bear witness. No fidelity can clasp your heart, but you fare like a weathercock which turns his face with every wind, and that is visible to all. Instead of blue you may wear nothing but green.

For your fickleness you should be put in a pillory, even more so than Delilah, Criseyde, or Candace;[5] for your only constancy is in changing. That vice nobody can root out of your heart. If you lose one lover, you can easily acquire two. All lightly clad for summer – you well know what I would say – instead of blue you may wear nothing but green.

Explicit.

---

[1] This poem and the following three poems are not fully accepted as authentically Chaucer's own work.

[2] Novelty. Chaucer's word is "Newfanglenesse," which is also the title given to the poem in some manuscripts.

[3] Servant. A lover (a servant of love).

[4] Blue . . .green. Blue is the color of faithfulness; green, unfaithfulness.

[5] Delilah, Criseyde, or Candace. All unfaithful lovers: Delilah to Sampson, Criseyde to Troilus, and Candace to Alexander.

COMPLAYNT D'AMOURS[1]

AN AMOROUS COMPLAINT MADE AT WINDSOR

I who am the most sorrowful man that ever yet lived in this world, who least knows a remedy for myself, thus begin my mortal lament against her who can bring me either life or death, but has no mercy or pity on her truest lover, and slays me for my fidelity.

I can do or say nothing to please you. For, alas and alack, surely it pleases you to laugh when I sigh, and thus you banish me from all my bliss! You have cast me on that pitiless isle from which never anyone can escape alive. This I have for loving you, sweet heart.

True it is and well I know, probably, that if it were possible to measure your beauty and goodness, I ought not to wonder even if you cause me woe; since I, the most unworthy man riding or walking on earth, dare always to place my thoughts so high, what wonder if you should show me no favor!

Alas, thus is my life finished! My death, I see, is my fate! Well may I sing, "In sorry time I spend my life!"[2] – damned be that song! For all my deadly plight, I say, it was mercy, pity, deep affection that made me in all my sorrow to love you dearly.

---

[1] This poem, like the one above and the two below, is not fully accepted as authentically Chaucer's own work.

[2] In sorry…life. This is the beginning of a little-known short contemporary poem that might be translated as follows: "My life is spent in sorry (sorrowful) time, and ever so I languish more and more, and even more still; until it is amended, I may not live; I am but lost, if I may not be granted her love; for surely I know it well."

And thus in despair, I live in love – no, but in despair I die! But shall I thus forgive you my death, you who without cause makes me suffer this sorrow? Yes, surely, I! For she has nothing to do with my folly, though she may cause my death. It is not by her will that I serve her!

Then since I am cause of my own sorrow, and since I endure this without her permission, then very briefly in a few words I may say it is no blame to her womanhood though such a wretch as I perish for her. Yet two things at all times slay me; that is to say, her beauty and my eyes.

So she is nevertheless the very root of my dismay and of my death as well. For with one word she might heal me, if she would promise to do so. Why then does she find gladness in my misery? It is her custom to find pleasure in seeing her servants die for her sake!

But surely, what makes me wonder most is this: since she is, in my judgment, the fairest creature that ever lived, the most benign and the best also that nature has created or shall as long as the world may last, why has she left Pity behind her this way. It was, in truth, a great fault in Nature.

Yet, by God, this is no defect in my lady; I would sorely blame only God or Nature. For though she may show me no pity, I ought not despise my lady's game, since she does likewise to other men. It is her pastime to laugh when men sigh; and I assent to all that gives her pleasure.

Yet, so far as I dare, I would with sorrowful heart beseech your gentle womanhood, that I might now venture to make known by words my sharp and bitter sorrow, so that for once you would read my complaint, about which I have been so fearful if through my ignorance I have said here any word to displease you.

As I hope for God's salvation, it would be the most hateful to me of all things to say a thing which might anger you. And to that day when I shall be laid in my grave you shall never find a truer servant. And though I have complained against you, forgive it me, my own dear lady!

I have ever been, and ever shall be, however I journey on, either to life or to death, your humble, true man. You are to me my beginning and end, the sun which illumines the bright and shining star.[3] By God and my word, it is my intent always and anew to love you freshly. Live or die, I will never repent of it!

I write this complaint, this woeful song and lament, on Saint Valentine's Day, when every bird shall choose his mate,[4] to her whose I am wholly and ever shall be, her who has never yet given me her mercy. And yet I will serve her evermore and love her best, though she may let me perish.

Explicit.

---

[3] Star. Probably Venus, since the next line mentions love.
[4] Saint Valentine's Day . . . mate. As noted also in "The Complaint of Mars," this is the subject of Chaucer's *Parliament of Fowls.*

MERCILESS BEAUTY[1]

❦

A TRIPLE ROUNDEL

I

Your two bright eyes will slay me suddenly; the beauty of them I cannot sustain, so keenly it strikes through my heart.

Unless your word will heal very speedily my heart's wound while it is still fresh, your two eyes will slay me suddenly: the beauty of them I cannot sustain.

Upon my word I tell you faithfully, you are the queen over my life and death, for by my death the truth shall be seen: your two bright eyes will slay me suddenly; the beauty of them I cannot sustain, so keenly strikes it through my heart.

II

Your Beauty has chased Pity from your heart in such a way that it does not help to complain, for Pride fetters your Mercy in his chains.

Thus you have purchased my death for guiltless me; I say the truth, I have no need to lie; your Beauty has chased Pity from your heart in such a way that it does not help to complain.

Alas, that Nature has placed in you so much Beauty that no man shall gain Mercy, though he may perish for the pain!

---

[1] This poem, like the two above and the one below, is not fully accepted as authentically Chaucer's own work.

Your Beauty has chased Pity from your heart in such a way that it does not help to complain, for Pride fetters your Mercy in his chains.

III

Since I who have escaped from Love am so fat, I intend no more to be lean in prison; since I am free, I regard Love less than a bean.

He may answer and say either this or that; I do not think about it, I speak just as I mean to speak. Since I who have escaped from Love am so fat, I intend no more to be lean in prison.

Love has struck my name from his slate, and he is stricken clean out of my books forevermore; there is no other course of action. Since I who have escaped from Love am so fat, I intend no more to be lean in prison; since I am free, I regard Love less than a bean.

Explicit.

A BALLAD OF COMPLAINT[1]

My heart neither knows how to nor is able to complain of half of the pain in my heart, nor what torment I have, even if I should forever be in your presence, lady of my heart, as truly as he who saved me also wished to make all Goodness and to engrave all Beauty in your person, and bid them both together ever to await, and always be where you were.

As surely he guide all my joys here and to you sad and true, as I am yours, and you, my life and cause of my good spirits, my death also, when you my pains renew, my world's joy, whom I will serve and follow, my entire heaven, and all my satisfaction, whom for to serve is set all my delight.

I beseech you in my most humble way to accept the value of this little poor poem, and because of my faithfulness despise not my service, and hold not in disdain not my dutiful attention, and do not allow me to suffer too long in this plight; I beseech you, lady of my heart, to hear my complaint, since I serve you, and ever will year after year.

---

[1] This poem, like the three above, is not fully accepted as authentically Chaucer's own work.

MINOR POEMS – ANELIDA AND ARCITE

ANELIDA AND ARCITE

*A*nelida and Arcite does not fit the description of the other works in this volume: it is not a dream poem and does not have the lyrical or occasional quality of the minor poems. It is a narrative that, following the French tradition of his day, moves into long sections of complaint similar to the complaints of Mars and Venus. *Anelida and Arcite*, probably written early in Chaucer's career (1370s), does resemble most of the tales from *The Legend of Good Women*, as it concerns a faithful woman and a deceitful man. It seems, however, to have hints of a larger plan, more like *The Knight's Tale* or *Troilus and Criseyde*.

In fact, *Anelida and Arcite* shares some of the same plot as *The Knight's Tale*, as both feature the character of Arcite. (Some believe that *Anelida and Arcite* was an early draft of *The Knight's Tale*). Both works also begin with exactly the same scene, namely, Theseus' return from the Scythian War with his new bride Hippolyta and her sister Emily. Both tales also move quickly to the aftermath of the Siege of Thebes when the merciless Creon seized power. Unlike *The Knight's Tale*, however, Arcite is not a prisoner of war and does not fall in love with Emily; instead he falls in love with the Armenian queen Anelida. Also unlike *The Knight's Tale*, there is no noble struggle for a woman's hand (though some have speculated that this might be part of the larger plan of the work), no grand tournament, no unusual twist of fate, and no making virtue of necessity.

In place of the broad action of *The Knight's Tale* and the philosophical discussions of love and fortune of *Troilus and Criseyde*, Chaucer offers us a finely detailed portrait of a loving and trustful woman and a cruel untrustworthy man

237

against the backdrop of a major moment of antiquity. In both the narration and the complaint, the psychology of love is explored in as much depth as any of Chaucer's best works on love. Though modern scholars have received the poem harshly because of the incongruity between the grand epic structure and the detailed personal complaint, they have doubtless underappreciated the strength and diversified approach of Chaucer's investigation into the psychology of a neglected lover as well as his attempt, as he so often does, at synthesizing or juxtaposing genres.

Unfortunately, the tale work was left unfinished. As no other complete versions of the story exist, we can only conjecture what the ending might be. If Anelida is like the heroines in *The Legend of Good Women* and Ovid's *Heroides* in her setting forth of her complaint against love, we might speculate that, like these many other women, her life ends tragically. Perhaps Chaucer was merciful, though, in leaving the work incomplete, so that we might imagine a better ending for one of Chaucer's most sympathetic characters.

ANELIDA AND ARCITE

THE COMPLAINT OF FAIR ANELIDA AND FALSE ARCITE

Fierce god of arms, Mars the red,[1] who in the frosty country of Thrace[2] is honored as patron of the land within your grisly, dreadful temple, be present, with Pallas,[3] your Bellona,[4] full of grace, and continue and guide my song! Thus I cry to you at my beginning. For it is sunk deep in my thought with pitiful heart to compose in English this old story, which I find in Latin, of Queen Anelida and false Arcite, that age, which gnaws upon and consumes all things, has very nearly devoured out of our memory, just as it has consumed many a noble tale.

Be favorable also, Polyhymnia,[5] who with your blithe sisters on Parnassus, near Helicon, not far from Cirra,[6] sing with memorial voice in the shade beneath the unwithering laurel; and let my ship come safe to the haven. First I follow Statius,[7] and after him Corinna.[8]

---

[1] Mars. The Roman god of war, brought together here with the ancient designation of Mars as the red planet.

[2] Thrace. The southeast tip of the Balkan Peninsula, including northeastern Greece, Bulgaria, and Turkey.

[3] Pallas. Athena, the goddess of war and wisdom.

[4] Bellona. Roman goddess of war, sometimes named as wife of Mars.

[5] Polyhymnia. Greek Muse of sacred poetry; also sometimes named as Muse of sacred hymn, dance, eloquence, pantomime, and agriculture

[6] Parnassus…Cirra. Mount Parnassus, the home of the Muses, in central Greece; Helcion, where Aganippe and the Hippocrene, two rivers sacred to the Muses, run; the town of Cirra, or Kirra, near Delphi, home of the Temple of Delphi, sacred to Apollo.

[7] Statius. Publius Papinius Statius (c. 45 – c. 96 AD), ancient Roman poet and author of the *Thebiad*, one of the probable sources of Chaucer's *Knight's Tale*. Depicted by Dante as one of his guides through the latter part of *Purgatorio*.

When Theseus[9] with long and arduous wars had overcome the fierce people of Scythia,[10] he came back to the homes of his country, crowned with laurel, in his chariot of beaten gold. At this the happy people one and all raised such a clamor that it rose to the stars, and did their utmost to honor him. Before this duke came trumpeters, in sign of high victory; and on his great banner was the image of Mars. In token of glory all could see many loads of treasure, many bright helmets, many spears and shields, many lusty knights and many joyous people, on horse and on foot, all around the plain.

He brought with him splendidly in a chariot of gold Hippolyta,[11] his wife, the hardy queen of Scythia whom he had conquered, with her fair young sister Emily;[12] and she illumined all the ground around her chariot with the beauty of her face, full of all generosity and grace. With all his triumph and thus laurel-crowned, in all the flower of Fortune's gift, I leave this noble prince Theseus riding on his way to Athens, and I will strive to bring in soon the story of the devious ways of false Arcite with Queen Anelida, of which I began to tell.

Mars, who through his furious wrathful course, to fulfill

---

[8] Corinna. Little-known ancient Greek poet (sixth century BC).

[9] Theseus. Ancient King or (or, in Chaucer's *Knight's Tale*, Duke, of Athens); military hero and slayer of the Minotaur of Crete and short-term lover of Ariadne (as told in *Legend of Good Women*), who on his return from conquering the Amazons, was beseeched by the women of Thebes to defeat the tyrant Creon who would not allow them to bury their husbands killed in the battle known as the "Seven Against Thebes." This scenario is also the beginning of The *Knight's Tale*.

[10] Scythia. North and northeast of the Black Sea and Greece. The Scythians had, to a small degree, mixed with the Amazons; Chaucer thus locates the Amazons in Scythia.

[11] Hippolyta. Queen of the Amazons.

[12] Emily. The focus of the attention of Palamon and Arcite, two noble knights found, still alive, among the dead of the battle of The Seven Against Thebes. This rivalry over the hand of Emily is the central action of Chaucer's *Knight's Tale*.

the ancient wrath of Juno[13], had set afire the hearts of the people of both Thebes[14] and Greece to kill each other with bloody spears, never rested quietly, but thrust among them both, now here, now there, and made them slay each other, so angered were they.

And when Amphiaraus and Tydeus as well as Hippomedon and Parthenopaeus were dead, proud Capaneus was slain (and the two wretched Theban brethren also), and King Adrastus[15] had gone to his home, Thebes stood so desolate and bare that no creature there knew any cure for its distress. And when the old Creon[16] saw how the royal blood was brought down, he held the city by tyranny and persuaded the gentle people of that country to be his friends and dwell in the town. So for love of him, and for fear, the people of noble blood were drawn to the town.

Dwelling in the town among all these people was Anelida, Queen of Armenia,[17] prettier than the shining sun. Her name so spread throughout the world that every creature had desire to look upon her; for, in truth, of all the women in this world's domain there was none like her. This queen was young, twenty years of age, of moderate stature, and of such beauty that nature rejoiced to behold her; and to speak of her constancy, she surpassed Penelope[18] and Lucrece.[19] And, if

---

[13] Juno. Roman goddess of women and childbirth (Greek, Hera); daughter of Saturn (Cronus), wife of Jupiter (Zeus), and mother of Mars (Ares) and Vulcan (Hepahaestus).

[14] Thebes. Ancient city in central Greece founded by Cadmus. One of the most important cities in Greek history and mythology.

[15] Amphiaraus...Adrastus. These six, along with Polynices, are the Argive warriors known as the "Seven Against Thebes." The two brothers are likely the sons of Oedipus, Polynices and Eteocles, whose dispute over the leadership of Thebes led to the battle in which they slew one another and after which Creon took control of the city.

[16] Creon. As noted above, the new leader of Thebes after the war.

[17] Armenia. Middle Eastern nation west of modern Turkey, east of Georgia, and north of Iran.

[18] Penelope. Wife of the Ithacan king Odysseus, whose adventures after the Trojan form the story of Homer's *Odyssey*. Penelope's patience in

she is to be comprehended in few words, nothing in her could have been bettered.

This Theban knight Arcite, to tell the truth, was also young, and a lusty knight too, but he was deceitful in love and in no way truthful, and more skillful than any in that art. With his cunning he won this bright lady; for so he assured her of his faithfulness that she trusted him above any creature.

What more should I say? She so loved Arcite that, when he was at any time absent, soon she felt her heart burst in two. For in her sight he bore himself humbly, so that she deemed she knew all his heart. But he was false. It was but feigned appearance, such artfulness as men have no need to learn. Nevertheless he had much work to do before he could win his lady, and swore he should die for distress, and should go out of his wits. Alack the while! For it was a grief and sin that she should have mercy on his sorrows; but the false and the true think in no way alike.

Arcite found her generosity such that all that she had, great or small, was his, and to no creature did she make a pleasant appearance beyond than was pleasing to Arcite. There was no fault to find in her; as she was so devoted to pleasing him that all that pleased him contented her. No type of letter was sent to her from any person concerning love, unless she showed it to him before it was burnt. She was so open and did all she could to hide nothing from her knight, lest he upbraid her with any charge of unfaithfulness. Without delay she obeyed his command.

And he made himself jealous over her, so that, when any man spoke to her, immediately he would pray her to swear

---

waiting twenty years for her husband's return is often cited as the epitome of patience.

[19] Lucrece. Roman noblewoman whose rape by Sextus Tarquinius, son of the seventh and last king of Rome, the Etruscan Lucius Tarquinius Superbus, spurred the Romans to reject the rule of the Tarquins and to begin the Republic. Her tale is told in *The Legend of Good Women*.

what those words were, or he would be displeased. Then she
thought that she had gone out of her wits; but all this was
only slyness and flattery. Without love, he pretended to be
jealous. And all this she took so meekly that in every wish of
his she found good reason, always loved him more and more
tenderly, and honored him as a king. With a ring was her
heart wedded to him. Her mind was so fixed to be faithful
that wherever he went her heart went with him. When she
should eat, her mind was so on him that she scarcely noticed
her food, and when she was brought to her rest, she thought
always of him until she slept. When he was absent, she wept
secretly. Thus lived fair Queen Anelida for false Arcite, who
did all this evil to her.

In his lust for novelty, because she was so lowly and true
to him, he took little delight in her constancy, and saw
another lady, a stranger and proud, and soon clad himself in
her color – I know not whether white, red, or green – and
was false to the fair Anelida. Nevertheless it was no great
marvel even if he were false, for since the time of Lamech[20]
so long ago it has been the nature of man to be as false in
love as ever he can be. Lamech was the first patriarch who
loved two women, and lived in bigamy; and, unless people
lie, he first invented tents.

This false Arcite, when he became false, had to pretend
somewhat to cover his treachery, like a horse that can both
bite and whine. So he accused her of treachery and swore he
discovered her double-dealing and that all she declared to
him was false. Thus this thief swore and went his way. Alas!
For pity and woe what heart could endure to tell her sorrow?
Or what man has the cunning or wit? Or what man could
remain in the room if I rehearsed to him the hell that the fair
queen Anelida suffered for the false Arcite, who brought her
all this pain?

---

[20] Lamech. Old Testament son of Methuselah and the father of Noah;
eighth generation of Seth, the third son of Adam and Eve. (Sometimes
named in the lineage of Cain.) His son Jabal was the first tent dweller.

She wept and wailed and piteously swooned, and fell as if in death to the ground like a stone. She writhed her limbs in knots. She spoke as if her wit were gone, and was all of ashen color. She spoke no other word, great or small, than, 'Mercy, my cruel heart, Arcite!' And this lasted until she was so spent that she could not sustain herself on her feet, but forever languished in this state.

Arcite had neither pity nor sorrow for this. His heart was elsewhere in new, blooming love, and did not deign to think on her woe; he cared not whether she swam or sank. His new mistress held him in so tightly by the bridle and under her lash that he feared every word like an arrow. Her coldness made him bow and bend, and turn or go as she wished; for never in her life did she grant him any grace for which he would wish to sing, but ever drove him on. Scarce did she care to know that he was servant to her ladyship, and lest he become proud she kept him in a humble state. Thus he served without fee or hire, and she sent him at times on land and at times by sea; and because she gave him his fill of coldness, she had him at her command.

All you prudent women, take example here from Anelida and false Arcite; because she wished to call him "dear heart," and was so meek, therefore he loved her little. The nature of man's heart is to delight in what is held back, so may God save me! For he desires what he cannot have.

Now let us return to Anelida, who day by day pined and languished. But when she saw that she gained nothing, one day, sorrowfully weeping, she thought to compose a complaint. And with her own hand she wrote it, and she sent it to Arcite, her Theban knight.

The Complaint of Anelida the Queen upon false Arcite.

The sword of sorrow, whetted with false pleasure, so pierces with the point of memory my heart, bare of bliss and black in hue, that all my dancing is turned into quaking, and my confidence into bewilderment, since it does not help to be loyal; for she who is truest, she who serves love and always devotes herself to one and changes to no new love, shall regret it most.

I know it myself as well as any; for with all my heart and might I love one a hundred thousand times more than myself, and called him my heart's life, my knight, and was all his, as far as was just. And when he was glad, I was happy; and his distress was soon my death. And he in turn pledged me his word, to declare me his lady evermore.

Now, alas! He is false, and without cause; and so pitiless of my woe that he does not stoop once by a word to bring peace to my sorrowful heart, for he is caught in another leash. He laughs at my pain as he wishes, and yet I cannot stop my heart from loving him forever. And for all this I know not to whom to lament.

Alack, this harsh hour! Shall I complain to my foe, he who wounded my heart and yet desires my harm to be greater? No, truly! Further, I will never seek any other help to probe my wounds. My destiny decreed this long ago; I will have no other medicine or teachings. I will forever be where I was once bound; what I have once said, may it be said forever.

Alas! Where is your noble gentleness, your words full of delight and humility, your devotion so humble, your watchfulness and your attentiveness to me, whom you called your mistress, your sovereign lady here in this world? Alas! And would you concede neither words nor kindly looks for me in my heaviness? Alas, I buy your love all too dearly!

Now surely, sweet, though thus without cause you are the cause of my mortal adversity, your manly reason ought to refrain before you slay your friend, and especially me, who never yet has in any way wronged you, so surely as I hope. May he who knows all things save my soul from woe! But because I showed you, Arcite, all that men would write me, and, saving my honor, had such zeal to please you, was so meek, kind, and generous – for all this therefore you put blame on me, and care not a mite for me, though through your cruelty the sword of sorrow would bite my woeful heart.

My sweet foe, why do you act this way? For shame! And do you think your reputation will be bettered to take a new love and be faithless? No! And to put yourself now into scandal and blame, and bring adversity and grief upon me, who (God well knows) ever loves you best? Yet return some day and be honest again, and then shall this that is now all wrong turn to mirth and be entirely forgiven, as long as I live.

Lo, dear heart, all this is to ask if I shall I make petition or a lament? Which is the way to make you true? For either I must have you in my chain, or you must separate us two by death; there are no other new courses between these. May God have pity on my soul, as you truly are slaying me with pains; that you may perceive from my hue without deceit.

For so far have I gone toward my death, I murder myself with my secret brooding. I weep, wake, fast, for pitiful sorrow over your cruelty. Nothing helps; I forsake all joys that I care for, I avoid company, I flee from gladness. Who may boast more of heaviness than I? And into this plight you have brought me, guiltless – for that I need no witness.

And should I petition you, and cast aside womanhood? No, rather death than do so foul a deed! And, being innocent, what need is there to ask mercy? And if I lament my wretched life, you do not care; that I know, without doubt. And if I profess to you my oaths to excuse me, a mock shall be my reward. Your manner flowers, but does not seed; long ago I should have seen that.

For even if I had you back tomorrow, I might as well withhold April from rain as expect you to make yourself steadfast. Almighty God, Sovereign of truth, where is the truth in men? Who has slain it? Anyone who loves them shall find them as secure as a rotten mast in a tempest. Is that a tame beast that will be glad to run away when he is least frightened?

Now have mercy, sweet, if I speak amiss; have I spoken ill, I pray? I know not; my wit is gone. I am like the song "Now Singing, Now Weeping"[21] for now I lament, and now I am mirthful. I am so bewildered that I am dying. Arcite has carried away the key to my entire world and my good fortune. For in this world there is no living creature in more restlessness than I, and nobody endures more sorrow. And if I sleep a little time, then it seems to me that your figure stands before me, clad in the azure of constancy, to profess again a new assurance of faithfulness and to pray me for mercy.

This wondrous vision I have through the long night, and in the day I die of fear. And of all this you care not a bit, in sooth. Nevermore are my two eyes dry, and I call upon your pity and your faith. But alack! They are too far to fetch! Thus my destiny keeps me a captive. And my wit is so weak, it cannot stretch to direct or guide me out of this fear.

Then, since I can do no more I end thus, and abandon hope now and forever. For I shall never more put my security in the balance, or learn the teachings of love. But as the swan, as I have long heard, sings in his pains before his death, so too I sing here my destiny or fate, how Arcite has pierced Anelida so sorely with the point of memory.

When Anelida, this woeful queen, had written in this fashion with her own hand, she fell into a swoon, her face as if dead, between pale and green. And then she arose and with a sorrowful visage vowed a sacrifice unto Mars within his temple, which was fashioned as you shall now hear.

[*Unfinished*]

---

[21] Now…Weeping. Chaucer uses the title "La Pleurchante" (the song of weeping), a thirteenth-century French lyric describing the shift from joy in love to misery, either in this world or the next.

ABOUT THE TRANSLATOR AND EDITOR

Gerard NeCastro is Professor of English at The University of Maine at Machias and Visiting Professor of English at The University of Maine. He teaches courses in Humanities, Creative Writing, Theater History, World Literature, Art History, Latin, Shakespeare, and Chaucer. He is the founder of Medica, The Society for the Study of Healing in the Middle Ages, and he has published on a variety of medieval and other subjects. For fifteen years, he has been the editor of *The Binnacle: The Literary Journal of Coastal Maine*. After many years of academic writing, translations, web pages, short stories, and poems, he has completed his first novel, *Columbine AS3*, and is working on his second, *The In-Law*.